The Business 2.0

B1+ INTERMEDIATE Student's Book

John Allison with Paul Emmerson

MACMILLAN

The Business 2.0
B1+ INTERMEDIATE

To the student

The objective of *The* **Business 2.0** is to help you learn two things: how to do business in English and the language you need to do it. The new language and structures are presented in the Student's Book whilst the eWorkbook provides language practice and extension.

Here is a summary of what you will find in each.

Student's Book

The modules

The Student's Book contains 48 modules in eight units. Each unit deals with a key sector of activity in the business world. There are six different types of module:

1 About business

These modules contain information and language for the topic area of each unit. The focus is on understanding the topic and the general sense of the texts – don't worry too much about details such as new vocabulary.

2 Vocabulary

These modules build on the important words and phrases associated with the topic and provide thorough practice.

3 Grammar

These modules help you practise the grammar in a communicative and meaningful way, in business situations relating to the unit topic. Before you start, read the 'Refresh your memory' box to remind yourself of the key grammar points. Use the Grammar and practice section at the back of the book for consolidation.

4 Speaking

These modules develop understanding and speaking skills in typical business situations. In these modules, you build up a checklist of useful expressions to use in the speaking activities. The activities themselves allow you to practise these expressions and your speaking skills in realistic situations with other people.

5 Writing

These modules provide practice for the most important types of document you will need to write at work. You analyse a model text, focus on key language and use both as a basis for doing a writing output activity.

6 Case study

The case studies provide an opportunity to apply all the language, skills and ideas you have worked on in the unit. They present authentic problem-solving situations similar to those you will meet in business.

Internet research

Every module includes an Internet research task to encourage you to explore the topic in more detail. The tasks can be done before or after working on the module. Remember that to search for an exact phrase, you may get more accurate results if you put quotation marks around it.

Other features

In addition to the eight main units, the Student's Book contains the following:

Business fundamentals

This opening section introduces you to basic business principles and vocabulary. It provides a solid foundation for you to build on in the course and will help you get the most out of all components of *The* **Business** 2.0.

Reviews

These units can be used in three ways: to consolidate your work on the units, to catch up quickly if you have missed a lesson, and to revise before tests or exams.

Additional material

This section contains all the extra materials you need to do pair- or group-work activities.

Grammar and practice

This section gives a useful summary of grammar rules with clear examples, and also provides further practice of the essential grammar points in this level of the course.

Recordings

Full scripts of all the audio recordings are provided, allowing you to study the audio dialogues in detail. However, try not to rely on reading them to understand the listenings – very often you don't need to understand every word, just the main ideas.

Glossary

In each module, there is a short glossary of words you may not know. The definitions for these are in the Glossary at the back of the book. Words in red are high-frequency items, which you should try to learn and use. The others, in black, are words you just need to understand.

eWorkbook

The **Business** 2.0 eWorkbook provides everything you would find in a printed Workbook, as well as extra multimedia resources. It is mainly intended for self-study or home study and contains material to support and enhance the activities in the Student's Book.

Language practice

This section contains activities to consolidate the language presented in the Student's Book. You can practise grammar, vocabulary, listening, pronunciation, reading and writing.

Watch

This section contains a video clip and worksheet to accompany each unit in the Student's Book. The video clips are episodes of a mini-drama that illustrate the communication and people skills in each unit. The exercises allow you to practise the functional language in the video

Tests

You can test yourself at any point in the course using the eWorkbook, by setting either the time or the number of questions. Your test scores are recorded for your reference.

Print and work

This section offers a pen-and-paper version of the activities in the Language practice section. You can also download the audio tracks required for these activities.

Grammar help

You can refer to this section for helpful grammar rules and examples.

Word lists

This section contains the key words and definitions from the Vocabulary modules in the Student's Book.

Dictionary

Use the Dictionary Tool to link to the *Macmillan Dictionary* online http://www.macmillandictionary.com.

Writing tips

This section provides explanations and exercises on aspects of writing, such as spelling, punctuation and paragraphing.

Listen

This section contains all the audio recordings from the Student's Book and eWorkbook, together with the audioscripts. You can download all the material in this section to a mobile device for listening on the move.

We sincerely hope you will enjoy working with *The* **Business** 2.0. Good luck!

John Allison
Paul Emmerson

Contents

Business fundamentals

- business structures
- types of companies

Company types and structures

Vocabulary

1 Look at the ways of classifying businesses. Which categories do the companies that provide these products and services belong to?

your Internet connection / your bicycle / spare parts for your car
your milk and cheese / your haircut / your dental care

Industry type	Primary	agriculture, fishing, forestry, mining
	Secondary	construction, manufacturing
	Tertiary/service	banking, tourism, entertainment
Business type	Sole trader	The business is owned by one person who is responsible for any debts.
	Partnership	Two or more people run the business; all partners share profits and losses.
	Limited liability (Ltd)	The company is responsible for any losses, not the owners; the company is private, i.e. shares cannot be sold to the public.
	*Public limited (PLC)	The company is owned by shareholders who receive dividends and gain or lose money if share prices go up or down.
Business model	B2B	business to business – companies sell to companies
	B2C	business to consumer – companies sell to individuals
	C2C	consumer to consumer – individuals sell to individuals
	B2B2C	third party vendors or consultants sell a company's products to consumers
	*A public limited company can also be known as a corporation (Corp) (Inc)	

2 Look at the business structures. Which do you think is best for these companies?

small family business / global online retailer / multinational conglomerate / medium-sized manufacturer

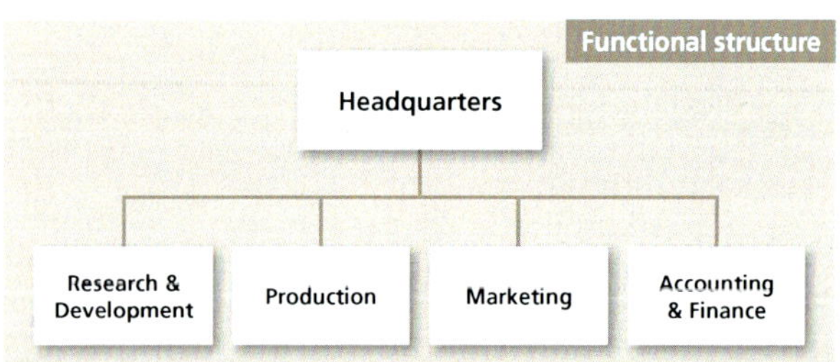

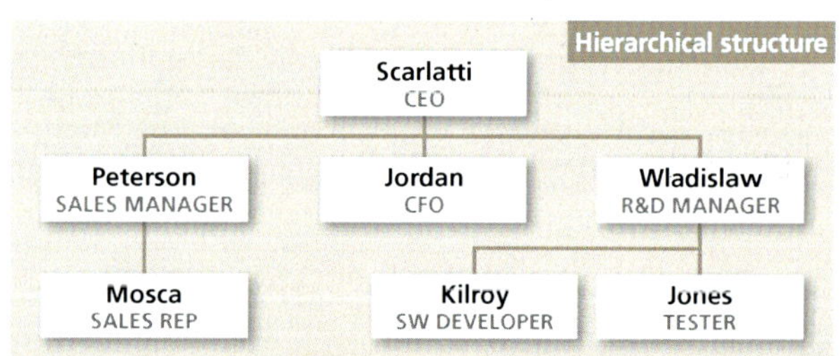

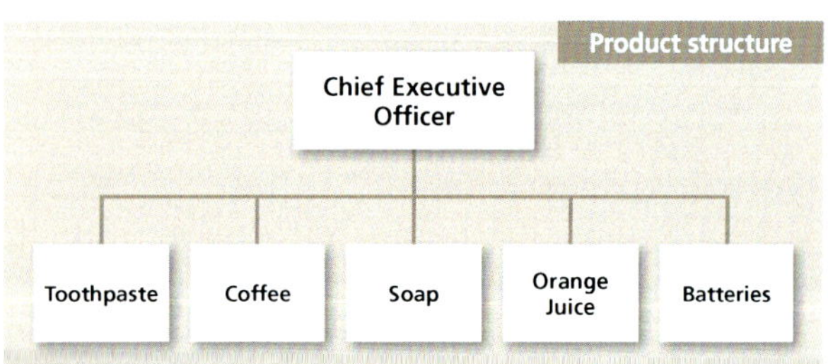

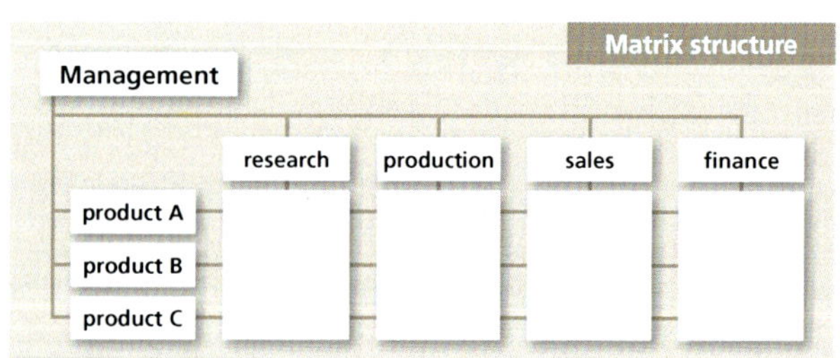

Listening

3 1:01–1:05 **Listen to five people talking about their businesses. Note each speaker's job, industry type, business model, type of business and company structure.**

e.g. *Speaker 1 - geologist - mining - B2B - multinational corporation - functional structure*

- profit and loss
- assets and liabilities

Company finance

Reading

1 Read the article below and choose the best summary:

a) Baker's Dozen makes healthy profits because its products sell well.
b) Baker's Dozen makes a heavy loss because its costs are out of control.
c) Baker's Dozen only just breaks even because its overall margin is too small.

THE Baker's DOZEN

Baker's Dozen Ltd's thirteen outlets bake and sell their own fresh bread and cakes. **Revenue** has risen quickly since the bakeries started selling to hotels and restaurants as well as the general public. Pastries and pies are selling well, but shareholders are finding annual results disappointing. It seems that there is very little left over to pay **dividends** or to reinvest in the business as **retained profit**. So what's the problem?

The company reports a healthy **gross profit**, since its **cost of goods sold** is low: raw materials (essentially flour, water, eggs and sugar) are cheap, and most bakery staff are on minimum wage. However, **operating profit** is much less impressive. As the business has expanded, **operating costs**, such as rent, electricity, administrative salaries, insurance and marketing have increased considerably. So **net profit after tax** has been a big disappointment, not to mention all the money that disappears in corporation **tax and depreciation** (the B2B market requires customized vans that lose value very quickly). In conclusion, it seems there's still profit to be made in baking, but it's certainly not easy money!

Vocabulary

2 Use the words in bold in the article to complete 1–9 in the table.

money from customers	1	revenue
cost of goods sold	2	direct costs, e.g. materials and labour
profit (or loss) after direct costs	3	gross profit
operating costs	4	other costs, e.g. administration, buildings, utilities
profit (or loss) after direct and other costs	5	operating profit
tax and depreciation	6	money paid to the government and loss in value of equipment
profit (or loss) after all costs and taxes	7	net profit after tax
Dividends	8	money distributed to shareholders
money reinvested in the company	9	retained profit

3 With a partner, put the assets and liabilities in the box in the correct category.

~~bank loans~~ buildings cars inventory invoices land
money invested in the company by the founders mortgages office furniture patents
production machinery raw materials retained profit unpaid customer invoices
unpaid insurance premiums unpaid salaries unpaid supplier invoices

Assets (what the company owns)		Liabilities (what the company owes)		
Current assets (cash and things that can be sold within one year)	Long-term assets (things that are used over more than one year)	Current liabilities (debts to pay back within one year)	Long-term liabilities (debts to pay back over more than one year)	Shareholders' equity (what's left after paying all debts)
			bank loans	

Business fundamentals

- supply chain logistics
- financial supply chain

Supply chain

Vocabulary

1 Complete the text about the supply chain responsible for Suzy's new computer with the company names from the chart.

PRODUCTS ▶

General Plastics Corp.	China Keyboards Ltd	Cherry Computer Inc	Electronic Distribution PLC	High Street PCs Ltd	Suzy
raw materials supplier	component supplier	manufacturer	wholesaler	retailer	customer

◀ ORDERS/MONEY

When Suzy's old PC breaks down, she can't imagine a weekend without her social network. So she goes down to (1) _________ and buys a new one. It's as simple as that. She doesn't need to know about the supply chain that makes it possible, or the multiple financial operations that will distribute her credit card payment to companies around the world.
On another continent, a new order of plastic granulate (made from crude oil) is being delivered to component suppliers (2) _________ by a (3) _________ truck. Suzy's new computer was only delivered to the store last week by FedEx, but they're already almost out of stock, so the inventory system automatically places an order for ten more with (4) _________. Every month, the manufacturer (5) _________, buys hundreds of thousands of components from suppliers like (6) _________, whilst distributors like (7) _________ order several hundred PCs to be able to supply stores all over the country. By the time Suzy gets her new PC set up, literally hundreds of people have contributed to keeping her online.

2 Complete the sentences about supply chains with the correct preposition from the box.

for from (x2) to to Ø with (x2)

1 Retailers order _________ wholesalers.
2 Wholesalers place orders _________ manufacturers.
3 Suppliers sell _________ their customers.
4 Manufacturers buy components _________ sub-contractors.
5 Commodity suppliers provide manufacturers _________ raw materials.
6 Trucks deliver goods _________ customers.
7 Customers pay _________ retailers, usually in cash.
8 Ultimately, the end-user pays _________ everything.

3 Complete the diagram of a financial supply chain with the words in the box.

delivery goods invoice

4 With a partner, draw a similar diagram to the one in Exercise 1 to show how you think the supply chain is organized for buying books or music online. Compare your ideas with another pair.

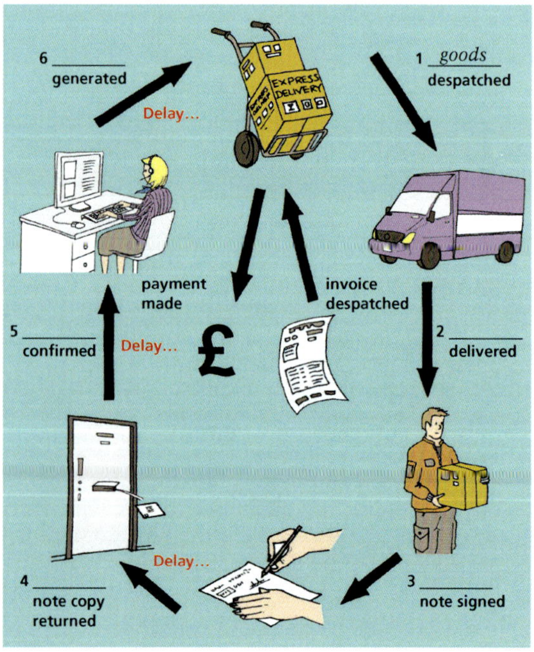

- CV information
- composing a cover letter

CVs and cover letters

Writing

1 **Use the headings in the CV below to create your own CV with your personal details.**

NAME: (Your first or given name(s) and family or surname)
Lina Ramírez Moreno

DATE OF BIRTH:

NATIONALITY:

CURRENT ADDRESS:

PERMANENT ADDRESS: (IF APPLICABLE)

EDUCATION: (year: from–to, starting with most recent) (names of institutions attended and qualifications obtained)
2010–2013 Oxford High School, Buenos Aires: International Baccalaureate Diploma

WORK HISTORY: (month/year: from–to, starting with most recent) (type of work, employer and responsibilities)
July–August 2012 holiday job, Big Jack's Pizza, Hong Kong
I worked as …, I was responsible for …

POSITIONS OF RESPONSIBILITY: (year: from–to, starting with most recent) (position and responsibilities)
2010–2011 Secretary of High School French Society
I organized …, I managed …

OTHER: (give details of language and IT skills, sports or cultural activities, driving licence, etc.)
good spoken French, MS Office and Adobe Photoshop, volleyball, clean driving licence

REFERENCES:
See next page

Speaking

2 **With a partner, exchange CVs. Ask and answer questions to find out at least *two* more pieces of information for each item.**

Which type of baccalaureate did you do?
What was the most difficult part of your job at Big Jack's Pizza?
Why did you choose volleyball?

Writing

3 **With a partner, put the phrases in bold in this cover letter in the correct order.**

Dear Ms Naqvi,
As a second-year student at Cracow University of Economics, [1]**am business experience gain I keen to** through a three-month work placement (July–September) with a leading international retailer like PC Warehouse.
[2]**extensive of have I knowledge** the PC market, and [3]**assembling considerable of computers experience** for family and friends. In addition, my university course in Customer Relationship Management [4]**a has in given interest me retailing strong**.
I will be a [5]**and highly hard-working intern motivated** and I feel sure that I can [6]**a contribution make your valuable organization to**. I am interested in all aspects of your business model, and [7]**accept any happy position to be would** you are able to offer me.
[8]**to answer any call I next questions week you will** you may have, but [9]**at contact time free to me any feel please** for more details or to arrange an interview. Thank you [10]**and time your consideration for**.
Sincerely yours,
Karol Kowalski

4 **Write your own cover letter for a job or work placement you would like to do.**

1 Corporate culture

- company culture
- unwritten rules in the workplace

Internet research

Search for the keywords *work fun*. Find out how companies are trying to create a fun atmosphere at work.

1.1 About business Work culture and placements

Discussion

1 With a partner, discuss what you would do in each situation and explain why.

You've just started working for a new company. Do you:
a) try to look as smart and professional as possible?
b) wear jeans and a T-shirt like all the other employees?
Why?
a) stop work at five o'clock like everyone else?
b) stay longer to finish your work?
Why?
a) share your ideas and opinions at staff meetings immediately?
b) say nothing like most of your colleagues?
Why?

Scan reading

2 Scan the article opposite to find:

a) what the monkey experiment demonstrated.
b) seven examples of unwritten rules.
c) what new staff learn about work culture and how they learn it.

Discussion

3 In small groups, discuss the questions.

1 What do you think organizations and companies can do to avoid negative unwritten rules?
2 What unwritten rules do you imagine you might encounter in your country as an intern in:
   - a government department?
   - a small public relations firm?

   Think about:
   - office etiquette, e.g. dress code, punctuality, personal calls, coffee and lunch breaks
   - relationships with colleagues, management and clients/business partners
   - autonomy and initiative
3 Which work culture above would you prefer to work in? Which would be the most difficult to adapt to? Why?

Listening for gist

4 1:06–1:07 Listen to Sandra, an American business student, and David, a British civil service manager, talking about problems they experienced with work placements. Answer the questions.

1 What problems did Sandra and David have?
2 What were the misunderstandings that caused these problems?

Listening for detail

5 1:06–1:07 Listen again. What mistakes did the students and the supervisors make in each case?

Brainstorming and presentation

6 In small groups, compare organizations where you yourself, your friends or members of your family have worked or studied. In what ways are their cultures different? Have these differences ever caused problems or misunderstandings?

Glossary PAGE 152

assignment
autonomy
bealing
dress code
etiquette
initiative
intern
pick up

Monkey BUSINESS?

Scientists put a group of five monkeys in a cage. At the top of a ladder, they hung a banana. As soon as a monkey climbed the ladder, he was showered with cold water; the group soon gave up trying to reach the banana.

Next, the scientists disconnected the cold water and replaced one of the five monkeys. When the new monkey tried to climb the ladder, the others immediately pulled him down and gave him a good beating. The new monkey learned quickly, and enthusiastically joined in beating the next new recruit. One by one, the five original monkeys were replaced. Although none of the new group knew why, no monkey was ever allowed to climb the ladder.

Like the monkeys in the experiment, every culture and organization has its unwritten rules. These rules are probably the single most influential factor on the work environment and employee happiness. Though many work cultures embrace positive values, such as loyalty, solidarity, efficiency, quality, personal development and customer service, all too often they reinforce negative attitudes.

'Like the monkeys in the experiment, every culture has its own unwritten rules.'

In many businesses, an unwritten rule states that working long hours is more important than achieving results. In one medium-sized company, the boss never leaves the office until it is dark. Outside in the car park, he checks to see who is still working and whose office windows are dark. Staff who risk leaving earlier now leave their office lights on all night.

Other common unwritten rules state that the boss is always right, even when he's wrong; if you're not at your desk, you're not working; nobody complains, because nothing ever changes; women, ethnic minorities and the over 50s are not promoted; the customer is king, but don't tell anyone, because management are more interested in profitability.

Often nobody really knows where these unwritten rules came from, but like the new monkeys, new recruits pick them up very quickly, despite the best intentions of induction and orientation programmes. The way staff speak to management, to customers and to each other gives subtle but strategic clues to an organization's culture, as do the differences between what is said, decided or promised, and what actually gets done. New staff quickly learn when their ideas and opinions are listened to and valued, and when it's better to keep them to themselves. They learn which assignments and aspects of their performance will be checked and evaluated, and whose objectives and instructions they can safely ignore. Monkeys may be more direct, but work culture is every bit as effective at enforcing unwritten rules as a good beating.

- company departments
- job titles
- describing responsibilities

1.2 Vocabulary Work organization and responsibility

Discussion

1 **Decide which word in each group is different from the others. Then compare your ideas with a partner.**

1 job task work project
2 manager boss deputy supervisor
3 colleague co-worker associate collaborator

Listening for detail

2 1:08 **Sam Shenton is a new intern at Warndar Techonologies, a software engineering company in Texas. Listen to Bertram Newman, her supervisor, explaining the company structure. Complete the organigram.**

Warndar TECHNOLOGIES

Merilyn Warner
CEO

David Darren
(1) COO

Administration	Marketing	(6) R&D	(8) Engineering Dep.	IT & Technical Support
Monica Overstreet (2) Finance Manager	*Bertram Newman* (4) Business Development Manager	*Douglas Pearson* R&D Manager	*Herb Monroe* Program Manager	*Roxane Pawle* (10) IT Manager
two (3) accountants	one Art Director one (5) PR officer two salesmen	seven (7) research scientists	two software engineers one (9) technical writer	one (11) Web developer two (12) Support engineers

3 1:08 **Listen again and answer the questions.**

1 Why is the organization simple now?
2 Why does Bertram say it's going to change?
3 What is the difference between the roles of the CEO and the COO at Warndar?
4 Who are Irysis and where are they based?
5 What happened about two years ago?
6 When did Roxane Pawle join Warndar? What happened to her predecessor?

4 **Match the parts of these sentences from the listening to complete ways of describing responsibilities.**

1 You're going to report
2 She also looks
3 She has two accountants working
4 David runs the business
5 Merilyn deals

a) on a day-to-day basis.
b) with strategy.
c) directly to me.
d) under her.
e) after finance.

6 Our Office Manager
7 He's responsible
8 Roxane is in charge
9 My role is
10 He liaises

f) to manage Marketing & Sales.
g) with me in Marketing.
h) for building our product package.
i) takes care of personnel.
j) of IT & Technical Support.

Internet research

CEO, COO, CFO ...
Search for the keywords *Chief Officer* to find more C ...Os. Make a list, dividing them into two categories, serious and humorous.

Prepositions

5 Complete the electronic newsletter by using each preposition once.

alongside as at in on under

INBOX | REPLY | FORWARD

This month Warndar News is delighted to welcome Sam Shenton, our new intern. Sam, who comes from Boston, joins the Marketing team and will be working (1) alongside Jake Smith and Saidah Hussain.
Andy Highlands has moved from R&D. He is now working (2) under IT Manager Roxane Pawle in IT & Technical Support. He replaces Fred Staples, who retired last month. Good move, Andy!
News of Jackson Tyler, our former IT Manager: after transferring to Washington and working (3) as Head of IT (4) at Sterns & Lowe, Jackson is now back in San Antonio. He was hired immediately, but only to work (5) in an Internet café. Jackson tells us it's just a temporary demotion; he is also working (6) on a business plan for a new social networking site. We wish him the best of luck!

Discussion and presentation

6 Work in groups of three. You want to open a private music school that offers music lessons to people of all ages. Decide:

- who is responsible for the areas in the box below.
- how many extra staff members you will need.
- who everyone reports to.

Draw an organigram of the company structure using the words from the box.

accounts advertising CD and music library cleaning and maintenance discipline educational policy instrument repairs insurance legal questions organizing concerts planning timetables public relations purchasing quality and complaints reception and office recruiting teachers registrations salaries sound systems transport and logistics

7 Work with a partner from a different group. Present your music school's organization using relevant phrases and vocabulary from the previous exercises.

Glossary PAGE 152

on a day-to-day basis
organigram
predecessor
take over

Defining words

8 With a partner, practise defining words relating to work organization.

Student A: turn to page 114.
Student B: turn to page 118.

1 Corporate culture

- past simple and continuous
- past perfect
- *should, ought to, it's a good idea to*

Refresh your memory

Past simple
He *worked*
completed actions

Past continuous
He *was working*
background situations

Past perfect
He *had already worked*
one past event before another

▶ **Grammar and practice** page 122

Advice structures

▶ **Grammar and practice** page 123

1.3 Grammar Past tenses and advice structures

Past tenses

Past continuous

1 **With a partner, take turns asking about and explaining these situations:**

1 A: I saw you at the meeting yesterday. Why were you sleeping?
B: *I wasn't sleeping actually. I was thinking. Deeply.*
A: So why were you snoring?
B: *I wasn't snoring! I was just laughing at the presenter's jokes.*

2 I heard you on the phone yesterday in the office. Why were you talking to your mother?
3 I heard you in a teleconference yesterday. Why were you shouting at your boss?
4 I saw you at the coffee machine yesterday. Why were you laughing at the new intern?
5 I saw you at your computer yesterday. Why were you playing a video game?
6 I saw you in the car park yesterday. Why were you kicking the CEO's car?

Past perfect and past simple

2 **Write endings for any *six* of the sentences below. Use the past simple or the past perfect as appropriate. Your partner has to guess which sentence the ending goes with.**

A: I had my first interview at university.
B: You had just passed your exams?
A: No, try again.
B: You had never been so nervous as when?
A: Right.
B: Why was that?
A: Because …

1 I had just passed my exams when …
2 When I got my first car …
3 I had already done several holiday jobs when …
4 The first time I came here …
5 I had never been so nervous as when …
6 I was completely lost on the first day because …
7 I hadn't felt so good for a long time when …
8 When I first met you I was surprised because …
9 I had just been on holiday at the seaside when …
10 When I heard the news …
11 I had just found a job when …
12 I'd never been so happy in my life as when …

Advice structures

3 **In small groups, take turns to ask for and give advice on the points 1–6 below. Use expressions from boxes A and C to give, accept and reject advice.**

A You should(n't) … It's (not) a good idea to … It's (un)wise to … It's important (not) to …

B Have you tried …? How about …? What about …? Why don't you …? Have you thought of …? You could always … You ought to … You might want to …

C Good idea. I'll try that. Yes, you're quite right. OK, point taken. You've got a point, (but …) I see what you mean, (but …) You may be right, (but …) I'm not sure about that. I don't think that will work. You're joking!

1 how to get a well-paid job
2 how to be popular in the office
3 how to manage your time effectively
4 how to keep customers happy
5 how to get a promotion quickly
6 how to manage stress

4 **Take turns to explain the problems 1–6 below and give each other advice on how to solve them. Use expressions from boxes B and C to give, accept and reject advice.**

1 a problem with your car
2 a problem with your computer
3 a problem with your teacher
4 a problem of money
5 a problem with a colleague or friend
6 a problem of time

Internet research

Search for the keywords *business jokes*. Which other tenses do business jokes use? Tell a joke in your own words, without using notes.

Listening for detail

5 1:09 **Listen to an after-dinner story. Number the events below in the order they happened.**

☐ The largest crocodile's mouth shut -snap- behind the CFO.
☐ There was a loud splash.
1 The CEO gave a party.
☐ The CEO showed the executives the pool.
☐ Everyone ran back to the pool.
☐ The CFO asked the CEO who was responsible.
☐ The CFO climbed out of the pool.
☐ The CEO challenged his team.

6 1:09 **Listen again and complete the sentences from the story.**

1 The boss ________ very well for himself, so he ________ the executives around his luxurious country house.
2 At the back of the house, he ________ the largest swimming pool any of them had ever seen.
3 They ________ to follow the CEO towards the barbecue when suddenly there ________ a loud splash.
4 Everyone ________ and ________ to the pool where the Chief Financial Officer ________ for his life.
5 The crocodiles ________ him when he ________ the edge of the pool.
6 He ________ climb out of the pool when he ________ the mouth of the biggest crocodile close shut -snap- behind him.

Telling a story

7 With a partner, tell a story in your own words using appropriate past tenses.

Giving advice

8 Match the beginnings of the sentences 1–10 with the endings a–f to make pieces of advice for new employees.

1 You should
2 It's unwise
3 It's a good idea
4 You should
5 You shouldn't

a) expect to finish on time every day.
b) learn to set goals.
c) dress appropriately.
d) to make too many personal phone calls.
e) to learn proper meeting behaviour.

6 It's a good idea to
7 It's important
8 You shouldn't
9 You should
10 You ought

f) accept responsibility for mistakes.
g) learn who does what and how things get done.
h) not to neglect forming effective relationships at work.
i) to reduce stress by balancing your life.
j) expect that you will like every task.

9 With a partner, take turns asking for and giving advice.

Student A: turn to page 114.
Student B: turn to page 118.

- adjectives to describe behaviour
- diplomatic expressions
- roleplaying a one-to-one meeting

1.4 Speaking Meetings one-to-one

Discussion

1 Do the questionnaire from a business magazine. Mark the statements *T* (true), *F* (false) or *D* (it depends). Then compare and justify your answers. Talk about how different cultural and business contexts affect your answers.

OFFICE ETIQUETTE Questionnaire

1. It is perfectly acceptable to call the boss by their first name.
2. You should never socialize with managers after work.
3. If a superior asks you to bring coffee for a visitor, you can tell them politely it's not your job.
4. Personal calls are acceptable only at certain times of the day.
5. Staying late at the office to finish your work is a sign of inefficiency.
6. In meetings it is advisable for junior staff to speak only when invited to do so.
7. It is OK to offer suggestions to superiors about how to improve the business.
8. It is not advisable to have a romantic relationship with a co-worker.

Listening for detail

2 1:10–1:11 Listen to two versions of a conversation between Tiffany, an intern, and Simon, her supervisor. Underline the words that describe Simon's behaviour. Then compare your answers with a partner.

Version 1 – Simon is:	Version 2 – Simon is:
objective impatient a good listener dogmatic diplomatic friendly firm understanding insincere authoritarian threatening weak frank	objective impatient a good listener dogmatic diplomatic friendly firm understanding insincere authoritarian threatening weak frank

3 With a partner, discuss the questions.

1. Why is Simon's communication style more effective in Version 2?
2. Are there situations when the style in Version 1 is more appropriate?
3. Would the two communication styles be a) acceptable and b) effective in your own language?

4 1:11 **In Version 2, Simon uses modal verbs, introductory phrases and negative questions to make his advice more diplomatic. With a partner, find suitable words to complete the useful expressions for being diplomatic in the checklist. Then listen again and check your answers.**

Useful expressions: Being diplomatic

Modal verbs

You __might__ want to ...	You could maybe ...	You'd do better (not) to ...

Introductory phrases

I think __perhaps__ ...	It ~~seemed~~ __seems__ to me that ...	Actually, I think ...

Negative questions

__Don't__ you think ...?	Wouldn't you agree that ...?
Wouldn't it be better (not) to ...?	Why __don't / didn't__ you ...?

Diplomatic advice

5 **Make these comments more diplomatic.**

1 You shouldn't disturb your co-workers.
2 You won't meet deadlines if you don't prioritize.
3 Delegate, or you'll never finish the job.
4 You shouldn't eat at your desk.
5 Don't make personal calls at work.
6 If you ignore your colleagues, don't expect them to help.
7 You'll make yourself ill if you don't take care of your life-work balance.

6 **With a partner, read the dialogue aloud. Then read it again, making it more diplomatic.**

A: You disagreed with the boss this morning. Not a good idea!
B: So what? I was right, he was wrong.
A: But you're always so aggressive!
B: And you should mind your own business!
A: You'll never progress in this company if you can't accept criticism.
B: So that's why you never got promotion, right?
A: Well, unless you change your attitude, don't expect any support from me.
B: Look, just forget it, OK? It's coffee time anyway.

Internet research

Search for the keywords *learn English*. What are the best e-learning resources for English available on the Web?

Roleplay

7 **With a partner, hold informal problem-solving meetings. Use diplomatic language to help you agree, unless you feel a more direct approach is necessary.**

Student A: turn to page 114.
Student B: turn to page 120.

1 Corporate culture

- report structure
- formal phrases
- writing a report

1.5 Writing A placement report

Discussion

1 **Henry, a marketing student, has just finished his placement at Cambro Corp. an engineering company in Littlehampton, New Jersey. He has to write a report on his experiences. Discuss what you think this report will contain and what style it will be written in.**

Model

2 **Read the extracts from different sections of Henry's report below. Choose the correct heading a–e for each section 1–5.**

a) Observations about the company
b) Appendix
c) Introduction
d) Professional achievements and conclusions
e) Experience during work placement

1 ________________

a six-month placement with Cambro Corp. under the supervision of Mr Geoffrey Thomson, Marketing Manager. The objective of the internship was to design, conduct and analyze the results of a market study for a new electronic gearbox.

2 ________________

response rate to the first mailshot was very poor. When customers were contacted by telephone, it became clear that many of them had not understood the first question. The order of the items was therefore modified and the response rate increased by 200% …

3 ________________

a long history of sponsoring local sports and cultural events. Cambro's reputation is one of its greatest strengths. To obtain a similar result through media campaigns would cost millions. This aspect of the company's marketing and PR policy was most impressive …

4 ________________

communication skills in particular. Developing and performing a market study in less than six months was a major challenge. Fortunately, I was able to apply the knowledge I had acquired in marketing in year two of my degree, and the results of my study were extremely well received. In future, I think it would be very helpful if …

5 … including the following documents:

A Daily journal B Thank you letter to Mr Thomson C Evaluation letter from Mr Thomson D Résumé E Cambro brochure and sales literature

Analysis

3 **Decide which section 1–5 of the report these topics should be in.**

1 ☐ Analysis of successes and failures
2 ☐ Objectives of the internship
3 ☐ Details of your responsibilities
4 ☐ Analysis of what you learned
5 ☐ Evaluation of the company as a potential employer
6 ☐ Suggestions for the future
7 ☐ Description of the company and how it is organized
8 ☐ Observations on the company's culture and policies

Internet research

How and where can you find an internship? Search for the keywords *find internships* to learn more.

Language focus

4 **Match Henry's informal diary entries 1–9 with the formal phrases used to talk about the same things in the report extracts in Exercise 2. Underline the formal phrases in the report.**

1 My boss is a guy called Geoff.

2 Today I called lots of customers.

3 I finally understood what the problem was!

4 So, I changed the questions around.

5 This is worth a fortune! Much better than paying for advertising.

6 … was cool!

7 It was really difficult and exhausting.

8 Thank goodness I'd learnt how to do a market survey!

9 Geoff was really happy with what I did.

Output

5 1:12 **Listen to a conversation between Jason, who has recently completed a placement at Diftco, an exporter of construction equipment in Birmingham, UK and his friend Alex. Take notes about Jason's placement in preparation for writing his placement report.**

6 **With a partner, organize your notes from Exercise 5 and Jason's notes below into the five placement report sections listed in Exercise 2. Then write Jason's placement report. Remember to use more formal language.**

- good rapport with export staff, warehouse staff more difficult
- equipment assembled and packed in warehouse
- double-check information – very important lesson!
- waste problem in warehouse – don't recycle enough
- remember to attach daily journal – journal.doc
- one of most profitable firms in region
- learnt bar code system – interesting
- too much routine paperwork – very boring!
- copies of letters to and from Ms Witten, supervisor
- most of time in Export Office, also checking containers in warehouse
- very tiring – need a holiday now!

Glossary PAGE 152

appendix
gearbox
mailshot
rapport
take the mickey
waste

1.6 Case study Counselling

Discussion

1 What kind of personal problems can interns or employees experience when working abroad? With a partner, brainstorm a list.

Listening for detail

2 1:13 Listen to an extract from a lecture on counselling skills and complete the handout.

COUNSELLING

Counselling = helping someone ________ a personal problem using their own ________

COUNSELLING SKILLS

☐ listening	☐ helping	☐ assisting	☐ solving (for them)
☐ manipulating	☐ persuading	☐ exploring problems	
☐ talking	☐ telling	☐ reassuring	

THE THREE PHASES OF COUNSELLING

Phase one = ________ Phase two = ________ Phase three = ________

3 With a partner, describe a situation when you helped someone with a problem, or when someone helped you. Did your experience correspond to what you heard in the lecture?

Counselling language

4 Match each phrase in the box with a counselling skill on the second handout below.

How did you feel? Why not start by *–ing* …? What's your first priority?
You were surprised? What would happen if (+ past tense)? Right.
So, to sum up, … So you're saying that …? What are the options?

COUNSELLING SKILLS CHECKLIST

Counselling skill	Description of skill	Useful phrases or body language
1 Asking open questions	Ask *who*, *why*, *what*, *where*, *how*, etc. to get them talking about the issues.	
2 Paraphrasing	Clarify your understanding by rephrasing what they said, and feed it back to them.	
3 Paying attention	Use positive body language to show that you are really listening.	look person in the eye, smile, nod head
4 Encouraging	Show you're interested by nodding and saying *Uh-huh*, *Mmm*, *Yeah*, *I see*, etc.	
5 Echoing	Encourage them to tell you more about a topic by repeating a key phrase or word.	
6 Summarizing	Show you have understood all they said by pulling it all together in two sentences.	
7 Establishing options	Get ideas from them on possible alternatives to resolve the problem.	
8 Asking hypothetical questions	Encourage the problem holder to think through the implications of their suggestions.	
9 Prioritizing	Establish which of the possible options the problem holder chooses to tackle first.	
10 Action-planning	Suggest a clear first step they can take to help them manage their problem.	

5 Add one more phrase of your own to each counselling skill in the handout in Exercise 4.

Internet research

Find out more about living and working in either Japan, the UK or the USA.

Roleplay

6 **Work in groups of three. Take turns being the problem holder, the counsellor and the observer.**

Problem holder

Problem holder A: turn to page 114.
Problem holder B: turn to page 118.
Problem holder C: turn to page 120.
Use the information given to respond to the counsellor.

Counsellor

Guide the problem holder through the three phases of counselling in Exercise 2. Use the counselling skills in the checklist in Exercise 4 to help the problem holder find solutions to their problems.

Observer

Observe the counselling session and take notes. Use the checklist in Exercise 4 to note which counselling skills the counsellor uses and how well they use them. At the end of the session, give the counsellor feedback to help them improve their skills.

eWorkbook
Now watch the video for this unit.

Writing

7 **Work with a partner. You are on a placement in a foreign country.**

a) Write an email to your partner explaining the problems you are having.
b) Exchange emails with your partner. Write a reply, giving your advice. Use some of the expressions in the box to show that you understand your partner's problems and to encourage them to think positively.

> I can see exactly what you mean about ... It can't be easy to ... when / if you ...
> You must be feeling very ... I know just how you feel. It's perfectly normal to feel that way.
> You have to keep things in perspective. I'm confident you'll be able to find a solution.
> I'm sure you'll bounce back.

Glossary PAGE 152

body language
bounce back
echo
headache
open question
outlook
paraphrase
perspective

2 Customer support

- call centres
- customer service technology

2.1 About business Call centres

Discussion

1 **From the customer's point of view, does it matter where a call centre is? With a partner, think of reasons why it is, or is not important.**

Scan reading

2 **Read the article opposite about call centres in the Philippines. Decide if statements a–f are *T* (true) or *F* (false).**

The Philippines have overtaken India as a business process outsourcing provider because …

- [F] a) millions of Filipinos emigrate every year.
- [T] b) changes to financial regulations have made setting up call centres more attractive.
- [T] c) call centre operators don't want to put all their eggs in one basket.
- [T] d) American customers understand Filipinos better than Indians.
- [F] e) most Filipinos' mother tongue is Tagalog.
- [F] f) Indian call centres only provide high-level consultancy services.

Summarizing

3 **Match the headings below with the correct paragraph in the text.**

1 Margin for improvement [E]
2 Culture change [A]
3 India's reality check [C]
4 Language of success [D]
5 Learning from India [B]

Reading for detail

4 **With a partner, discuss the significance of these words and phrases from the article. Decide whether they represent strengths or weaknesses, threats or opportunities for the Philippines and complete the SWOT chart.**

- bars, restaurants and shopping malls
- to bus employees to and from work
- replace up to half their staff
- four million college graduates
- consultancy projects
- national language
- unreliable infrastructure
- experienced managers
- cultural links
- tax breaks
- night shifts

	helpful	harmful
internal factors	Strengths cultural links	Weaknesses
external factors	Opportunities	Threats

Listening

5 **1:14 Cloud computing now offers a third alternative to domestic or outsourced call centres. Listen to an interview with the head of customer relations at Groupon®, a 'deal of the day' website company, talking about new technology they use. Answer the questions.**

1 How does Natterbox deal with calls from important clients?
2 How does Natterbox match callers to the best customer service agent?
3 What is special about Groupon's call centre staff?
4 How does Natterbox avoid customer frustration?
5 How could cloud-based computing change call centre staff's lives?

Roleplay

6 **Work in groups of three. Your company provides an online music-streaming service to customers all over the world. Hold a meeting to decide where to set up your new call centre. Choose one of the three roles and prepare your arguments before you begin.**

Role A: low-cost country - turn to page 114.
Role B: your own country - turn to page 118.
Role C: cloud-based approach - turn to page 117.

Internet research

Search for the keywords *call centre racist abuse* to learn about racism experienced by call centre operators. What can be done to combat this type of abuse?

Glossary PAGE 152

bus (verb)
copycat
tax break
tax holiday
twentysomething

MANILA CALLING

A Times have changed in the Philippines. In a traditionally poor, deeply religious and conservative country, suddenly twentysomethings are spending freely in bars, restaurants and shopping malls as they start or leave their night shifts. After decades of exporting its labour force to richer countries, Manila is turning the tables in the business process outsourcing market.

B In the Philippines, emigration is a long-established tradition. Every year, a million Filipinos leave their islands, hoping for a better life in Asia and the Middle East. As welcome as the $10b (5% of GDP) they send home to their families may be, a decade ago there were worries that emigration was slowing the country's development. In its search for ways to encourage foreign investment and growth, the government turned to India's call centre industry. Copying the Indian model, Manila introduced tax breaks and incentives for telecoms companies as well as sponsored training schemes to help students fine-tune their language and communication skills.

C At the same time, Indian call centres were becoming a less attractive investment for American and European businesses. Not only were their generous tax holidays coming to an end, but irritations like unreliable infrastructure and having to bus employees to and from work were increasing. In addition, the opportunity to spread risk by diversifying into the Philippines came at a time when Indian outsourcing operators were having to replace up to half their staff every year.

D The Philippines' copycat strategy has been so successful that American customers are now far more likely to be talking to a Filipino helpline adviser than an Indian. With revenues of nearly $11 billion, Philippine outsourcing now employs 650,000 people, almost twice as many as India. What's more, operators believe their customers are likely to be more satisfied with the service they receive from well-educated young Filipinos who grew up listening to American pop music and reading American comics. A US colony until independence in 1946, the Philippines has maintained strong cultural links with its former masters: in a country where the national language, Tagalog, is not most people's mother tongue, English is a second, rather than a foreign language.

E Not satisfied with outselling the market leader, the Philippine government hopes to double the market to $26 billion in the next five years. However, staying on top of the pile may prove harder than getting there: as it grows, the new outsourcing industry is discovering how much more difficult it can be to find experienced managers and competent engineers than to hire young English-speaking helpline advisers. India, on the other hand, with four million college graduates a year, is moving upmarket. Margins for more complex financial and engineering consultancy projects are much higher than for simply handling customer calls. In the longer term, Indian operators may be happy to leave Filipinos to pick up the phone while they pick up the pace on more profitable assignments.

Manila is turning the tables in the business process outsourcing market

2 Customer support

- personal qualities
- describing problems
- phrasal verbs for phoning

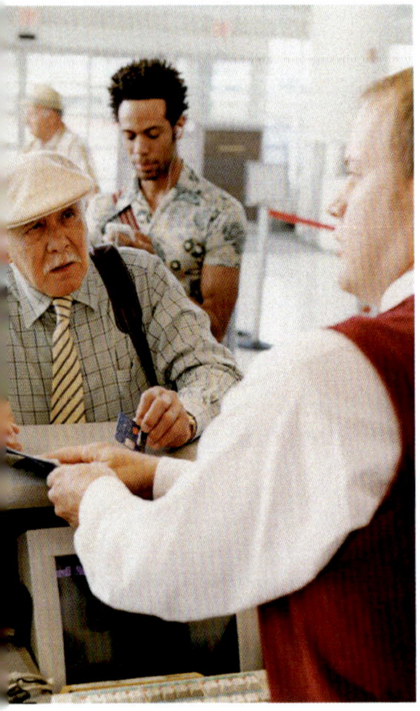

2.2 Vocabulary Customer service and telephoning

Adjectives

1 With a partner, decide whether these adjectives are most likely to be used to describe customers, helpline operators or both. Write *C* (customers), *H* (helpline operators) or *B* (both) next to each word.

annoyed cheerful difficult frustrated grateful helpful knowledgeable patient persuasive pleasant reassuring satisfied sympathetic upset

Listening for attitude

2 1:15–1:22 Listen to eight extracts from helpline conversations and choose appropriate adjectives from Exercise 1 to describe the speakers.

Describing problems

3 Decide which device each of the sentences can refer to and tick (✓) the appropriate columns.

	car	photocopier	PC	mobile phone
1 When I switch it on, nothing happens.		✓	✓	✓
2 It broke down on the way to work.				
3 It keeps crashing.				
4 There's something stuck inside.				
5 I can't switch it off.				
6 It's not working properly.				
7 It won't start.				
8 It's out of order.				
9 I think it's a complete write-off.				
10 The battery's dead.				

Collocations

4 Choose the best verb from the box to complete each collocation. Use each verb once only.

arrange diagnose escalate exchange give identify sort out talk

1 ____________ the symptoms
2 ____________ the fault
3 ____________ a problem
4 ____________ the customer through the process
5 ____________ the problem to a supervisor
6 ____________ a visit from our technician
7 ____________ the product
8 ____________ a full refund

Antonyms

5 Match each verb with its opposite.

1	connect	a)	disconnect
2	insert	b)	fasten
3	lift out	c)	push in (to)
4	release	d)	remove
5	replace	e)	remove
6	screw in	f)	switch off
7	turn on	g)	unscrew

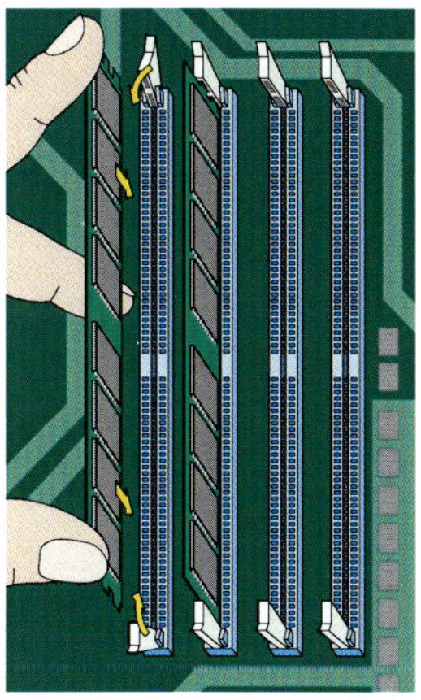

6 Complete the instructions for upgrading a PC memory module using 12 of the verbs from Exercise 5.

First, (1) _________ the PC. Do not (2) _________ the power cable, so that the PC remains earthed. Then (3) _________ and (4) _________ the side-panel. Next, (5) _________ the retaining clips at each end of the old memory module. (6) _________ the old memory module. Carefully (7) _________ the new memory module and (8) _________ it firmly _________ the slot. (9) _________ the clips at each end. (10) _________ and (11) _________ the side panel. Finally, (12) _________ the PC and check that the new memory is recognized.

Phrasal verbs

7 Match each verb with the correct definition.

1	hang up	a)	renew a call	5	hold on	e)	make a note
2	speak up	b)	connect	6	get through	f)	stay on line
3	call back	c)	talk louder	7	get back to	g)	make contact
4	put through	d)	terminate a call	8	take down	h)	return a call

8 Complete the crossword with the phrasal verbs from Exercise 7.

1 I can't hear you very well. Could you ______ ______, please?
2 I'm going to ______ ______ ______ to my supervisor.
3 I'll just ______ ______ your name and address.
4 We tried to contact you yesterday, but we couldn't ______ ______.
5 We'll ______ ______ ______ you as soon as we solve the problem.
6 All our lines are currently engaged. Please ______ ______ later.
7 Could you ______ ______ a moment, please?
8 It's a terrible line. Could you , and try again?

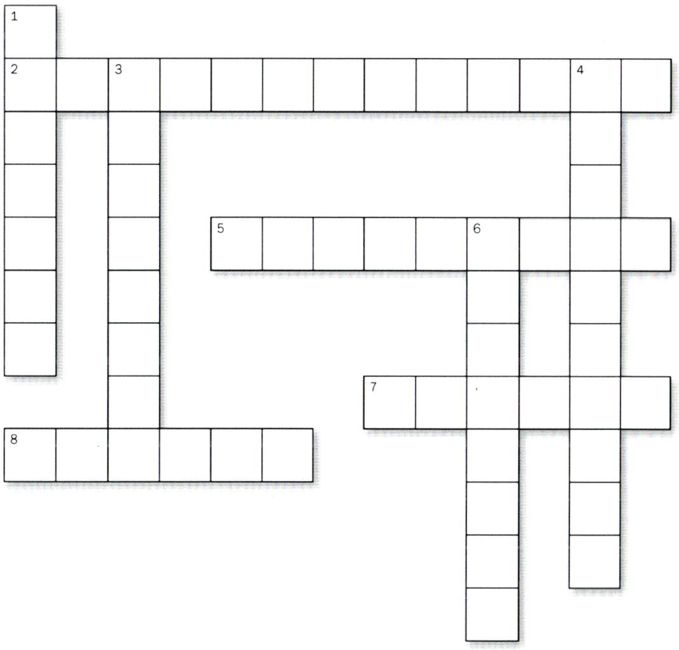

Glossary PAGE 153

clip
earth (verb)
retain
side-panel
slot
upset

Internet research

Search for the key words *golden rules of customer service*. Compare your findings with your own 'golden rules' from Exercise 9.

Discussion

9 In small groups, brainstorm ten 'golden rules' of customer service. Then present your 'golden rules' to another group.

2 Customer support

- *Yes/No* questions
- *Wh-* questions
- *have to, might have to, need to*

Refresh your memory

***Yes/No* questions**
auxiliary verb + subject + main verb

***Wh-* questions**
question word + auxiliary verb + subject + main verb
except if *who*, *what* or *which* is the subject: no auxiliary is needed

▶ **Grammar and practice** page 124

2.3 Grammar Questions and instructions

Listening

1 1:23 **Listen to some people playing *Guess the Product*. Try to guess what the mystery product is along with the contestants. Then continue listening to check your answer.**

2 1:23 **Listen again and complete the questions.**

1	____________________	on TV?	No, it isn't.
2	____________________	for work?	Yes, you do.
3	____________________	in every office?	Yes, you would.
4	____________________	in your pocket?	Yes, you can.
5	____________________	twenty years ago?	No, it didn't.
6	____________________	electricity?	Yes, it does.
7	____________________	speak to people?	No, you don't.
8	____________________	with computers?	Yes, there is.
9	____________________	more than $30?	No, it doesn't.
10	____________________	to store data?	Yes, you can.

3 **In small groups, take turns choosing a mystery product and play *Guess the Product*.**

Asking questions

4 **Work in small groups of As or Bs. Write a question for each answer in your list below.**

A

- 365
- about €25,000 a year
- about 10km
- about two years ago
- at home
- Barack Obama
- by offering a discount
- Coca-Cola®
- coffee
- once a quarter
- since the 1990s
- Steve Jobs
- the Olympic Games®
- to buy food and drink
- 20 minutes or so

B

- about 300m
- at least an hour
- between €30 and €50 a month
- Bill Gates
- by advertising the product
- 52
- for about five years
- Formula One™
- in a restaurant
- last year
- mobile phones
- Nelson Mandela
- once a year
- to meet friends
- Toyota

5 **Work in pairs, A and B. Close your books and ask each other the questions you prepared in Exercise 4, in any order. Score one point for each correct answer.**

Internet research

What's the best way to learn English? How long will it take? Do I have to learn grammar? How can I learn more vocabulary? Search for the keywords *FAQ learning English* to find the most frequently asked questions and some of the answers.

Making requests

6 Complete these requests with *fax* or *faxing*. Then put them in order 1–6 from the most direct (1) to the most polite (6).

☐ Do you think you could possibly ________ me the details, please?
☐ Would you mind ________ me the details?
☐ Can you ________ me the details?
☐ I was wondering if you would have any objection to ________ me the details?
☐ ________ me the details, will you?
☐ Could you ________ me the details, please?

7 Which one of these responses is not appropriate for all the requests in Exercise 6. Why?

a) I'm afraid my fax is out of order.
b) I'll do it straight away.
c) I'm sorry, but I'm not in the office.
d) I'm a bit short of time, actually.
e) No, no problem.

Roleplay

8 With a partner, take turns beginning these telephone roleplays and responding. Choose suitable forms for your requests, according to the answer expected, and give appropriate answers. Ask your:

- colleague to send you an email to test your new address.
- boss to give you an advance on next month's salary.
- supplier to postpone a delivery by one week.
- supervisor to write a reference for your job application.
- friend to lend you their laptop for the weekend.
- customer to call back later when the sales manager comes back from lunch.
- bank manager to lend you a million dollars.
- supplier to upgrade the office coffee machine, at no charge.

Giving instructions

9 Complete Steve's side of the telephone conversation using *don't, might have to, 'll have to, 'll need to, don't have to* or *needn't*.

Steve: OK, Pete. First of all, you open the printer. No, wait a minute, (1) ________ just open it. Select 'change cartridge' from the menu.
Pete: ________________________________
Steve: Er, yes, of course you (2) ________ switch it on, otherwise you can't use the menu!
Pete: ________________________________
Steve: No, that's all right, you (3) ________ switch the PC on, just the printer.
Pete: ________________________________
Steve: So now you gently remove the old cartridge. (4) ________ force it. If it's difficult, you (5) ________ pull it back first, then upwards.
Pete: ________________________________
Steve: OK. So now you can install the new cartridge. You (6) ________ remove the adhesive tape first, but be careful you (7) ________ touch the printed circuits – they're very fragile.
Pete: ________________________________
Steve: Right. It'll ask you if you want to align the new cartridge, but you (8) ________ bother. Usually it's fine as it is.
Pete: ________________________________
Steve: Oh no, (9) ________ throw the old cartridge away. You can recycle them.
Pete: ________________________________
Steve: No, that's all right, Pete. You (10) ________ worry. Just buy me a coffee some time!

10 1:24 Write Pete's side of the conversation. Then listen and compare your version with the recording.

11 Choose something you don't know how to do from the list below.

- change the oil in your car
- organize a press conference
- upgrade the processor in your PC
- publish your website
- (your own idea)

Find someone who knows how to do it and ask them to explain what to do. Ask questions and/or reformulate their answers to check that you understand.

2 Customer support

- expressions for giving instructions
- handling a technical problem

2.4 Speaking Dealing with problems by telephone

Giving instructions

1 **With a partner, practise giving instructions by describing a symbol so that your partner can draw it. Do not look at each other's pages during the exercise.**

Student A: turn to page 114.
Student B: turn to page 119.

Listening

2 1:25 **Listen to a software helpline conversation and answer the questions.**

1 What is the customer's problem? 2 What help does the operator give?

3 **With a partner, decide which expressions in the telephone language checklist below were in the conversation, a or b. Then listen again and check your answers.**

Telephone language

	a)	b)
1	I'm just putting you on hold for a moment.	Please hold the line.
2	Dean speaking.	This is Dean.
3	What can I do for you?	How can I help you?
4	What exactly seems to be the problem?	Could you explain the problem you're having?
5	The line's bad.	It's not a very good line.
6	Could you speak up a little?	Can you talk a bit louder?
7	I'll connect you to ...	I'll put you through to ...
8	The number is engaged.	The number's busy.
9	Can I get her to call you back?	Could I ask her to get back to you?
10	So you're on ...	So, your number is ...
11	Could I have your name, please?	What's your name, please?
12	You're welcome.	Not at all.

Improving a conversation

4 **With a partner, read this conversation aloud.**

Helpline: Superword helpline, wait a minute ... Yeah? What's your problem?
Customer: I'm having trouble with PDF files. I can't print them.
Helpline: What? I can't hear you.
Customer: I said I can't print PDF files.
Helpline: Oh. I don't do PDFs.
Customer: Well, could you connect me to someone who does?
Helpline: Can't. The PDF expert's gone out for lunch. Give me your name and we'll call you later.
Customer: Oh, all right. It's Gearhirt. Jamila Gearhirt.
Helpline: Er, come again?
Customer: That's G-E-A-R-H-I-R-T.
Helpline: OK.
Customer: All right. Well, I'd appreciate it if you could call me as soon as possible. Goodbye.
Helpline: Yeah, right.

1 Decide how the conversation could be improved.
2 Practise your improved version.
3 Now change roles, turn to page 115 and do the same with a similar conversation.

Handling problems

5 1:26 **Listen to another helpline conversation, which is based on a true story, and answer the questions.**

1 What is the customer's problem? 2 What is the operator's solution?

Internet research

Go to the BBC World Service Radio Player (http://www.bbc.co.uk/worldservice/index.shtml) and find a radio programme about one of your interests. Listen extensively, then tell a partner about the three most interesting points in the programme.

6 1:26 **With a partner, find suitable words to complete the expressions in the customer support checklist below. Then listen again and check your answers.**

Useful expressions: Customer support

Explaining the problem

I'm having __________ with Word.
It doesn't __________.
It __________ accept anything when I type.
Nothing __________.
I __________ type anything.
I'm having difficulty connecting to the Internet.
It keeps crashing.

Diagnosing the causes

Was it __________ properly before that?
What does your screen __________ like now?
Have you __________ hitting 'Escape'?
Did you __________ Word?
Can you __________ the cursor around?
Does your __________ have a power indicator?
Have you installed any new software?
What happens if you press 'Control – Alt – Delete'?

Giving instructions

Could you __________ on the back of the monitor?
Now you just __________ to follow the cord to the plug.
I __________ you to look back there again.
I'd like __________ to go and get them.
Then I __________ you to take it back to the store.
You'll have to adjust the settings in the control panel.

Promising help

I'll __________ someone call the electricity company.
I'll get our technical expert to help you.
We'll get back to you in a couple of hours.
I'll have a technician call as soon as possible.

Roleplay

7 **With a partner, use the chart to roleplay helping a colleague with the technical problems below. Take turns being Student A and Student B.**

- You can't print your report.
- Your mobile phone doesn't work.
- The video projector doesn't work.
- There are no lights in your office.
- Your car won't start.
- Your laptop is frozen.
- (your own problem)

Student A	Student B
Explain the problem. →	
	← Diagnose possible causes.
Answer Student B's questions. →	
	← Give instructions.
Problem solved?	
Yes. / No. →	Promise help.
(Yes.) Thank Student B.	

eWorkbook
Now watch the video for this unit.

Cartoon from Dilbert.com 28/5/05

Glossary PAGE 153

Come again?
crash
freeze

2 Customer support

- levels of formality
- email expressions
- writing emails

2.5 Writing Formal and informal correspondence

Discussion

1 **With a partner, discuss what differences you would find in your own language between formal correspondence, e.g. a letter to your bank or your legal advisor and informal messages, e.g. an email to a friend.**

Model

2 **Read the four emails below and answer the questions.**

1 Which email is from:

[4] a customer service department? [1] a junior colleague?
[3] a senior colleague? [2] a customer?

2 Which two emails are formal? Which two are neutral/informal?

INBOX | REPLY | FORWARD

1

Dear Ms Reckett, formal
I am writing with regard to a computer problem. You may remember we met at the office Christmas party, and I believe you mentioned having a similar problem with your laptop. Unfortunately, I have dropped mine and the screen is cracked. I was wondering if you could give me any advice on getting it repaired? I would very much appreciate any help you might be able to give me.
Yours sincerely,
James Blair

INBOX | REPLY | FORWARD

2

Dear Sir or Madam, formal
I am writing to enquire about having a television repaired. The set is a Goodson 42" LED TV which we bought 18 months ago and therefore is unfortunately no longer under guarantee. Currently we have a picture but no sound.
I would be very grateful if you could give me the address of an authorized repair centre in the Greater Manchester area. Thank you for your help.
Yours faithfully,
J. Roebotham (Miss)

INBOX | REPLY | FORWARD

3

Hi James, informal
Thanks for your mail. Bad luck about the laptop. Mine was a write-off – had to get a new one! Why don't you try Harrowson's in Oldham? They're usually good. Hope this helps.
Cheers,
Margaret
P.S. Of course I remember you. Give me a ring next time you're in town and we'll go for a drink!

INBOX | REPLY | FORWARD

4

Dear Miss Roebotham, informal
Re your email of 10 September: your TV is in fact covered by a two-year manufacturer's guarantee. Can you just send the set back in its original packing and we will repair or exchange it ASAP. Don't hesitate to get back to me if you need any more information.
Regards,
Max Hurst
P.S. Are you by any chance the Jenny Roebotham I knew at Manchester Business School in 06/07?

Internet research

The advantages of email are obvious – but what risks must companies consider? Search for the keywords *email risk policy* to find out.

Glossary PAGE 153

accounts payable
ASAP
crack
duplicate
inconsistency
patch
Trojan (horse)
write-off

Language focus

3 **Find expressions in the four emails in Exercise 2 to complete the table.**

	Formal	Neutral/Informal
Greeting	Dear Ms	Hi
	Dear Sir or Madam	Dear Miss
Opening	I am writing with regard to	Thank for your email
	I am writing to enquire about	Re your mail
Requests	I was wondering if you could	Give me a ring
	I would be very gratefol if you could	Can you just ?
Closing	I would very much appr. any help	Hope this helps
	Thank for your help	don't hesitate to get back to me
Salutation	Your sincerly	Cheers
	Yours faitfully	Regards

4 **Read the next four emails the people in Exercise 2 sent and answer the questions.**

1 Which two writers have changed style? Why?
2 Find and correct the two inconsistencies of style in each email.

INBOX | REPLY | FORWARD

5 Dear Mr Hurst,
Thanks for your email of 12 September. I am afraid you have mistaken me for my cousin, who attended Manchester Business School.
I am very pleased to learn that the TV set is still under guarantee. Unfortunately, I no longer have the original packaging, so I think it would be preferable if I deliver the TV directly to your repair centre after work. Could you possibly let me know the opening hours?
Cheers,
Jane Roebotham

INBOX | REPLY | FORWARD

7 Dear Miss Roebotham,
I am writing with reference to the repair of your Goodson TV750. Our Manchester repair centre is open from 9am to 6pm from Monday to Saturday.
I've attached a leaflet with the details and a map.
Hope this helps.
Yours sincerely,
Max Hurst
P.S. Please accept my apologies for confusing you with your cousin.

INBOX | REPLY | FORWARD

6 Hi Margaret, informal
Thanks for your email. I wasn't sure if you'd remember me – it was quite a party, wasn't it? Funnily enough, I will be in town next Thursday so perhaps we could have that drink? I would be very grateful if you could let me know if you are free around 6.30? Looking forward to seeing you.
James
P.S. I would like to express my gratitude for your help with the computer. I'm getting it fixed tomorrow.

INBOX | REPLY | FORWARD

8 James,
Re next Thursday. It will be lovely to see you. Actually, my husband will be in Indonesia that week, so I need to be at home to look after the cats. I was wondering if you would mind coming over to our place? I've attached a map – get back to me if it's not clear.
Yours sincerely,
Margaret

Output

5 **Work in groups of three to write and reply to business emails using appropriate styles.**

Student A: page 115.
Student B: page 116.
Student C: page 119.

2 Customer support

- customer feedback
- job satisfaction
- presenting recommendations

2.6 Case study Cybertartan Software

Discussion

1 **What annoys you most as a customer?**

waiting for service · products that don't do what they claim · high prices · hidden costs · planned obsolescence · deadlines not respected · incompetent service · poorly translated instructions · being put on hold · other?

With a partner, discuss what you as a customer can do about these problems.

Scan reading

2 **Read the email from Hamish Hamilton, CEO of Cybertartan Software and answer the questions.**

1 What are his four problems?
2 How are the problems linked?

INBOX | REPLY | FORWARD

For your next project, I need you to take a look at our Kirkcaldy contact centre. Our Q4 customer satisfaction survey is disastrous (see charts and report extract attached) and this represents a major risk to our corporate image and future sales. We have serious recruitment problems and a high staff turnover. These two problems are obviously linked. I suggest you talk to Laurie McAllister, our HR Manager there. I'd like you to come up with some proposals but without significantly increasing costs, which are another problem. Currently we estimate that on average a customer call costs us £4.50. We cover this from the call charge (currently £0.50 per minute), which is why we keep customers on hold for around six minutes. They spend about the same time with an adviser, although if possible we need to reduce this because at the moment we can't take enough calls. Obviously, we can't afford to increase salaries. I'm counting on you to come up with some creative ideas; get back to me as soon as you can.

Best regards, Hamish

Customer satisfaction Q1

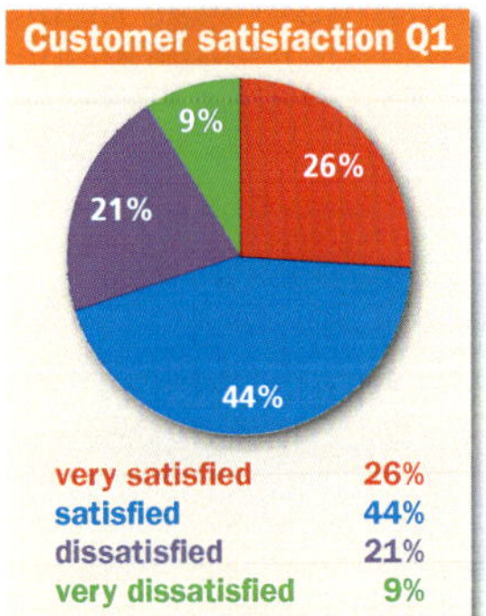

Customer satisfaction Q4

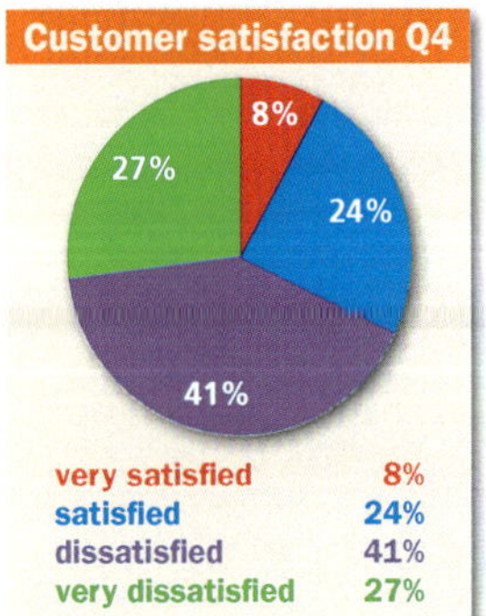

TOP FIVE REASONS FOR CUSTOMER DISSATISFACTION		
1	Difficult to get through to customer adviser	76%
2	Time spent on hold	65%
3	Several calls needed to solve problem	53%
4	Cost of calls	49%
5	Can't get help by email	32%

Reading for detail

3 **Mark these statements *T* (true), *F* (false) or *D* (it depends).**

1 Hamish Hamilton is probably writing to an external consulting group. ☐
2 The Kirkcaldy contact centre has satisfied employees and dissatisfied customers. ☐
3 The contact centre is losing money at the moment. ☐
4 If the centre employs more advisers, its income will increase. ☐
5 More than two thirds of customers were satisfied or very satisfied in Q1. ☐
6 The number of both dissatisfied and very dissatisfied customers tripled in Q4. ☐
7 About half of their customers would be prepared to pay for support if their problems were solved quickly. ☐

Internet research

What is the FLSA? What are employees' rights on meal and rest breaks in the USA? Are they similar to those in your country? Search for the keywords *meal rest breaks* to find out.

Listening for detail

4 1:27 **Listen to part of an interview with Laurie McAllister, HR Manager at the Kirkcaldy contact centre. In her opinion, what is the biggest problem for advisers?**

5 1:27 **Listen again. What are the effects on the contact centre of the following?**

1 Employees have poor working conditions and low job satisfaction.
2 The workload is heavier than before.
3 The bus service is inadequate.
4 Desks are shared with colleagues on other shifts.
5 Software products have become very complex.
6 Advisers don't get enough training.
7 The shift system is inflexible.

Solving problems

6 **Work in small groups. You are the consultants that Hamish Hamilton wrote to in Exercise 2. Hold a meeting to discuss the agenda below.**

Kirkcaldy Contact Centre

AGENDA FOR CONSULTANTS' MEETING

The situation

Isolate the problems and prioritize them as:

a) important and urgent
b) important but not urgent
c) not important.

Solutions

Brainstorm solutions to the problems prioritized as a) and b) above.

- Review company policy on customer services?
- Review company policy on working conditions for advisers?

Recommendations

Define recommendations for short- and long-term policy.

Glossary PAGE 153

come up with
from the horse's mouth
obsolescence
shift
staff turnover
swap
triple

Writing presentation slides

7 **Prepare slides to present to Cybertartan Software summarizing your recommendations. For each problem, make recommendations, give reasons for these and outline the expected results.**

Presentations

8 **In your groups, present your recommendations and take questions from the class.**

Review 1

Corporate culture

1 Make expressions about internships by matching each verb with a phrase a–f below.

1 Incorporate … ☐
2 Enhance … ☐
3 Relate … ☐
4 Be assessed … ☐
5 Be supervised … ☐
6 Offer … ☐

a) … your academic study to the workplace.
b) … work experience into a university degree.
c) … by your institution through reports, appraisals, etc.
d) … closely by someone from the workplace and a university staff member.
e) … your career prospects by doing an internship.
f) … permanent employment to a student after graduation.

2 Match each word in the box with its definition below. Then translate the words into your language.

appraisal	commitment	deadline	etiquette
insight	outcome	overview	predecessor
threaten	workload		

1 a date by which you have to do something ________
2 an ability to understand something clearly ________
3 an opinion about how successful someone is ________
4 the amount of work that a person has to do ________
5 enthusiasm, determination and loyalty ________
6 a set of rules for behaving correctly ________
7 a description of the main features of something ________
8 the person who had a job before someone else ________
9 the final result of a process, meeting, etc. ________
10 to tell someone you might cause them harm ________

3 Underline the correct preposition in each expression.

1 be in charge *to* / *of* / *from* a department or project
2 be involved *on* / *in* / *for* doing something
3 be responsible *to* / *for* / *with* an area of work
4 deal *with* / *on* / *for* an area of work
5 have somebody working *of* / *under* / *on* you
6 liaise *for* / *to* / *with* someone about an area of the business
7 look *through* / *with* / *after* an area of work
8 report directly *to* / *for* / *under* somebody
9 run the business *from* / *with* / *on* a day-today basis
10 take care *with* / *of* / *for* an area of work

4 Complete the sentences with expressions from Exercise 3 so that they have the same meaning.

Maria (1) is ______ ______ ______ / (2) is ______ ______ the marketing side of the business.

She (3) ______ ______ / (4) ______ ______ / (5) ______ ______ ______ the marketing side of the business.

5 Mark these statements about work organization *T* (true) or *F* (false).

1 A task is bigger than an assignment. ☐
2 A line manager has a higher position than a project leader. ☐
3 A branch is bigger than a division. ☐
4 *COO* stands for Chief Organization Officer. ☐
5 The Public Relations officer will often work in the Marketing Department. ☐
6 Personnel is a function of Human Resources. ☐
7 *R&D* stands for Resources and Deployment. ☐
8 A parent company owns several smaller companies called *subsidies*. ☐
9 *Purchasing* is a more formal way of saying *buying*. ☐
10 Company structure can be shown visually using an 'organichart'. ☐

6 In each sentence, put one verb in the past simple (*did*), one in the past continuous (*was/were doing*) and one in the past perfect (*had done*).

1 While I ________ (work) in my father's business I ________ (start) to understand the importance of marketing – I ________ (never/think) about it before.
2 I ________ (already/be) in the job for two months when I first ________ (speak) to the big boss, the CEO; I nearly hit his car as I ________ (park) mine!

7 Complete the expressions for giving diplomatic advice (in bold) by filling in the missing letters.

1 **Ac_ _ _ _ _ _, I think** there's a better way to do this.
2 **It s_ _ _ _ to me that** there has been a misunderstanding.
3 **You m_ _ _ _ want to** ask Sue for her opinion.
4 **You c_ _ _ _ maybe** try a different approach.
5 **D_ _'_ you think that** making personal calls at work creates an unprofessional atmosphere?
6 **W_ _ _ _ _'_ you agree that** it's important to meet all our deadlines?

8 Match these words related to report writing with their definitions below.

description	observation	analysis
suggestion	evaluation	

1 examining something in order to understand it ________
2 a statement about what something is like ________
3 considering something in order to discover how good or bad it is ________
4 a comment about something you have seen, heard or felt ________
5 an idea or plan that you offer for someone to consider ________

Review 2

Customer support

1 In each set of four below, match an adjective on the left with a noun on the right to make collocations about working conditions.

1 clean	customer
2 satisfied	environment
3 high	meals
4 subsidized	staff turnover
5 heavy	rate
6 hourly	staff
7 competent	job
8 dead-end	workload

2 Make adjectives from these nouns.

1 annoyance ________
2 competence ________
3 frustration ________
4 gratitude ________
5 help ________
6 knowledge ________
7 persuasion ________
8 reassurance ________
9 satisfaction ________
10 rudeness ________

3 The collocations below are useful in customer support. Cross out the one verb that does not collocate with the noun.

1 *deal with / look into / push in / sort out* a problem
2 *describe / identify / replace / treat* the symptoms
3 *diagnose / locate / offer / repair* the fault
4 *escalate / exchange / launch / replace* the product
5 *ask for / call / give / offer* a full refund
6 *escalate / fax / refer / replace* the problem to a supervisor

4 In this customer support dialogue the verbs in bold are all in the wrong places. Put them in the correct places.

Helpline operator: Before I can **locate** the problem, I first need to **escalate** exactly where the fault is.

Customer: OK, no problem, we can do that. But if it's still not working properly, can you **sort out** the product, or at least **replace** me a refund?

Helpline operator: Yes, that's possible, but I'm not authorized to do it. I would first have to **give** the problem to my supervisor.

5 Complete this useful phrase for after sales service using the letters in brackets.

'I'll ____ into it, ____ it out, and ___ back to you tomorrow.' (gklrstteooo)

6 Complete the sentences typical of customer support telephone calls 1–10 using the prepositions in the box.

down	down	in	into	on	on
through	through	up	up		

1 We tried to contact you, but we couldn't get ________.
2 The machine broke ________ after only a few days.
3 Replace and screw ________ the side panel.
4 When I switch it ________, nothing happens.
5 I'm going to put you ________ to my supervisor.
6 I'll just take ________ your details.
7 Push the new module ________ the slot.
8 Please hold ________ a moment while I find your records on our database.
9 The line is bad. Please hang ________ and I'll call you back.
10 The line is bad. Could you speak ________, please?

7 Read the definitions and complete the words by filling in the missing letters.

1 computer screen m_ _ _ _r
2 a row of icons on a computer screen too_ _ _r
3 something you hope your computer doesn't do c_ _ _h
4 make a computer more powerful up_ _ _de
5 something that goes in a printer ca_ _ _ _dge
6 connect to the electricity supply p_ _g in
7 send a document with an email a_ _ _ch
8 someone who a business sells to c_ _ _ _ _ _r
9 someone who a business buys from s_ _ _ _ _ _r
10 a written promise that a company will repair something you buy from them g_ _ _ _ _ _ _e

8 Complete the email using the words in the box.

appreciate	attached	could	further
get back to	grateful	hesitate	regard
urgently	would		

INBOX | REPLY | FORWARD

Dear Mr White
I am writing with (1)________ to my order placed online last week. It still hasn't arrived. I (2)________ be (3)________ if you (4)________ ship the order immediately. For your reference, I have (5)________ a copy of the confirmation you sent me. Do not (6)________ to (7)________ me if you need any (8)________ information.
I would (9)________ a quick response as these items are needed (10)________.
Best regards
J Garcia

9 The extracts below come from an email between colleagues at a customer contact centre. Use one word to fill each gap. The clues in brackets will help you.

1 I ________ you to take a look at our Metz contact centre. (**clue**: not *want*, but a similar single word more often used in a business context)
2 Our ________ customer satisfaction survey is disastrous. (**clue**: how business people often write *fourth quarter*)
3 This represents a major ________ to our corporate image. (**clue**: it means *the possibility that something bad may happen!*)
4 These two problems are obviously ________. (**clue**: not *connected*, although the meaning is the same)
5 I ________ you talk to Marie Pinon. (**clue**: the meaning is close to *recommend*, although less definite)
6 I'm ________ on you to come up with some ideas. (**clue**: not *relying*, although the meaning is the same)

3 Products and packaging

- wrap rage
- package design

Internet research

Search for the keywords *universal design packaging* to find out about Universal Design and its impact on packaging.

3.1 About business Packaging

Discussion

1 **With a partner, think of three examples of products which are packaged well or badly, and say why. Think about protection, identification, transport, storage, display and security.**

Listening for gist

2 1:28 **Listen to an interview with Charlie Wang, President of New China Packaging, a design consultancy based in Taipei, and answer the questions.**

1 Why does he think packaging is so important?
2 What is special about New China Packaging's approach?

Listening for detail

3 1:28 **Listen again and mark these statements *T* (true) or *F* (false).**

1 Branding is not enough to differentiate almost identical products.
2 Business guru Jack Trout thinks that companies overcommunicate their difference.
3 Most customers decide which product to buy before going to the store.
4 In the past, design teams were not told about financial and manufacturing problems so as not to limit their creativity.
5 Creative ideas are often simplified and adapted because focus groups don't like them.
6 The task force can't leave their hotel until every member of the team is enthusiastic about the new concept.
7 Consumers are not always conscious of what they need.
8 New China Packaging's task forces need months or years to deliver a consumer-validated package.

Discussion

4 **What do you think the advantages and disadvantages of using a cross-functional task force might be for the following situations?**

1 Interviewing new job candidates
2 Briefing software consultants who are designing new systems for the company
3 Setting up special deals with important customers
4 Creating new in-company training programmes

Scan reading

5 Read the article and answer the questions.

1 What is wrap rage?
2 Who suffers from it?
3 What triggers it?
4 What are the underlying causes?

Paraphrasing

6 Reformulate these phrases from the article in your own words.

1 *to reduce theft from shops* (line 10)
2 *the most common triggers of wrap rage* (line 22)
3 *even fighting to remove price tags … can raise blood pressure* (line 26)
4 *pure provocation to the ecologically-minded* (line 28)
5 *there's light at the end of the tunnel* (line 29)
6 *The bottom line is that if they don't react, they risk losing sales …* (line 32)

Discussion

Glossary PAGE 153

focus groups
frustration
interface with
provocation
rage
resistant
trigger
wrap

7 You have invented a new children's toy – MP-Bunny, an electronic rabbit which dances, talks and plays children's favourite songs. In small groups, discuss how you will package it. Think about the questions below.

1 What different materials could you use? What are their advantages and disadvantages?
2 What design elements will you incorporate? Think about shape, colour, photos, logos and text.
3 How will your packaging make your product look different from other electronic toys?

Present your packaging solution to another group.

WRAP RAGE

SURVEYS show that intense frustration and even injury caused by modern packaging is on the increase, especially amongst seniors. Seventy per cent of over 50s admit to injuring fingers, hands and shoulders as a result of 'wrap rage', a new term used to describe the irritation and loss of self-control experienced when struggling to open wrapping.

In recent years manufacturers have been under increasing pressure to keep food items sterile, to provide child-proof packaging for dangerous or toxic household cleaning products, to protect products during transport and to reduce theft from shops. At the same time, they are forced to keep costs to a minimum. As a result, packaging has become ever more resistant to fingers, nails and even teeth. In their frustration with plastic packs, which defeat all attempts to open them, even with scissors, consumers use all kinds of tools and knives. At best, the product inside the packaging is at risk; at worst, it is hardly surprising that 60,000 people a year are injured in Great Britain alone.

'… consumers use all kinds of tools and knives …'

Some of the most common triggers of wrap rage are processed cheese packages, tightly wrapped CDs, child-proof tops on medicine bottles, and milk and juice cartons. Ring-pull cans are particularly problematic for older fingers and delicate skin. Even fighting to remove price tags from items bought as gifts can raise blood pressure, and unnecessary overpackaging is pure provocation to the ecologically-minded.

However it seems there's light at the end of the tunnel. Manufacturers are listening to customers' complaints, and some have begun to research and invest in more consumer-friendly packaging. The bottom line is that if they don't react, they risk losing sales if customers simply stop buying products with packaging that offers too much resistance.

3 Products and packaging

- measurements
- product description
- expressions for product presentations

3.2 Vocabulary Specifications and features

Discussion

1 Put these stages of product development into the most likely chronological order.

- [6] Beta test the product by users in typical situations.
- [5] Conduct market studies to test the concept.
- [8] Launch the product.
- [4] Draw sketches and build mockups.
- [7] Go into production.
- [3] Draw up specifications for the product.
- [1] Generate new ideas in focus groups and brainstorming meetings.
- [2] Screen out unfeasible or unprofitable ideas.

Reading for detail

2 Read the information on the FedEx® Box and FedEx® Tube and complete the product specification summaries below.

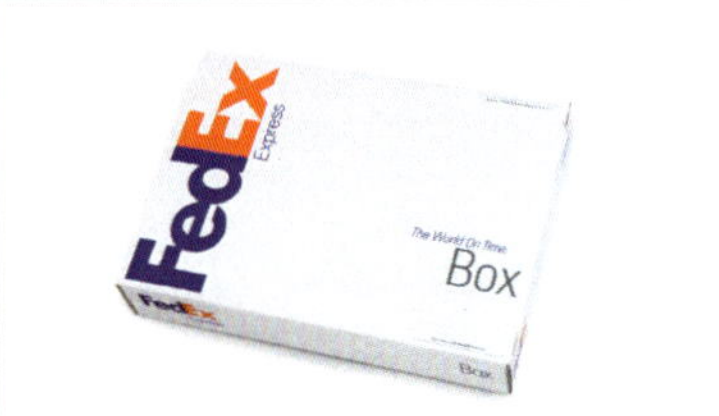

Inside dimensions

for Large FedEx Box **are**

width x length x height

31.4 x 45.4 x 7.6

For shipments weighing maximum 9 **kg**

Inside dimensions

for FedEx Tube **are**

96.5 x 15.2 x 15.2

long **wide** **high**

Maximum weight allowed 9 **kg**

1 The large FedEx Box is 31,4 cm wide and 45.4 cm long. It is 7.6 cm high. When empty, the box weighs 400 g; it can be used to ship small parts or computer printouts up to 9 kg in weight.

2 The FedEx Tube is 96.5 cm in length and 15.2 cm in width and height. With a capacity of 450 g when empty, it can be used to ship plans, posters, blueprints, etc. weighing up to 9 kg.

Describing products

3 Describe the dimensions of objects in your pockets or your bag. Your partner should try to guess what they are.

Collocations

4 Match the nouns in the box with the compound adjectives they most often collocate with.

design devices materials packaging personal stereos technology

energy-saving labour-saving	devices	child-resistant tamper-resistant	packaging
fire-retardant water-resistant	materials	future-proof fool-proof	technology
waterproof shockproof	personal stereos	eye-catching attention-grabbing	design

Internet research

What are the best ways of recording and learning vocabulary? Search for the keywords *recording vocabulary* and make a list of possible techniques. Rank the techniques on your list from the most to the least useful for you personally.

Listening for gist

5 1:29–1:34 **Listen to six conversations. Use collocations from Exercise 4 to describe what is being discussed.**

6 1:35 **Listen to a presentation of the ChartTech i3. What are its three main features?**

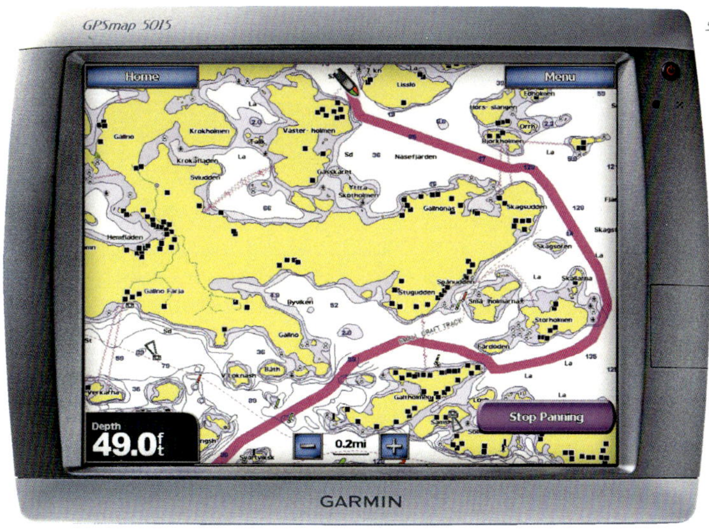

Listening for detail

7 1:35 **Listen again and complete these expressions for structuring a product presentation using the correct preposition from the box.**

about	back	by	on	to	up	with

1 I'm here today to tell you ______ (the ChartTech i3 ...).
2 Let's start ______ (Touch Screen Command).
3 Moving ______ to (what's below the water ...).
4 Can I just turn ______ (communications)?
5 I'll just sum ______ (the ChartTech i3's three main features ...).
6 Let's just go ______ to (our midnight fishing trip).
7 I'd like to finish ______ (inviting you to ...).

8 **Match the expressions in Exercise 7 with their function in the presentation a–d.**

a) Beginning the presentation ☐
b) Moving to a new point ☐
c) Returning to a point made earlier ☐
d) Ending the presentation ☐

Presentation

9 **Work in small groups. Use the vocabulary and expressions in the previous exercises to present the specifications and features of an electronic device of your choice.**

Glossary PAGE 153

attention-grabbing
bird's-eye view
blueprint
chart
fool-proof
mockup
overlay
retardant
tamper with

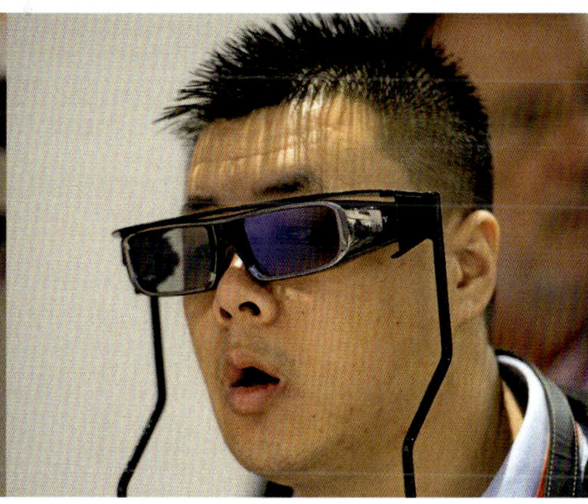

3 Products and packaging

- relative clauses
- *a/an*, *the* and no article
- noun combinations

3.3 Grammar Relative clauses, articles and noun combinations

Refresh your memory

Relative clauses
who: people
which: things
that: people or things, but not after a comma

Grammar and practice page 126

Articles
a/an: non-specific or not previously mentioned
the: specific, unique or previously mentioned
no article: generalizations

Grammar and practice page 126

Noun combinations
The main noun comes at the end. Any others describe it.

Grammar and practice page 127

Defining relative clauses

1 **In small groups, answer these business trivia questions.**

1 What was the communications device that was invented by John Logie Baird?
2 Who was the woman who is famous for her research on radioactivity?
3 What was the business process that was introduced by Henry Ford?
4 Who was the man who invented radio?
5 What was the business model first developed by Martha Matilda Harper in 1891?
6 What was the revolutionary pointing device which was invented by Douglas Engelbart in 1963?

2 **In your groups, write your own business and technology trivia quiz using the formulae 'Who was the man/woman …' or 'What was the product/device/process/model …'. Use the Internet if you have a connection. Then challenge another group.**

Non-defining relative clauses

3 **With a partner, take turns making sentences and adding relative clauses about famous people, products and organizations. How much information can you add?**

A: *Steve Jobs was the co-founder of Apple®.*
B: *Steve Jobs, who was from California, was the co-founder of Apple.*
A: *Steve Jobs, who was from California, was the co-founder of Apple, which is famous for high-end electronic products like the iPhone.*
B: *Steve Jobs, who was from California, and whose parents adopted him at birth, was the co-founder of Apple, which is famous for high-end electronic products like the iPhone.*

1 Steve Jobs, Apple (iPhone)
2 Oprah Winfrey, The Oprah Winfrey Show (Harpo Studios®)
3 Walt Disney, Walt Disney Co. (Mickey Mouse)
4 Mark Zuckerberg, Facebook (Facebook)
5 Ben Cohen and Jerry Greenfield, Ben & Jerry's (Yes Pecan)
6 Jeff Bezos, Amazon (Kindle)
7 Sergey Brin and Larry Page, Google (Google Earth)
8 Richard Branson, Virgin (Virgin Galactic)
9 Muhammed Yunus, Grameen Bank (micro-credit)
10 Victoria Beckham, Beckham Brand ('Intimately Beckham' perfumes)

Discussion

4 **Which of the people in Exercise 3 have had the biggest influence on the business world? Choose your top three.**

Articles

5 **Complete texts about important products and inventions with *a/an*, *the* or – (no article).**

Some popular products take a long time to get to the marketplace.

- In 1485, Leonardo da Vinci made detailed drawings of ___ parachutes. He also made sketches of ___ helicopter and ___ tank. ___ first helicopter that could carry ___ person was flown by Paul Cornu at ___ beginning of ___ twentieth century. During ___ First World War, ___ tanks were first used in ___ France in 1917.
- ___ Bar codes were invented by Silver and Woodland in 1948. They used ___ light to read ___ set of concentric circles, but it was two decades before ___ arrival of ___ computers and ___ lasers made ___ system practical.
- ___ first computer was built in 1943, more than 100 years after Charles Babbage had designed ___ first programmable device. In 1998, ___ Science Museum in London built ___ working copy of ___ Babbage machine using his original plans and ___ materials that would have been available at the time. It worked just as Babbage had intended.

Expanding notes

6 1:36 **When writing notes in English, pronouns, articles and common verbs like *be* and *have* are often omitted. Listen to a product review and write the words you hear which the customer omitted in the notes below.**

Easily best phone so far. Perfect phone for basic user. Already bumped and dropped few times but still going strong. Battery life incredible. Overall real workhorse. No frills, but does what cellphone needs to do. Rating 5/5.

7 1:37–1:38 **With a partner, expand these notes written by customers into full product reviews. Then listen and compare your versions with the recordings.**

1 *Hate the phone. Too small – can't open flip cover with one hand. No screen on outside to see caller identity. Reception – horrible. Drops calls probably 30% of time. Very long key delay, incredibly annoying. Anxiously awaiting day can upgrade and get rid of monstrosity. Rating 0/5.*

2 *Had phone about three weeks like size and design. Features good too. Easy enough to use, and survived couple of drops. However, alarm clock won't work anymore. Not too sure about internal antenna. Hate having full signal when making call, only to have dramatic drop when put phone to head. Everybody says telecom company's fault, not phone, or maybe just got bad one. We'll see. Going to try 9200 next. Rating 3/5.*

Internet research

Open an online dictionary by searching for the keywords *online dictionary*.
Search for the noun *information*. Is information countable or uncountable? What is its informal form? Which prepositions is it used with? What typical collocations and constructions is it used in?
Browse several online dictionaries and find out what other features they offer. Vote to find out which online dictionary the class prefers.

Defining words

8 **Complete the definitions by matching the noun combinations 1–4 with the appropriate relative clauses a–d.**

1 Decision-making tools are tools
2 Feature-packed spreadsheets are spreadsheets
3 An industry-standard battery package is a pack of batteries
4 Market studies are investigations

a) that have many different functions.
b) that companies conduct to identify customer needs.
c) that you evaluate choices and options with.
d) whose specifications comply with industry norms.

Glossary PAGE 154

bump
drop calls
empowerment
flip cover
get rid of
no frills
rating
workhorse

Definitions game

9 **In small groups, divide into As and Bs.**

As: turn to page 115. Bs: turn to page 121.

3 Products and packaging

- structuring a presentation
- hooks and objectives
- presenting a product

3.4 Speaking Presentations – structure

Brainstorming

1 What are the qualities of a good lesson, lecture or presentation? With a partner, draw up a checklist.

Listening for gist

2 1:39 Listen to Version 1 of a presentation of the Pingman, a new personal GPS tracking device which can be used to locate children, elderly people, animals or mobile staff. Compare the presentation with your checklist.

3 With a partner, discuss how the presentation could be improved.

Listening for detail

4 1:40 Listen to Version 2 of the presentation and answer the questions.

1 How does the presenter get the audience's attention and interest?
2 What is the objective of the presentation?
3 How long will the presentation last, and what is the next step?
4 What does the presenter say about questions?
5 What subjects will be covered in the three sections of the presentation?
6 Which part of the presentation do we not hear?
7 What does the presenter do at the beginning of the conclusion?
8 What does the presenter ask the audience to do?
9 How do the audience know when to applaud?
10 What aspects of presentation technique have improved in Version 2?

5 1:40 With a partner, find suitable words to complete the useful expressions in the checklist. Then listen again to Version 2 and check your answers.

Useful expressions: Structuring a presentation

Hook

__________ you like to know …?
What would you do if …?
__________ __________ would it be worth to …?
Somebody once said …

Objective

I'm here this morning to __________ the Pingman, …
My objective today is …
The goal of this meeting is …

Agenda

Feel __________ to interrupt me.
I've divided my presentation into three __________.
__________ of all, I'm going to …
__________ that, I'll be talking about …
__________, I'd like to present …
I'll take any questions at the end.

Summary

I'd like to __________ up the presentation and move on to …
__________, I explained why …
__________, I presented the different specifications …
Last, but not __________, I have given you …

Call for action

These are the __________ why I am asking you to …

Close

Thank you very much for your __________.
Thank you for listening.
If you have any questions, I'll do my best to answer them.

Internet research

Search for the keywords *presentation tips* to find answers to the questions below.

1 How long should a good presentation be?
2 What should you research before a presentation?
3 What are the most important parts of a presentation?
4 What are the best ways to practise a presentation?
5 Which colours and fonts should you use in your slides?
6 How should you deal with hostile questions?
7 What's the latest presentation technology available?

eWorkbook
Now watch the video for this unit.

Glossary PAGE 154

hook
lecture
overwhelmingly
ping
tracking
wrap up

Pronunciation

6 1:41 **Decide where the speaker should pause in this extract from the presentation. Before each pause, mark whether the speaker's voice should go up ↗ or down ↘, as in the examples. Then listen and compare your answers.**

I've divided my presentation into three sections. ↘ First of all, ↗ I'm going to remind you of the background to this project and the current offer on the market. After that, I'll be talking about the prototype, and the data we've collected from tests, focus groups and market studies. Finally, I'd like to present a business plan; this will demonstrate why we expect a return on investment that is without precedent for our company. Is everybody happy with that agenda?

7 **Underline the key syllables and key words which should be stressed, and draw a line between words which should be linked (_), as in the example below.**

I've di<u>vi</u>ded my presen<u>ta</u>tion_into <u>three</u> <u>sec</u>tions. First_of_all, …

8 1:41 **Listen again and compare your answers. Then practise reading the extract with correct intonation, stress and linking.**

Presentation

9 **In small groups, prepare the introduction and conclusion of a presentation of one of these new products to a group of department store buyers.**

- a flexible tablet PC that can be rolled up to fit in a pocket
- furniture which changes colour and temperature depending on the light and room temperature
- a T-shirt which displays a text message that can be modified from a mobile phone
- your own product idea

Think about the following questions.

Hook: What is the most surprising, exciting or unusual aspect of your product?
Objective: Why are you making the presentation and what do you hope to obtain?
Agenda: How will you organize your presentation and what will happen after the talk?
Summary: What are the highlights of your talk?
Call for action: What do you want your audience to do now?
Close: How can you avoid an embarrassing silence at the end of your presentation?

10 **In your group, present your introduction and conclusion and answer any questions. (Assume the body of the talk has been presented.) The rest of the class are the buyers. As a class, vote for the best product presentation.**

3 Products and packaging

- structure analysis
- features and benefits
- writing a product description

3.5 Writing A product description

Discussion

1 **Read the items in the box and identify the four features of this car and the four corresponding benefits to consumers. Then discuss the questions below.**

ABS air-conditioned comfort alloy wheels automatic climate control
head-turning good looks power on demand safe braking and cornering
3.0l V6 engine

1 What do you look for in a car – features or benefits? Why?
2 When you buy a computer, a mobile phone, or software, are you more interested in its features or benefits? What about other products?

Model

2 **Read the product description and list the main benefits of using OpenOffice.**

OpenOffice.org.3

Great software ... Easy to use ... and it's free!

A OpenOffice.org 3 is the leading open-source office software suite. It is available in many languages and works on all common computers. It stores all your data in an international open standard format and can also read and write files from other common office software packages. It can be downloaded and used completely free of charge for any purpose.

A new approach to office productivity software

B OpenOffice.org 3 gives you everything you'd expect in office software. You can create dynamic documents, analyze data, design eye-catching presentations, produce dramatic illustrations and open up your databases. You can publish your work in Portable Document Format (PDF) and release your graphics in Flash (SWF) format – without needing any additional software.

C If you're used to using other office suites – such as Microsoft Office® – you'll be completely at home with OpenOffice.org 3. However, as you become used to OpenOffice.org 3, you'll start to appreciate the extras that make your life easier. You can of course continue to use your old Microsoft Office files without any problems – and if you need to exchange files with people still using Microsoft Office, that's no problem either.

What's in the suite?

D WRITER – a powerful tool for creating professional documents. You can easily integrate images and charts in documents, create everything from business letters to complete books and web content.
CALC – a feature-packed spreadsheet. Use advanced spreadsheet functions and decision-making tools to perform sophisticated data analysis. Use built-in charting tools to generate impressive 2D and 3D charts.
IMPRESS – the fastest way to create effective multimedia presentations. Your presentations will truly stand out with special effects, animation and high-impact drawing tools.
DRAW – produce everything from simple diagrams to dynamic 3D illustrations and special effects.
Find out more – try it today!
Get OpenOffice.org 3 now!
Go to www.openoffice.org for an introduction in Flash format.

Analysis

3 **Number the five sections in the box in the order they appear in the OpenOffice.org text above.**

background compatibility details of features and benefits
invitation overview of benefits

Internet research

Search for the keywords *open source software* to learn about free software, including games. Choose one product, and write a short description; try to 'sell' your software to your classmates.

Language focus

4 **R&D departments often focus on describing features, while marketing departments prefer to describe benefits to consumers. Read the eight features described by R&D and underline their corresponding benefits in the text in Exercise 2.**

1 Open source code application available to download (Paragraph A)
It can be downloaded and used completely free of charge for any purpose.
2 Fully integrated suite of office applications (Paragraph B)
3 Supports PDF and SWF publishing without plug-ins (Paragraph B)
4 Intuitive user interface (Paragraph C)
5 Fully compatible with other document formats (Paragraph C)
6 Image integration capability (Paragraph D)
7 Built-in 2D and 3D charting tools (Paragraph D)
8 Diagram and special effects functions (Paragraph D)

5 **Reformulate the product features of the Creole Audio Manager, pictured on the right, in terms of benefits.**

1 Fully integrated multi-format audio and video player
Creole gives you everything you'd expect from an audio player; watch and play video and music in all popular formats.
2 Downloadable shareware
3 Full PC and Mac compatibility
4 Music search, download and organizer features
5 Online radio and TV capability
6 Built-in CD burning tool
7 Intuitive user interface and foolproof operation
8 Karaoke function

Glossary PAGE 154

alloy
benefit
feature
intuitive
plug-in
quibble
stand out

Writing

6 **Write a product description of the Torrent tablet PC using the notes below. (Alternatively, use a product of your choice.) Focus on the benefits to consumers, adding any details you feel are appropriate.**

Background	New Torrent now available – all features of Apple® iPad at a fraction of the price. Smaller, lighter, stronger.
Overview of benefits	Only 1cm thick, ultra-light, unlimited free cloud storage, access to movies, TV, albums, books, magazines, newspapers, 50,000+ apps.
Details of features and benefits	Attention-grabbing design Shock proof, water-resistant aluminium case and Gorilla Glass screen Intuitive touch-screen interface 18cm x 12cm x 1cm, 345g 64 gigabytes storage 15 hour autonomy WiFi and 3G GPS Screen resolution 1024x768 Front and rear camera, headphone jack, USB port. Android OS and browser Office software Battery life 12hrs 2-year guarantee
Invitation	2-week no quibble money-back guarantee

- product differentiation
- formulating a development strategy
- presenting recommendations

3.6 Case study Big Jack's Pizza

Discussion

1 **In one minute, list as many fast-food businesses as you can. How does each of them try to differentiate itself from its competitors?**

Scan reading

2 **Read the documents and answer the questions.**

1 What sort of company is Big Jack's Pizza? franchisee
2 Who is Jack Jr? President & CEO
3 What is Big Jack's USP (unique selling point)? 24/7 home delivery
4 What proportion of Big Jack's customers eat in the restaurants? 28+4%
5 What is the company's development strategy? relaunch products
6 What is the biggest threat to the company? Pizza Hut and other
7 What do customers like and dislike about Big Jack's? nearby, availability, taste
8 What four changes is Jack Jr suggesting?

Big Jack's Pizza

Big pizzas, big value!

23 stores in Hong Kong, Kowloon and New Territories
dine-in, parties, takeout or 24/7 home delivery

Call us now on 2893 6161
Become a Big Jack's franchisee - call 2893 5468

INBOX | REPLY | FORWARD

Re: Marketing meeting tomorrow
Billie, Mick,
I've attached the latest figures and customer-feedback summary, which seem to confirm what we discussed last time. Restaurant sales are holding up but, as expected, our takeout and delivery revenues are down again this month.
If we want to defend our market share against Pizza Hut and the other international majors, and attract new franchisees, we desperately need to relaunch our product.
So, here's the agenda for the meeting:
1 a new, more exciting range of pizzas
2 new promotional ideas
3 a new or updated logo and color scheme
4 a new box for takeout and delivery
Looking forward to hearing your ideas on all these points tomorrow.
Jack Jr
President & CEO

Why did you buy a Big Jack's pizza?

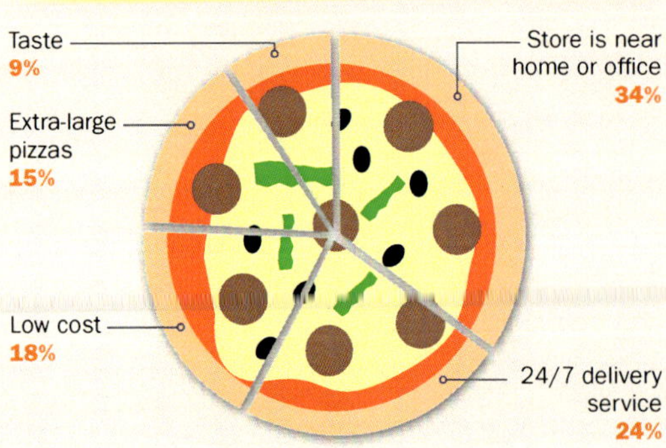

Big Jack's Pizza Revenues

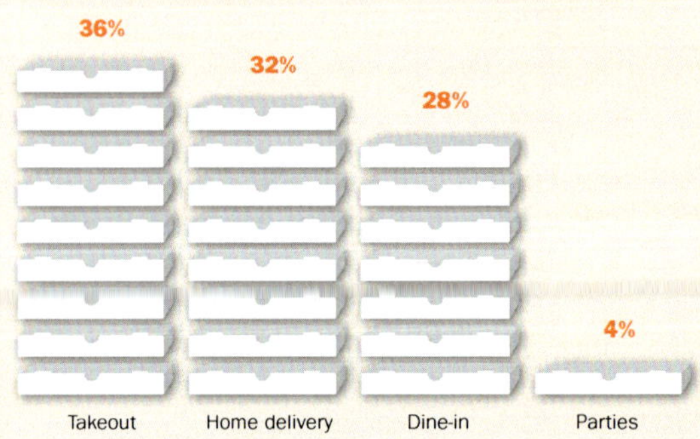

Internet research

Search for the keywords *pizza box advertising* to find out how companies are using a new way to get their messages into the home.

Glossary PAGE 154

BOGOF
chequered
dine-in
franchisee
fusion cuisine
gourmet
slide
strengthen
threat
USP

Listening for gist

3 1:42 **Listen to an extract from the marketing meeting at Big Jack's. What two decisions are made?**

Listening for inference

4 1:42 **Listen again and list the ten suggestions made by Billie and Mick. Which ones does Jack like?**

5 **Match the diplomatic phrases on the left with their real, more direct, meanings on the right.**

1 Of course, but we can come back to that later?
2 Can we move on to point two?
3 Well, Billie, it's been done before, but I guess we could do that. Why not?
4 I'm sorry?
5 I'm not sure that's a direction we really want to go in.
6 That's more the kind of thing I had in mind.
7 I think you feel strongly about this?
8 Things have changed since Big Jack's time.
9 This is all very interesting, but …
10 I trust you'll agree.

a) It's not a wonderful idea, but it's a possibility.
b) It's not a priority right now.
c) It's a bad idea.
d) I don't want to waste more time on this.
e) I know we disagree about this.
f) Big Jack's is old-fashioned.
g) What are you talking about?
h) It's not exactly what I wanted, but better than your previous ideas.
i) I've decided, whether you like it or not.
j) This isn't relevant.

Brainstorming and presentation

6 **Work in small groups as consultants to Big Jack's Pizza and do the following tasks.**

1 Read the brief below from Big Jack's Pizza.
2 Brainstorm and select the best ideas.
3 Prepare a presentation to the company's management.
4 Present your recommendations and take questions from the class.

Big Jack's Pizza wishes to strengthen its brand and improve its packaging. Please provide advice on the following points:

- **a new range of fusion cuisine pizzas: exciting names needed for at least five pizzas**
- **new promotional ideas**
- **a new or updated logo, color scheme and slogan**
- **a new box or box design for takeout and delivery.**

Estimated impact of implementing changes on packaging and advertising costs:

- **change logo + 2%**
- **three-color printing + 1%**
- **four-color printing + 2%**
- **non-standard box shape + 2%**
- **non-standard box materials + 2%.**

NB Big Jack's will not accept an increase of more than 5%.

Recurrent negative customer comments:

'The pizzas all taste the same.'

'Big Jack's is old-fashioned – it's time for a change.'

'The pizzas are too big; I can never finish them.'

'The slices slide around in the box and get stuck together.'

'No different from other pizza houses – same pizzas, same colors, same box, same price.'

4 Careers

- careers, jobs and vocations
- managing your career

4.1 About business Career choices

Discussion

1 **Mark your position on the scales below. With a partner, explain and justify your choices.**

I have no idea how my career will develop.	◄—+—+—+—+—►	I have a clear idea of my career path.
I expect to work for one company all my life.	◄—+—+—+—+—►	I expect to work for several different companies in my life.
Money, status and a comfortable lifestyle are my priorities.	◄—+—+—+—+—►	Job satisfaction, variety and being useful to society are my priorities.

Internet research

Search for the keywords *personality profile test* and do at least one online test. Compare your results with a classmate and discuss how well they describe your personality.

Predicting and listening

2 1:43 **You are going to hear a talk for university students about how to choose a career. In part one, Charlie Schumann, a popular careers coach, talks about two things you *shouldn't* do, and two things you *have* to do. Before you listen, try to predict what those things might be. Then listen and check your predictions.**

Listening for detail

3 1:43 **Listen to Part 1 again and mark these statements *T* (true) or *F* (false).**

1 Schumann says you should choose something you love doing and that feels right for you. ☐
2 She recommends going to the Himalayas to learn martial arts. ☐
3 Myers Briggs (MBT®) and Keirsey are Kung Fu experts. ☐
4 You don't need to research a lot of careers, only those that suit your personality profile. ☐
5 Facebook and Google+ are a great place to read about potential career choices. ☐

4 1:44 **Listen to Part 2 of the talk and answer the questions.**

1 According to Schumann, which of these factors are more likely to make you happy? Money, variety, fame, autonomy, beauty, recognition, team spirit, job security, helping people.
2 What are 'flow' activities?

Discussion

5 **In small groups, discuss your reactions to these statements from the talk.**

1 'This is maybe the one time in your life when you need to be totally selfish'.
2 'Tests like Myers Briggs or Keirsey are not a hundred per cent reliable'.
3 'Having more money doesn't actually make you any happier'.
4 'Jobs that let you experience that 'flow' (are) the key to … your ideal career'.

Scan reading

6 **Read the article opposite and find which two tips can be summarized as:**

1 Move towards your long-term goal in small, easy stages.
2 Make sure that preconceived ideas about success and failure are not preventing you from reaching your goals.

Summarizing

7 **Summarize each of the eight remaining tips in one sentence. In small groups, compare your sentences with other people and choose the best summary for each tip.**

Glossary PAGE 154

earth-shattering
inertia
jump in at the deep end
pick someone's brains
posse
start the ball rolling
stay put
treadmill

Ten Tips for Creating a Career That LIGHTS YOUR FIRE

Have you ever found yourself so excited about something that the energy it generates just seems to pull you along? Imagine feeling that every day in the work you do. It's possible! Begin exploring your passions and discovering ways, big or small, to incorporate them into your life.

1 GET TO KNOW YOURSELF – Before you start off in pursuit of a career that really lights your fire, take some time to do some serious self-exploration. Make a list of all the things in your life that you have really enjoyed. It could be work or play, an event, a period of time in your life, etc. Pick one and start digging into the reasons why. Get beyond what you love doing, and break it down into the underlying characteristics. Think of it as identifying your passion's building blocks.

2 BRAINSTORM – Once you have a picture of the things that light your fire, brainstorm ways you could incorporate them into your life. Write them down alone or with friends, in one session or on a small pad of paper you carry with you. Above all, be creative. You never know what crazy idea is going to spark the Big One.

3 EXPLORE – Ask, ask, ask! Once you have identified some things you think you might be interested in, identify people who are knowledgeable in those areas and contact them. Explain that you are exploring your options and ask if you can pick their brains. You'll get some fantastic insights if you make this a habit, not to mention making some great contacts along the way.

4 BABY STEPS – The fear of jumping in the deep end of the passion pool keeps many people from swimming at all. Remember there's a shallow end too, so you can still enjoy splashing in the water. Look for baby steps you can take that will bring your passion into your life and keep you moving towards your long-term goal.

5 IDENTIFY YOUR OBSTACLES – What things are getting in your way? Make a list. Maybe they're real financial obstacles, or perhaps the need for more training. Maybe they are internal. What's stopping you? Fear? Self-doubt? Simple inertia? We all have voices in our heads that are always telling us 'You can't do that', 'You're not good enough', 'What will they think?', etc. Identifying and acknowledging those voices is the first step in taking their power away.

6 CREATE A PASSION POSSE – In my interviews with people who have followed their dream, the most commonly mentioned success factor has been the support of the people around them. Friends, family and colleagues can all be a great source of support and inspiration. It can be an informal support network, or a regularly scheduled meeting to exchange ideas and brainstorm solutions to challenges.

7 RE-EXAMINE YOUR DEFINITIONS OF SUCCESS AND FAILURE – What is your definition of success? Is it getting in the way? Our culture places a lot of emphasis on material accomplishments, status, etc.

Unfortunately, that gets in the way of real happiness for a lot of people, who choose to stay on the treadmill in pursuit of that version of success. Perhaps you're not at a point where you can or want to change that definition of success. That's OK; don't. Instead, try identifying one or two less common ways of identifying 'success' – ones that come from the heart – and try to move towards them as well.

Our definition of failure, which tends to be all or nothing, also gets in the way. If you try something and it doesn't pan out, how do you see that? Is it a failure? Or is it an opportunity to learn? If you 'fail' in an effort to move toward your passion, it's not really failure. Think of it as a step in the right direction. Taking a longer term view can help with this.

8 MAKE A PLAN – Whether it's a high level overview or a step by step action plan, it is up to you – you know how you work best. Creating a plan will force you to think things through and add some comfortable structure to something that can seem very up in the air and undefined.

9 ACT! TODAY! – The fact is, the time will never be right. Something is always going to be less than optimum. Don't wait! Do something right now that will move you toward your passion. What two things can you do right away that will start the ball rolling? They don't need to be earth-shattering, they just need to happen.

10 COMMIT TO MAKING IT HAPPEN – Let it out of your brain and into the open. Say, 'I am going to do this.' Say it out loud to yourself. Say it to a friend. Put it in writing and put it where you can see it. Once it's out in the open it will have room to grow. And that's exactly what you want!

4 Careers

- job benefits
- recruitment and employment verbs
- skills and qualities

4.2 Vocabulary Careers, personal skills and qualities

Discussion

1 **Rank these benefits from the most (9) to the least desirable (1), in your opinion.**

Christmas bonus   company car   free accommodation   free medical insurance   luncheon vouchers   pension plan   profit-sharing   sports and social facilities   stock options

Careers and employment

2 **Put the events in Josef Gutkind's career in logical order.**

Part 1

- [1] Before graduating, Josef **applied for** jobs in 20 companies.
- [ ] Wilson Brothers **offered** Josef **a position as** a management trainee.
- [ ] His first interview was successful and he **was short-listed for** a second interview.
- [ ] When Wilson's got into difficulties, Josef was **made redundant**.
- [ ] Two years later he **was appointed** Logistics Manager.
- [ ] He was invited for an **interview** at Wilson Brothers.

Part 2

- [ ] In his early fifties he **took a sabbatical** to write a book.
- [ ] Josef quickly **found a new job**, but **was dismissed** after arguing with his boss.
- [ ] The book was a best-seller, and Josef **resigned from** the firm.
- [ ] While he was **unemployed** Josef studied for a master's degree.
- [ ] He **retired** from business and now lives in the south of France.
- [ ] Thanks to the masters on his CV, Josef **was hired by** a firm of consultants.

3 **Use appropriate expressions in bold from Exercise 2 above to complete these job interview questions. Change the form as necessary.**

1 Could you tell me exactly why you _________ _________ from OQP?
2 Were the departments merged before or after you _________ _________ Quality Manager?
3 After the factory closed, was it difficult to _________ _________?
4 Have you _________ _________ jobs in other companies in the area?
5 If you _________ _________ for a second interview, would you be able to come to our head office in London?
6 How would you feel if we _________ you _________ as a product manager?

4 **Now correct these sentences from a biography. The words in bold have been mixed up. Put them back in the right places.**

1 Aisha's résumé was impressive; she was **dismissed** without even attending a first interview.
2 At the second interview, Aisha did so well that she was **made redundant** on the spot.
3 A few years later, she wrote her first novel while she was **unemployed**; it sold only 400 copies.
4 Aisha was an unconventional journalist who preferred to work at night; after arriving four hours late for a meeting she was **hired**.
5 When the editor in her next job refused to publish a controversial article she had written, Aisha immediately offered to **retire** but the editor refused to let her.
6 However, when the newspaper was taken over by a larger competitor, Aisha was **short-listed**.
7 After difficult times while she was **on sabbatical**, she was finally able to live in comfort when her sixth novel became a best-seller.
8 She was 74 when she finally decided to **resign** from writing novels.

Internet research

Search for the keyword *mentoring* to find out how a mentor can help employees with their personal development.

Collocations

5 In each set of five below, match a verb 1–10 with a noun a–j to make collocations for describing skills and qualities.

1 take	a) a commitment to
2 make	b) initiative
3 be	c) good working relationships
4 work	d) a good listener
5 build	e) to strict deadlines
6 work	f) a busy workload
7 make	g) ownership
8 manage	h) closely with
9 possess	i) a valuable contribution to
10 take on	j) strong negotiating skills

6 Use eight of the collocations from Exercise 5 to complete the sentences below. Change the verb form if necessary.

1 I enjoy taking initiative, and I keep my promises; when I ____________ to a project, I always deliver.
2 I have a lot of experience in ____________ both product development and sales teams, and can adapt to their different working styles.
3 I have excellent organizational skills, and I hate being late – so I have no problem with ____________.
4 I liaise with government officials: fortunately, I ____________.
5 I'm used to ____________; I'm good at multitasking, and coping with pressure is no problem.
6 I often ____________ of projects with multi-million dollar budgets.
7 I believe I can ____________ any work group.
8 I ____________, so I build good working relationships with colleagues.

7 Which two answers in Exercise 6 could you give to each of these questions?

a) Are you able to take responsibility? ☐☐
b) Are you a good communicator? ☐☐
c) Are you a good time manager? ☐☐
d) Are you a good team worker? ☐☐

Listening for gist

8 1:45 Listen to an extract from a human resources review meeting. Mark these employees as high-fliers (+) or as concerns (-).

Rachel Ratcliff Paul Stevens Michael Diegel Shane Garney

Taking notes

9 1:45 Listen again. Take notes on the problem, causes and possible solutions for Rachel, Michael and Shane.

	Rachel	Michael	Shane
problem			
causes			
possible solutions			

Glossary PAGE 155

controversial
flag (verb)
headhunter
liaise with
multitasking
on the spot
unconventional
wannabe

Discussion

10 In small groups, decide what you would do about Rachel, Michael and Shane.

- present simple, present continuous
- present perfect, present perfect continuous

Refresh your memory

Present simple
I *work* best late at night.
permanent or recurrent present actions or situations

Present continuous
I'*m not working* on anything special at the moment.
temporary present actions or situations

Present perfect simple
I've never *worked* in sales, but I *have worked* in a café.
life experience up to now, or present result of a past action

Present perfect continuous
I'*ve been working* too hard – I'm exhausted!
action in progress up to now

▶ **Grammar and practice** page 128

4.3 Grammar Present tenses

The bluffing game

1 **Complete the sentences below with information about yourself that other students don't know. Use the present simple, present continuous, present perfect simple and present perfect continuous. Four of your sentences should be true, the other four should be untrue.**

1 I often …
2 I don't usually …
3 At the moment, I'm …
4 Right now, I'm not …
5 I've never …
6 I've already …
7 Recently, I've been …
8 For some time now, I haven't been …

2 **In groups, take turns reading your sentences out and answering other students' questions. The group has to decide whether you are telling the truth or bluffing. Who is the best bluffer?**

Present perfect and past simple

3 **You and your partner work for an international recruitment agency. Your clients are looking for:**

1 a Spanish-speaking science graduate
2 an undergraduate with marketing experience
3 a graduate accountant, to be a future finance director
4 a French-speaking graduate in business
5 an arts undergraduate with experience in the Far East
6 a Portuguese-speaking graduate with experience in sales.

You have each interviewed and tested five candidates. Exchange information with your partner and decide together which candidates are most suitable for each request.

Student A: use the information below.
Student B: turn to page 117.

Candidate	Graduation	Work experience	Management potential test
Mr Salmon	next summer, Chemistry	pullover sales in Mexico	B
Ms Bianco			
Mrs Grey	next June, Marketing	nurse in New York	B
Miss Rose			
Mr Da Silva	last December, MBA	own business in Brazil	C–
Mr Green			
Mr Schwartz	last October, Accountancy	banks in Geneva, Monaco, Portugal	A+
Miss Plum			
Ms Violeta	next spring, History	holiday club in Thailand	B
Mr Braun			

Internet research

Search for the keywords *English grammar practice* to explore the many websites offering grammar explanations and exercises. In class, hold a vote to find your favourite grammar site.

Listening: present perfect simple and continuous

4 1:46–1:55 **Listen to situations 1–10 and match them with the pictures A–J.**

5 1:46–1:55 **Listen again and write down what has happened or has been happening in each situation. Then compare your ideas with a partner.**

Asking questions

6 **With a partner, take turns interviewing each other for a job.**

Student A: turn to page 115.
Student B: turn to page 118.

Glossary PAGE 155

assault course
hand
knock over
relevant
undergraduate
You're kidding

4 Careers

- preparing for interviews
- answering interview questions
- roleplaying a job interview

4.4 Speaking Job interviews

Discussion

1 How would you answer the following interview questions?

1 Where do you see yourself in five years' time?
2 How do you motivate people to do their best?
3 What are your weaknesses?
4 Can you give an example of a situation you found stressful, and how you coped with the stress?

Listening

2 1.56–1.59 Listen to extracts from four job interviews A–D. Which candidate(s):

1 give(s) concrete examples from their experience?
2 ask(s) questions to make sure they answer the interviewer's question?
3 structure(s) the answer in two parts?
4 turn(s) a question about a negative point into an opportunity to emphasize a positive quality?

3 1.56–1.59 Listen again and complete the checklist of useful expressions for answering job interview questions.

Useful expressions: Answering interview questions

Asking for clarification or reformulating

I'm sorry, could you expand on what you mean by …?
Do you __________, …?

Structuring your answer

I'd like to answer that in two ways: firstly, … secondly, …
I think there are two important __________ to this question …

Talking about yourself

I __________ what I learned.
I see __________ as a top performing employee in a leading company.
I plan to __________ experience and learn new skills.
I would be ready to __________ up to a position with more responsibility.
I realized that knowing how well you're __________ is essential to staying motivated.
I'm __________ that there are areas that I can improve on.
I don't feel that I have any __________ weaknesses.
I would say that organization is one of my __________.
I __________ to finish the project on time.

Playing for time

That's a very interesting question. I would say …
That's a difficult question to __________; let's __________ that …

Giving concrete examples

Let me give you an example of what I mean.
Take …, for __________.

Validating your answer

Is that what you wanted to know?
Does that __________ your question?

Internet research

Search for the keywords *interview advice tips* to find out how to succeed in job interviews.

4 The candidates in Exercise 2 used these expressions. Put the words in **bold** in the correct order.

1 I applied **what learned I**.
2 I'm able **being unpopular with to cope**.
3 I see myself **performing as top a a employee company in leading**.
4 I plan **experience to gain new and skills learn**.
5 I would be ready **more a move to position up with to responsibility**.
6 I realized that knowing **well you're how motivated essential doing is to staying**.
7 I'm aware **there that on that areas are can I improve**.
8 I don't feel **weaknesses I any have that significant**.
9 I would say **my organization is that one of strengths**.
10 I managed **on finish to the time project**.

5 Read the quotation and mark the interview questions a–h as type 1 or type 2 questions.

> The good news is that there are only two interview questions. That is, regardless of what you're asked, the employer really only wants to know:
> 1 What value can you add to my enterprise as an employee (and can you prove it)?
> 2 Why do you want this job?

a) What are your strengths and weaknesses?
b) Why do you want to work for us?
c) What is your greatest achievement?
d) How do you make sure things get done?
e) Why do you want to leave your present job?
f) Tell me about a time when you successfully handled a difficult situation.
g) What sort of environment would you prefer not to work in?
h) What are the most difficult kinds of decisions for you to make?

With a partner, ask and answer the questions using expressions from Exercises 3 and 4, inventing any details as necessary.

Glossary PAGE 155

achievement
cope with
rapport
regardless of
strengths
weaknesses

eWorkbook
Now watch the video for this unit.

Roleplay

6 With a partner, roleplay an interview for one of the jobs below.

Interviewer
Interview the candidate for the job they have chosen. Invent further information about the job as necessary. For each of your questions, note whether the answer is satisfactory or not. At the end of the interview, give the candidate feedback on how well they performed.

Candidate
Let the interviewer lead the conversation initially, but try to develop an exchange by asking questions about the job and the organization.

Multinational oil company

seeks **future managers** to lead development teams for alternative energies in Norway, Indonesia and South America.

Strong leadership and communication skills essential.

Motivating compensation package.

For details visit www.nuenergeez.com

Leading consultancy requires business graduates to train as **auditors** and **consultants**

Vacancies in London, Paris, New York, Tokyo
Candidates should be analytical, independent and able to develop a rapport with clients in all sectors
Competitive salary and benefits
Send CV to Jane O'Hara – johara@acc.jobs.org

Music major seeks dynamic **tour managers** to organize and manage promotional tours for top pop, rock, and R&B acts

80% of time on tour
Successful candidates will have strong intercultural, negotiation, people- and crisis-management skills
Salary and performance-related bonus
Contact Sue – sue.rhodes@mjmc.biz

- CV structure
- appropriate language
- writing a CV

4.5 Writing A CV

Discussion

1 **Discuss why you agree or disagree with the following statements about writing CVs or résumés.**

1 You should never use more than one page.
2 You should describe your experience first, then your qualifications.
3 You should list five or six people who can be contacted for a reference.
4 You should always include a photograph.

Model

2 **Decide in what order you expect the following categories to occur in a CV. Then read the CV below to check.**

general additional skills   personal details   positions of responsibility
qualifications   references   voluntary roles   work experience

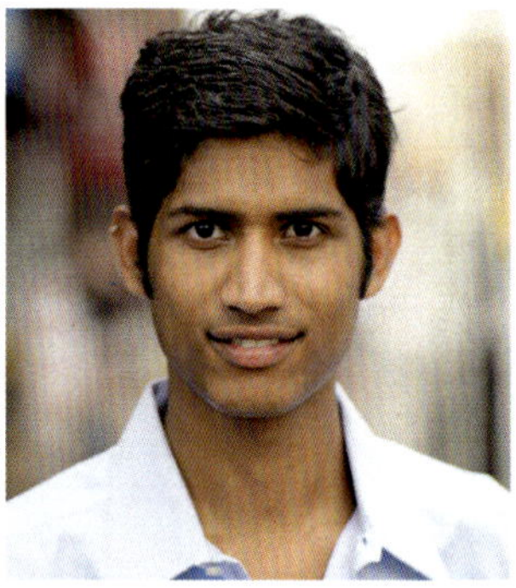

Robert Khan

Date of birth	29 April 1991
Nationality	British
Current address	27 Keats Road, London SE4 3KL (until 30 June)
Tel:	020 8088 8965
Permanent address	247 Newmarket Road, Norwich NR4 1ET
Tel:	01603 443143

EDUCATION

2010–2013	BA in Business Studies at Chelsea School of Business (Exam results to date 2:2; Expected final grade 2:1)
2007–2010	Norwich School: 3 'A' levels: Economics (A), Maths (B), History (C)
2003–2007	Norwich School: 10 GCSEs, including Maths and English

WORK HISTORY

Jan–June 2012	*Work placement, Atherton Consultants* I played an integral part in a team of consultants working on IS projects. This position required familiarity with networking solutions and Web design and involved liaising with a client's parent company in Germany.
July–Sept 2011	*Vacation Trainee, Jardine, White & Partners* I coordinated an office reorganization project.
2010–2011	*Sales Assistant, Kaufhaus des Westens, Berlin* I was responsible for managing the outdoor exhibition of camping equipment. I ran a language training programme for members of the department.

POSITIONS OF RESPONSIBILITY

2011–2012	*President of CSB Students' Union* I represented over 400 members in faculty meetings and organized and chaired conferences with visiting speakers.
2011 to present	*Captain of CSB Squash Team* I run training sessions and am responsible for organizing matches and motivating the team.

OTHER

Fluent German
Advanced computer literacy: Office software, networking and Web design
3rd trombone in the London Students' Jazz Orchestra
Clean driving licence

REFERENCES

See next page

Internet research

Search for the keywords *résumé style* to find out about different résumé styles to consider, including *functional*, *skills* and *chronological* styles.

Analysis

3 Underline all the verbs in Robert's CV in Exercise 2. What do you notice?

Language focus

4 Read the CV again. How has Robert formulated the following information in more appropriate language?

1 I sometimes phoned people in Germany.
2 I'm good with computers.
3 I was the contact for the removal company for the transfer to new offices.
4 I gave some colleagues some English lessons.
5 I spoke on behalf of 400 students in meetings with teachers.
6 I was the general assistant to the computer consultants.
7 I sold tents.
8 I had to learn how to set up a LAN.
9 I'm the only member of the team who believes we can win.
10 My job was to introduce the speakers and thank them at the end.

Output

5 Read the facts about Justine Collier and organize the information under the five headings used in Robert Khan's CV. Then write Justine's CV using relevant language and expressions from Exercise 4.

- Voluntary work since 2008 – OUTLOOK, charity for disabled children – parties, visits, etc.
- Play violin in string quartet
- University basketball team – my job to bring drinks
- 2005–2007 Northern High School 'A' level Maths (A), Economics (B), French (B)
- Secretary, Newcastle Junior Chamber of Commerce in 2009 – minutes of meetings, monthly newsletter, etc. Sometimes phoned VIP to invite to receptions, etc.
- June–Sept 2004 Holiday job, Newcastle Social Security; entered personnel data into new HR management software. Confidential, very boring. Visitor from Spanish government, three days.
- References – tutor, Mr. Bowers, Newcastle University, Mrs Broadbent, Principal, Northern High School
- Typing speed 90 wpm
- Justine Dominga Collier
- 14 Green Street, Newcastle NE13 8BH   Tel: 01879 122 7789
- Oct–Mar 2005 Internship Arbol Oil: finance department, small jobs, learned accounts software, email from S America
- Bilingual Spanish
- 4/11/89, Auckland NZ
- 2007–2010 BA Economics, Newcastle University (maybe 2:1 if I'm lucky)

6 Write (or update) your own CV.

4 Careers

- taking a gap year
- applying for a placement
- placement interviews

Internet research

Search for the keywords *gap year* to read about some of the ways students (and other age groups) are using their gap years.

4.6 Case study Gap years and career breaks

Brainstorming

1 **Brainstorm the advantages and disadvantages of taking a year off before or after university or in mid-career. How many different ways of spending a gap year can you think of?**

Listening

2 2.01–2.06 **Listen to six interviews with people who took a gap year and answer the questions.**

1 When and where did they take their year out?
2 Were their experiences positive, negative or mixed? Why?

Scan reading

3 **Read the advertisement and answer the questions.**

1 Who can apply for a gap-year placement, and when?
2 What are the four benefits of a gap-year placement mentioned in the advertisement?
3 What kind of work is available?
4 Do you get paid/have to pay?
5 How do you apply?

Want to change the world, or just want a change?

Whether you are still a student or already in work, a gap-year placement is a unique opportunity to broaden your horizons, enhance your CV and step back from your studies or career to decide what you want to do with your life. Perhaps more importantly, a gap-year placement is the chance to do something concrete and tangible to help people in need in underprivileged areas of the world.

Placements are designed for people over 17 years of age, and run for six or nine months throughout the world. All placements begin with an intensive orientation course to help you find your feet; for some countries, an optional ten-day intensive language course is recommended. Participants work as volunteers in sectors such as education, conservation, medical support and care work. Food and accommodation are provided, but participants pay their own travel costs.

To apply, choose your destination and complete and send in the application form (downloadable from our website www.gapyearplacement.org) together with your CV.

Please note that, due to an increasing number of applications, places cannot be guaranteed. Shortlisted candidates will be invited to attend a selection interview in their country of residence.

Reading and discussion

4 **Read the four descriptions of gap-year placements. With a partner, explain which one(s) you'd prefer to go on, and why. Why wouldn't you like to go on the others?**

Writing and roleplay

5 **You are going to take turns interviewing and being interviewed for www.gapyearplacement.org. First complete the application form, then follow the steps below.**

application form

www.gapyearplacement.org

Name: ________________________________

Current occupation: ________________________

A Describe your previous participation in any organization, your experiences in other countries and your contact with persons of other nationalities, races and cultures.

____

____

B What are your main reasons for spending a year abroad and why have you applied for a gap-year placement?

____

____

C What is your preferred destination and type of voluntary work?

____

____

1 Divide into A Groups and B Groups of four students each.
2 Three students from Group A interview one student from Group B. At the same time, three students from Group B interview one student from Group A. Use the completed application forms above (and CVs, if available) for the interviews.
3 When the first interview is finished, a different person from each group goes to the other group to be interviewed. The interview panel will, therefore, be slightly different each time.
4 When all the interviews are finished, decide in your groups which candidates have been successful.
5 Group A and Group B join together and give the candidates feedback on why their applications have or have not been successful.

Glossary PAGE 155

eco-
find your feet
step back
tangible
underprivileged

Care Work in South Africa

Population: 45 million
Official Language: 11 official languages, including English and Afrikaans
Placement: Schools for 4 to 18 year olds with special needs
Job: Classroom assistant in a special needs school, providing classroom support and working on an individual basis with children with mental and physical disabilities.
Working week: 45 hours, some evening duties.

Conservation in Malaysia

Population: 24 million
Official Language: Bahasa Melayu
Main Religion: Islam
Placement: Conservation work
Job: Various conservation projects: construction and maintenance of trails, identification of species, eco-tourism projects, organic farms, animal sanctuaries, turtle-conservation projects. Work is physically demanding.

Care Work in Costa Rica

Population: 4 million
Official Language: Spanish (Indian languages and Patois also spoken)
Main Religion: Roman Catholic
Placement: Care work
Job: Care-work placements in homes for children with disabilities or orphanages: assisting individual children, organizing activities, helping with lessons or assisting at meal times. Intensive Spanish language course recommended.

Teaching in Tanzania

Population: 37 million – over 129 tribes
Official Language: Swahili and English
Main Religion: Christianity and Islam
Placement: Teaching in primary or secondary schools
Job: Teaching five days a week: all subjects, including sport and drama. Participants must have excellent English. Four weeks' school holidays per year.

Review 3

Products and packaging

1 Fill in the missing vowels in these adjectives.

1 Today's marketplace is highly c_mp_t_t_v_.
2 Packaging has to be _ttr_ct_v_, _ff_ct_v_ and d_st_nct_v_.
3 Packaging is cr_t_c_l to make sure there is _ff_c_ _nt use of l_m_t_d shelf space.
4 An _r_g_n_l idea can turn out to be _mpr_ct_c_l for reasons of t_chn_c_l limitations.

2 Complete the sentences using words from the box.

chance	communication	field	issues	
needs	process	sale	solution	view

1 Packaging is the manufacturer's last ________ to seduce the customer.
2 Many products are identical from the consumer's point of ________.
3 Most purchasing decisions are made at the point of ________.
4 The principal problem is a lack of ________ between the people involved in the design and development ________.
5 There are different groups of experts, all working in their own specialized ________.
6 Production people know nothing about consumer ________.
7 The manufacturing people deal with the technical ________ as and when they arise.
8 Our task forces can deliver an optimal ________ in one week, sometimes less.

3 In each set of four below, match a verb on the left with a phrase on the right to make collocations about product development.

1 generate	the product onto the market
2 screen out	new ideas in focus groups
3 launch	specifications for the product
4 draw up	unfeasible or unprofitable ideas
5 conduct	production on a large scale after tests
6 draw	market studies
7 go into	sketches and build mockups
8 test	the product by using it in typical situations

4 Fill in the missing letters to complete these nouns about dimensions.

1 It's 45 cm **long**.	=	Its l______ is 45 cm.
2 It's 31 cm **wide**.	=	Its w____ is 31 cm.
3 It's 8 cm **high**.	=	Its h_____ is 8 cm.
4 It **weighs** 9 kg.	=	Its w_____ is 9 kg.

5 Match each word in the box with its definition 1–5. Then translate the words into your language.

benefit	feature	function	specification
USP (unique selling point)			

1 the thing that makes a product special or different from others ________
2 an important, interesting or typical part of something ________
3 a detailed instruction about how something should be made ________
4 an advantage that you get from something ________
5 the job that something is designed to do ________

6 Join the sentences using *who* (for people), *that* (for things) or *whose*.

1 Here's the email. I got it this morning.
Here's the email that I got this morning.
2 Here's the email. It arrived this morning.
____
3 The team leader is an interesting man. He comes from Spain.
____
4 The team leader is an interesting man. I met him yesterday.
____
5 The team leader is an interesting man. His background is in IT.
____

7 Put brackets around any examples of *who* or *that* that are not necessary in Exercise 6.

8 Make noun phrases from the following definitions.

1 A cycle for developing a product is a *product development cycle.*
2 A document that shows you have insurance for travel is a ________.
3 A concept for the design of packaging is a ________.
4 A product used for cleaning households is a ________.

9 Choose the correct word(s) to make phrases for a product presentation.

1 After that, I'll *go / go on* to present …
2 And now, if you have any questions, I'll do my best to *answer / respond* them.
3 My *reason / objective* today is …
4 *Final / Finally*, I'm going to …
5 First of all, *I / I'll* talk about …
6 Thank you for *listening / your listening*.
7 I've divided my presentation *by / into* three sections.
8 Please *make / feel* free to interrupt me.
9 So, in summary, these are the *reasons / motives* why I am asking you to …

10 Put phrases 1–9 from Exercise 9 into the order that you would probably hear them.

11 Rearrange the words to make diplomatic phrases used in a meeting.

1 can / to / that / later / come / back / we?
____
2 we / want / to / go / in / that's / a / direction / I'm / not / sure.
____
3 that's / the / more / mind / of / thing / I / had / in / kind.
____

Review 4

Careers

1 Finish each phrase about careers with the best collocation from a–h.

1 make a career	a) application
2 reach your long-term	b) bonus
3 prefer money rather than job	c) choice
4 learn new	d) experience
5 gain	e) goal
6 get a performance-related	f) placement
7 send off a job	g) satisfaction
8 apply for a gap-year	h) skills

2 Fill in the missing letters in these words which all have a meaning similar to *goal*.

1 clear / annual / production / sales t_____s
2 limited / clear / specific / business o________s
3 the overall / main / sole / underlying __m

3 Match each word in the box with its definition below. Then translate the words into your language.

aptitude background experience
know-how knowledge skill

1 knowledge that you need to be able to do something
2 information that someone knows
3 an ability to do something well, especially because you have practised it
4 knowledge or skill you get from being in different situations
5 the type of education, experience and family that you have
6 a natural ability to do something well or to learn it quickly

4 The expressions in the box refer to losing your job.

be dismissed be fired be laid off
be made redundant be sacked

1 Which three suggest it was your fault?
2 Which of these three is more formal?
3 Which two expressions suggest it was not your fault?
______, ______
4 Which of these two is British English? ______

5 Fill in the missing letters in these words about careers.

1 be sh__ __ __-li__ __ __d for a second interview
2 re__ __ __n from a job because you have a better offer in another company
3 a__ __ __ __d an interview on Friday morning
4 be p__ __ __ __ __ __d to a more senior position after some time in the company
5 be h__ __ed by a company after a successful interview
6 a__ __ __y for a job in a company

6 Put each verb into the correct form: present simple (*do / does*), present continuous (*am / are / is doing*), present perfect (*have / has done*) or past simple (*did*). Each form is used twice.

'I'm really busy this morning – I (1) ______ (interview) three candidates for that sales job – the second one is outside now. Yesterday was even worse. I (2) ______ (interview) five candidates in two hours, and none of them were any good. Let me see, over the last ten days I think I (3) ______ (interview) 16 candidates. Just imagine! And every time I (4) ______ (interview) someone there's a CV to read, questions to prepare, records to keep. It just never ends. Right now, I (5) ______ (need) a break. (6) ______ (anyone/see) that travel brochure about holidays in the Seychelles? I know I (7) ______ (put) it somewhere. Wait a minute. There's no-one here. I (8) ______ (talk) to myself.'

7 Put each verb into the correct form: present perfect (*have / has done*) or present perfect continuous (*have / has been doing*).

1 I ______ (write) my CV all morning, and finally I ______ (finish) it.
2 I ______ (write) four job applications this week. One day I must get lucky – I ______ (try) to find a job for ages.

8 Make nouns from the adjectives and verbs below.

1 strong (adj) ______
2 weak (adj) ______
3 responsible (adj) ______
4 perform (v) ______
5 commit (v) ______
6 achieve (v) ______

9 Use each noun from Exercise 8 to complete these questions from a job interview. Some have a plural form.

1 What are your main functions and duties in your present job? What are your ______?
2 How does the company know you are doing a good job? How do they measure your ______?
3 What are the positive things you can bring to the team? What are your ______?
4 And what would you say are your ______? Come on, be honest now.
5 What is the one thing you are most proud of in your present job? What is your greatest ______?
6 If we offer you this job, what kind of ______ will you have to the company? Will you be looking for another job after a year or two?

5 Making deals

- online and offline retailers
- social networking in retail

Internet research

Visit two or three of these sites: Foursquare.com, Booyah.com, Shopkick.com, Stickybits.com, Gowalla.com, Loopt.com, Brightkite.com, Facebook Places. Which service appeals to you most? Why?

5.1 About business Retailing

Discussion

1 In small groups, discuss these questions.

1 Do you prefer shopping in a bricks-and-mortar store or online? Why?
2 Do you do research online before buying in a store, or look at products in store before ordering online? Does it depend on what you're buying?
3 Have you used services like Facebook Places and Foursquare?
4 How do you see the future of retailing? Is there room for both bricks-and-mortar and e-commerce?

Scan reading

2 Read the article opposite quickly and choose the best summary.

Retailers are using Internet services
a) to attract social networking users to their websites.
b) to improve their conversion rates by having customers scan bar codes.
c) to acquire data about customers and their lifestyles.
d) to increase foot traffic and make personalized offers.

Reading for detail

3 Read the article again and decide whether these statements are *T* (true) or *F* (false).

1 The advantage offline retailers have over online stores is that they can easily know who their customers are and adapt to their needs. ☐
2 Visitors to an e-commerce site are more likely to make a purchase than people who walk into a store. ☐
3 Smartphone apps allow users to tell their friends where they are in return for exchanging information with retailers. ☐
4 Manufacturers could increase sales by persuading shoppers to handle their products. ☐
5 Big brands are unconvinced about the efficiency of using social media apps. ☐
6 Competing to collect virtual titles can become an obsession for some shoppers. ☐

Discussion

4 Explain the significance of the following phrases:

e-commerce doesn't let go easily (line 4)
app-mania came flying to bricks-and-mortar's rescue (line 11)
all-important foot traffic (line 19)
if that seems somehow less than essential (line 27)
powerfully addictive experiences (line 58)
to hook users into a self-perpetuating race to … their individual identity (line 60)

Listening

5 2:07 **Listen to a shopper answering questions in a survey on social media and shopping. Complete the questionnaire.**

How interested are you in services like Facebook Places and Foursquare? Please give each option a rating between 0 (no interest) and 5 (very interested).

1 checking in to shopping venues so your friends know where you are ☐
2 winning gift certificates or prizes after a certain number of check-ins ☐
3 receiving information on special deals from stores ☐
4 checking in to a product by scanning a bar code ☐
5 becoming the mayor of your favourite coffee-shop or the queen of lipstick ☐

Glossary PAGE 155

bricks-and-mortar
claws
hit

Discussion

6 Interview a partner. Ask questions to complete the questionnaire in Exercise 5. Compare and discuss your answers.

Retail finds its new best friend in social media marketing

EVERY ONLINE SHOPPER knows that a single internet purchase will be followed by an uninterrupted stream of offers tailored to their profile and tastes. Once it's got its claws into your digital ID, e-commerce doesn't let go easily. Make a cash purchase in a mall on the other hand, and you leave the retailer none the wiser about who you are, what kind of products you prefer or whether you'll ever set foot in their store again.

Until very recently, offline stores were at a distinct disadvantage when it came to knowing their customers. But just when the retail battle seemed almost lost, app-mania came flying to bricks-and-mortar's rescue. The consumer's love-affair with smartphone apps has not only saved physical retail's bacon, it may even be turning the tables in its favour. Because in-store conversion rates are far higher than the very small percentage of e-commerce hits that actually make a sale, if apps get shoppers through the door, high street stores know they're winning.

So just how is app-mania boosting that all-important foot traffic? Old friends like Facebook and new services like Shopkick and Foursquare provide offline stores with online data on their visitors by encouraging users to check in via their apps as they move around town. Stores and service outlets can track consumer behaviour, recognize returning customers and send them personalized offers. In return, app users can let their friends know exactly where they are and what they're buying. If that seems somehow less than essential, they can also collect points, and win vouchers and prizes.

Other new services are taking advantage of smartphone technology and real-world store visits to push individual brands and products. Services like Barcode Hero® and Stickybits™ invite users to compare prices, post product reviews and win prizes by scanning bar codes in stores. 'When we get a pack or a can off the shelf and into the consumer's hands, there's a very strong chance they'll actually purchase that product, enjoy it, and become a regular customer' says a brand manager for a household name in food products.

After an initial period of scepticism, the majors have been persuaded to get involved by serious user numbers (Foursquare has over three million). High street retailers like Walgreens, Starbucks™ and Gap® and service providers like American Express® are running app-based campaigns, while major brands like Pepsi, Lipton and Campbells® are also investing in social media. With a potential one billion Facebook users checking in to local businesses through 'Facebook Places', physical retailers can finally compete with e-commerce on equal terms. Savvy shoppers however have already seen loyalty cards, coupons, stamps and air miles come and go: will they be willing to keep checking in to venues and scanning bar codes? The results of new marketing concepts borrowed from digital gaming suggest they will.

One of the strongest motivators in social media is status and identity: collecting points to obtain virtual titles like 'duchess of books' or 'queen of lipstick' combines the powerfully addictive experiences of social media, interactive competition and shopping, allowing high street names and big brands to hook users into a self-perpetuating race to connect to others and affirm their individual identity. Like it or not, virtual browsing and real world shopping are converging; in social media marketing, retail has found its new best friend.

'Once it's got its claws into your digital ID, e-commerce doesn't let go easily.'

- collocations for negotiating
- e-tail transactions

Internet research

Search for the key words *principled negotiation* to find out about a popular approach to negotiation.

5.2 Vocabulary Negotiating and retailing

Discussion

1 'You can do everything in an e-store that you can do in a high-street store, except touch the product.' Do you agree? What can you do in an e-store that you can't do in a high-street store?

Collocations

2 Complete the collocations for negotiating by choosing the correct noun from the boxes for each group of three verbs.

a discount   an order   a price   a proposal   the benefits   the details

place take fill	1 an order	bring down quote state	2 a price	offer ask for grant	3 a discount
see sell explain	4 the benefits	sort out discuss go over	5 the details	make firm up reject	6 proposal

a compromise   a deadline   a deposit   costs   fee   negotiation

subject to open to under	7 negotiation	pay require put down	8 a deposit	a monthly an annual an entrance	9 fee
hidden extra fixed	10 costs	meet miss extend	11 a deadline	seek offer find	12 a compromise

Listening

3 2.08–2:15 **Listen to eight extracts from negotiations. What's happening in each case? Complete the descriptions with an appropriate verb or expression from Exercise 2.**

Extract 1: A supplier is taking an order.
Extract 2: A buyer is trying to bring down the price.
Extract 3: A buyer is asking for a bigger discount.
Extract 4: A seller is rejecting a proposal.
Extract 5: A negotiator is saying that availability is open to/subject to negotiation
Extract 6: A seller is asking the buyer to ______ deposit. put down
Extract 7: A customer is complaining that a supplier has missed the deadline.
Extract 8: A negotiator is offering a compromise.

Write two similar extracts illustrating two more of the collocations. Read them to a partner, who should try to identify the collocations you are referring to.

Pronunciation

4 2:16–2:20 **Listen to these phrases you heard in Exercise 3. Each contains examples of /ə/(schwa), the neutral sound used for unimportant, unstressed sounds, for example the first and last sounds in the word *another*. <u>Underline</u> the /ə/ sounds in each phrase.**

1 five hundred at 12 euros a box
2 two and a half thousand
3 an extra 2%
4 five or six weeks a year
5 We usually ask for 20% now.

Now practise saying the phrases with the correct pronunciation.

5 Put these steps in an e-tail transaction into the correct chronological order.

- ☐ The product is shipped to the customer's address by mail or express carrier.
- ☐ The seller exchanges the product or gives a refund.
- ☐ The customer goes to the check-out and pays by credit card.
- ☐ The website records the transaction and generates an invoice.
- ☐ The customer selects the product and places it in a cart.
- ☐ The customer sends the faulty product back under guarantee.
- ☐ The customer's credit card account is debited.
- ☐ The customer clicks on the link to the seller's site.
- ☐ The customer browses the site and identifies the product which interests him.
- ☐ The website sends an instruction to the warehouse to ship the product.

6 In each email, correct the words in bold which a computer virus has mixed up.

1

INBOX | REPLY | FORWARD

Dear Sir or Madam,
I am writing to complain about the service from your lowlowprice.biz website. Last month I ordered a DVD; you then took three weeks to ship the (a) **site**. While I was waiting for delivery, I browsed another (b) **product**, which advertised the same DVD for only half the price. I have also priced the (c) **credit** on several other sites, all cheaper than yours. Finally, when I checked my bank statement, I noticed that you have debited my (d) **product** card twice! Please correct this error as soon as possible.
Mary Brotherton

2

INBOX | REPLY | FORWARD

Dear Ms Brotherton,
Please accept our apologies for the errors you have experienced. Unfortunately, our computer recorded your (a) **link** twice, and therefore generated two (b) **refunds**. Usually our prices are the lowest on the Web; when this is not the case, we are happy to give full (c) **product**. Please send the (d) **transaction** back and we will credit your account for the full amount. (Click on the (e) **invoices** below for the return address.)
Customer Service Department
www.lowlowprice.biz

Discussion

7 Tell a partner about a time when you had difficulty reaching an agreement in a negotiation with someone. Talk about the different stages in the discussion, and if and what you eventually agreed. Use the words and the expressions in the box to help you.

be prepared to	clarify	consider	discuss	point out	propose	reach an agreement

- *If* + present simple + *will*
- *If* + past simple + *would*
- *recommend, advise, suggest*

Refresh your memory

First conditional
if + present simple, (*then*) + *will* + *do*
likely future events

▶ Grammar and practice page 130

Second conditional
if + past simple, (*then*) + *would* + *do*
unlikely future events

▶ Grammar and practice page 131

recommend/suggest/ advise
recommend/suggest something
recommend/suggest something to someone
recommend/suggest (not) doing something
recommend/suggest (that) someone do something
advise someone (not) to do something
advise (not) doing something

▶ Grammar and practice page 131

5.3 Grammar Conditionals and recommendations

Discussion

1 Read the questionnaire and think about your answer to each question; be careful to use the correct grammar structures. Then, with a partner, compare your answers; tell your partner if you think their answer is right or not.

Customer care questionnaire

You've just started a new job selling sportswear and equipment.

1. What do you advise when a customer can't decide between a cheap and an expensive product? how often do you want to use
2. What do you say if a customer asks for a discount?
3. What do you recommend doing if a customer is angry?
4. What would you do if a customer injured her foot by dropping weight training equipment on it?
5. What will you do if a customer breaks a valuable piece of equipment? insurance
6. What would you say if a customer said you knew nothing about sport?
7. What do you suggest doing if a customer asks you for your personal phone number?
8. What would you do if a customer complained about your attitude? apologise
9. What will you do if you accidentally short-change a customer? apo
10. What would you do if a customer made racist or sexist remarks?
11. What do you recommend if a customer brings back a set of golf clubs and demands a refund?
12. What would you do if you saw a customer steal some expensive running shoes? police
13. What do you do if the item the customer wants is out of stock?
14. What will you say if a customer asks why your prices are higher than online stores?
15. What would you do if a customer left their credit card in the store?

Internet research

Search for the keywords *negotiation quotes* to find quotations about negotiating by experts and famous historical figures.

Reformulating

2 Reformulate these sentences using the words in bold.

1 We can only deliver by 1 July if we receive a 30% deposit within ten days. (**unable**, **unless**)
We are unable to deliver by 1 July unless we receive a 30% deposit within ten days.
2 Our production manager will agree to make the changes, as long as you supply a prototype. (**willing**, **providing**)
3 We might consider a larger discount, on one condition: that you pay in advance. (**reluctant**, **unless**)
4 We would not wish to sponsor the exhibition unless we had a large stand in the entrance hall. (**prepared**, **but only if**)
5 Providing we can get the sub-components in time, we will be able to meet the deadline. (**unless**, **impossible**)
6 If, and only if, several other top CEOs were present, our president would agree to attend. (**as long as**, **available**)

Discussion

3 With a partner, ask and answer these questions, following the example.

1 Would you recommend working abroad for a few years and, if so, where?
I would certainly recommend it, providing it was a good career move and, personally, I would suggest going to an English-speaking country. What do you think?
2 Would you advise working for non-profit organizations and, if so, which ones?
3 Would you recommend that people work part-time?
4 How would you advise a manager who wants to be popular?
5 What do you suggest young people do to become millionaires?

Listening

4 2:21 Two colleagues in a sales department, Jan and Petra, are negotiating a list of responsibilities they have to share. Listen and write *J* (Jan) or *P* (Petra) next to the points they agree on.

- ☐ tennis tournament with customer
- ☐ run exhibition stand in Kazakhstan
- ☐ conference in Madagascar
- ☐ team-building course in Siberia
- ☐ relocate call centre manager to India
- ☐ take holiday in August
- ☐ take holiday in January
- ☐ open office at 6am
- ☐ close office at 10pm
- ☐ supervise intern for six months
- ☐ share office with PR Manager

Negotiating

5 With a partner, try to negotiate an agreement on the remaining points in the list above.

5 Making deals

- negotiating technique
- expressions for bargaining and offers
- roleplaying a negotiation

5.4 Speaking Negotiations – bargaining

Discussion

1 **In one minute, negotiate the sale of your bicycle/computer/musical instrument/other item to a partner.**

Did you win or lose the negotiation? Why? Is there always a winner and a loser?

Listening

2 2:22 **Listen to Part 1 of a negotiation and answer the questions.**

1 What does Harry Petersen's company do?
2 What services are included in the package Ingrid's company offers?
3 How does Harry intend to deliver products?
4 How will Holman Multimedia charge for their services?
5 What are the advantages for Harry of working with Holman Multimedia?
6 What is the next step?

3 2:23 **Listen to Part 2, Version 1. What important mistake does Harry make?**

4 2:24 **Listen to Part 2, Version 2 and answer the questions.**

1 How has Harry improved on Version 1?
2 What conditions does Ingrid ask for to:
   - bring down the monthly fee?
   - guarantee a maximum down time of 24 hours per month?
   - have the site up and running by next month?
3 What terms do Harry and Ingrid agree?

5 2:24 **With a partner, find suitable words to complete the useful expressions for bargaining in the checklist. Then listen again and check your answers.**

Useful expressions: Bargaining

Tentative offers

I might ______ be able to bring it down a little, but ______ if we had a three-year contract.
I might consider reducing the price if you increased your order.

Compromising

Would you agree to a compromise?
Is that an acceptable compromise?
… let's ______ the difference.

Firm offers

I am ready to sign a contract today if you can guarantee the price for two years.
… so we're happy to guarantee less than 24 hours per month, as ______ as you choose our platinum service level.
I can pay six months in advance, on ______ that you have the site online in two months.

Counteroffers

I'd be ______ to agree to a three-year contract, ______ you could guarantee a maximum down time of 24 hours per month.
I suppose we ______ do it, providing you ______ a year's fees in advance.
It would be difficult for me to increase my order unless you guaranteed the price for two years.

Which tenses are used in the condition (*if/unless*) clauses of the tentative offers, counteroffers and firm offers above, and why?

Internet research

Search for the keywords *cross cultural negotiation* to find out how cultural differences affect international negotiations.

Bargaining

6 Work with a partner to negotiate the following situations. Change roles for the second negotiation.

1 Student A: You have to give a presentation to the sales team tomorrow morning, but you booked an important client meeting at the same time. Ask B to give the presentation for you.

Student B: This is the second time this has happened in two months. You think A should be more organized, so if you agree, negotiate something valuable in return.

2 Student A: You have to work with an auditor on Friday afternoon, but your boss has booked you on an all-day training course. Ask B to look after the auditor for you.

Student B: You were planning to take Friday afternoon off as you are going away for the weekend, so if you agree, negotiate something valuable in return.

Use the following format to structure your negotiations:

Student A		Student B
Ask a favour.	→	Make a tentative offer.
Make a counteroffer.	↙ →	Make a firm offer.
Propose a compromise.	↙ →	Agree, go back to the beginning or break off negotiations.

Pronunciation

7 Stressing keywords is important in making clear that your first offers are tentative and hypothetical. Underline the two keywords that are stressed in each of these examples.

1 I might possibly be able to bring it down a little, but only if we had a three-year contract.
2 I might consider reducing the price, if you increased your order.
3 I'd be reluctant to agree to a three-year contract, unless you could guarantee a maximum down time of 24 hours per month.

8 2:25–2:27 **Listen and check your answers in Exercise 7. Then practise saying each sentence.**

Negotiating

9 With a partner, practise negotiating an e-tailing package.

Student A: look at the instructions below.
Student B: turn to page 121.

Student A
Harry Petersen's Application Service Provider, Holman Multimedia, has gone out of business, taking with it Harry's site which was turning over a thousand dollars per day.

Harry needs to hire a new provider. This time he is determined to negotiate a contract which will protect his business if there are problems. Harry has asked you to negotiate with another supplier, Easytail. He has given you a list of points to negotiate below. Try to obtain more 'Ideals' than 'Unacceptables'.

	Ideal	Acceptable	Unacceptable
Set-up time	< 3 weeks	3 weeks	> 3 weeks
Cost	less than Holman	same as Holman	more than Holman
Payment terms	> 30 days	30 days	< 30 days
Contract	6–12 months	12–18 months	> 18 months
Penalties if site is offline	> 50% of average turnover	50% of average turnover	< 50% of average turnover
Penalties if contract is broken	50% of turnover for 2 months	50% of turnover for 1 month	< 50% of turnover for 1 month

Glossary PAGE 155

down time
lead time
package
reluctant
tentative

5 Making deals

- proposal structure
- options and contingencies
- writing a proposal

5.5 Writing A proposal

Discussion

1 **Discuss your views on mailshots and spam. Mark your position on the scale.**

They make good business sense. ←—+—+—+—+—→ They're a waste of money.

Model

2 **Read the proposal below and answer the questions.**

1 What service does the proposal offer?
2 Which four benefits does it offer?
3 How much does the service cost?
4 Why should the customer choose this provider?

Dear Mr Bellows,

Thank you for taking the time to talk to me by telephone today. As agreed, please find below a proposal for our PZpay merchant account, which I believe will resolve all your online payment problems.

Your website currently generates five to ten orders per day. You expect this to increase steadily with the introduction of a new range of products. You are looking for a flexible, inexpensive and transparent payment system which will allow you to deal directly with your customers and control your cash flow.

We recommend the PZpay Pro small business merchant account, which can process up to 75 orders per day. If your sales volume were to expand more quickly than anticipated, you would be able to upgrade to PZpay Corporate with no additional set-up fee.

PZpay Pro will gain prestige and respect for your e-business, since customers will make their credit card payments directly on your website. PZpay is totally transparent, giving you total control of your sales, cash-flow and administration fees. In the unlikely event of a dispute with a customer, you alone would decide whether to refund your customer's payment. Our charges are amongst the lowest on the market, meaning that your business will be more profitable from day one.

We provide everything you need to set up PZpay on your website within 48 hours. Should you however encounter any difficulties, our helpline is available 24 hours a day, seven days a week to assist you.

With more than 1,800 satisfied members in 26 countries, PZpay is the fastest-growing merchant account provider on the Web. I will be happy to put you in touch with other PZpay users in your region.

The monthly fee for PZpay Pro is just $12, with minimum transaction fees of only $10. You will find full details of our terms and conditions in the attached quotation.

We look forward to having you as a member: to apply, simply fill out the application form at http://pzpay.com. If you have further questions, please feel free to call or email me.

Sincerely yours,
Clemmie A Buckton

Internet research

Search for the keywords *how to write direct mail* to find out more about writing to sell.

Analysis

3 Read the proposal again and number these sections in the order they appear in the proposal.

☐ Solution: State the options you recommend, and any contingency plans.
☐ Benefits: Sell your solution by pointing out its advantages for the customer.
1 Introduction: Refer to previous contact with your customer, state the purpose and contents of the document and summarize the objective of the proposal.
☐ Conclusion: Encourage the customer to take the next step.
☐ Qualifications and references: Justify your ability to do the job.
☐ Process and schedule: Explain procedures, lead time and after-sales service.
☐ Needs/Background: Review the reasons for the proposal and the customer's needs.
☐ Costs: Give a breakdown of the investment, or refer to a separate quotation.

Language focus

4 Your small business designs and builds multimedia websites. In small groups, supply suitable endings/beginnings for these options and contingencies.

1 If you would like to see similar projects we have managed, ______________.
2 In the unlikely event that you were less than 100% satisfied with the result, ______________.
3 Should you require on-site support, ______________.
4 ______________, I would be delighted to organize a demonstration on your premises.
5 ______________, we would provide a replacement while your server was repaired.
6 ______________, our engineers can reform an upgrade on-site.
7 ______________, we require a deposit of 25%.

Glossary PAGE 156

cash flow
contingency plan
mail order
merchant account
set-up fee

Output

5 Read the notes from a sales meeting with a prospect, and write a proposal to supply a new website. Invent any details as necessary.

Prospect
Ms Nash-Williams

Company
'Poster Passion' – they sell posters of pop stars, rock bands, sports, etc. by mail order and via the Internet. Customers are mostly teenagers.

Needs
Current website was designed by a friend five years ago – very static and boring.
No movement, no sound. Basically just a catalogue and price list.
Sales are dropping – competitors have more interactive sites. Wants something more exciting with music, guided tour, etc.
Perhaps games to attract visitors?
Give details of how we work, references, prices, etc.
Very concerned about after-sales – explain how we support them if anything goes wrong.

5 Making deals

- planning an incentive trip
- negotiating a package

5.6 Case study St John's Beach Club

Discussion

1 **Some companies reward their best sales staff with gifts, trips or additional pay, hoping that such benefits will serve as an incentive to improve sales. What do you think are the advantages of such sales incentive programs? Are there any disadvantages?**

Reading

2 **Read the memo and answer the questions.**

1 Who can go on the incentive trip?
2 Is this the first time the company has organized such a trip?
3 When and why was the memo sent?
4 What sort of customers does the St John's Beach Club aim to attract?

Ashton Pharmaceuticals – Memo

To: All sales reps
Re: Incentive trip

Just a quick reminder that our top ten performers will win an all-expenses paid holiday for two in the sun. As usual, our destination is the Caribbean, and this year we have chosen the St John's Beach Club in Antigua (see attached brochure). So if you haven't yet made it into the top ten, and you want to be on the beach this December, there's still time to record really excellent figures in Q4!

Good luck!

Malcolm Roberts

Sales Director

Internet research

Search for the keywords *employee incentive programmes* to find out more about motivating employees. Hold a vote to see which incentives the class find most motivating.

Listening for detail

3 2:28 **Listen to a conversation between Malcolm Roberts and Loretta Harding, CEO of Ashton Pharmaceuticals. Mark these statements *T* (true) or *F* (false), and say why.**

1 The conversation takes place in Malcolm's office.
2 Malcolm and Loretta are going on the trip.
3 Charles is probably the CFO.
4 Last year's budget was about $26,500.
5 Malcolm is going to negotiate with the St John's Beach Club.
6 There will be between 22 and 26 participants.
7 Malcolm hopes to stay in Antigua for ten nights.

4 2:28 **Listen again and complete these sentences.**

1 Loretta would get to know the sales team better if ________________.
2 If they only talked to one travel agent, ________________.
3 Loretta thinks the agents may give a free upgrade if ________________.
4 If they can negotiate a really good package, Malcolm ________________.
5 They'll stay longer than a week if ________________.

Negotiating

5 **Divide into travel agents (A) and buyers (B). Each buyer negotiates with two different travel agents to get the best possible deal for Ashton Pharmaceuticals' incentive trip to the St John's Beach Club. When you have finished negotiations, compare your scores to see who got the best deal.**

Student A: turn to page 115.
Student B: turn to page 119.

eWorkbook
Now watch the video for this unit.

6 Company and community

- ethical corporations
- CSR policies and programmes

6.1 About business Corporate social responsibility

Discussion

1 Brainstorm a list of groups of people a company has a responsibility towards. What conflicts of interest are there between the different groups?

Scan reading

2 Read the credo below and identify the four groups of people that Johnson & Johnson prioritize.

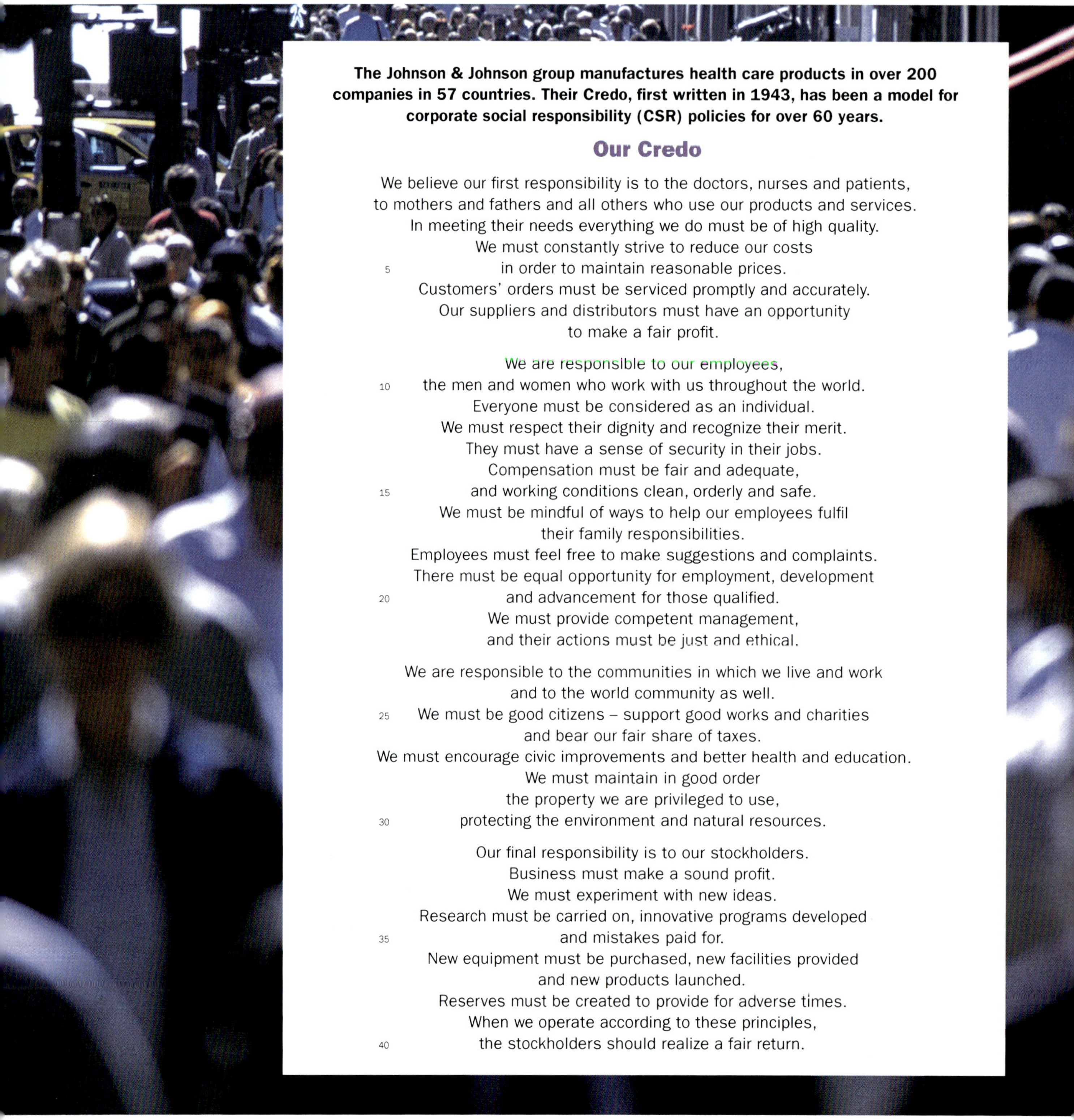

The Johnson & Johnson group manufactures health care products in over 200 companies in 57 countries. Their Credo, first written in 1943, has been a model for corporate social responsibility (CSR) policies for over 60 years.

Our Credo

We believe our first responsibility is to the doctors, nurses and patients, to mothers and fathers and all others who use our products and services. In meeting their needs everything we do must be of high quality. We must constantly strive to reduce our costs in order to maintain reasonable prices. Customers' orders must be serviced promptly and accurately. Our suppliers and distributors must have an opportunity to make a fair profit.

We are responsible to our employees, the men and women who work with us throughout the world. Everyone must be considered as an individual. We must respect their dignity and recognize their merit. They must have a sense of security in their jobs. Compensation must be fair and adequate, and working conditions clean, orderly and safe. We must be mindful of ways to help our employees fulfil their family responsibilities. Employees must feel free to make suggestions and complaints. There must be equal opportunity for employment, development and advancement for those qualified. We must provide competent management, and their actions must be just and ethical.

We are responsible to the communities in which we live and work and to the world community as well. We must be good citizens – support good works and charities and bear our fair share of taxes. We must encourage civic improvements and better health and education. We must maintain in good order the property we are privileged to use, protecting the environment and natural resources.

Our final responsibility is to our stockholders. Business must make a sound profit. We must experiment with new ideas. Research must be carried on, innovative programs developed and mistakes paid for. New equipment must be purchased, new facilities provided and new products launched. Reserves must be created to provide for adverse times. When we operate according to these principles, the stockholders should realize a fair return.

Internet research

Search for the keywords *Starbucks™ bean stock* and *Starbucks standards business conduct* or *CSR* to find out more about the social performance of other companies.

Reading and discussion

3 Read Johnson & Johnson's credo again and discuss what is meant by:

1 *maintaining reasonable prices* (line 5)
2 *making a fair profit* (line 8)
3 *fair and adequate compensation* (line 14)
4 *just and ethical actions* (line 22)
5 *our fair share of taxes* (line 26)
6 *a fair return* (line 40)

4 Discuss the questions relating to Johnson & Johnson's credo opposite.

1 Which 'good works and charities' (line 25) should multinational companies support?
2 What kind of 'civic improvements' (line 27) should the company encourage?
3 How should the company protect 'the environment and natural resources' (line 30)?
4 Are there any points in the credo you disagree with or items you would like to add?
5 Does a credo really change the way a company operates or is it just good PR?
6 Do small businesses have the same responsibilities as multinationals?

Listening

5 2:29–2:30 **Listen to an interview with Estela Maldonaldo, an Argentinian entrepreneur who has built a successful chain of ethical beach cafés.**

Part 1

Listen to Part 1 and decide if the following statements are *T* (true) or *F* (false).

1 Beach Hut's cafés are well-known for their fair trade coffee.
2 Estela believes socially responsible businesses cannot pay shareholders a lot of money.
3 Beach Hut's founders wanted to demonstrate that big corporations have their priorities wrong.
4 Estela believes that happy customers make happy employees.

Part 2

Listen to Part 2 and delete one incorrect item in italics from each statement.

1 Beach Hut reduces its carbon footprint by using *solar panels / biodegradable packaging / hybrid vehicles*.
2 Working with local businesses means Beach Hut can *reduce transport costs / keep prices low / source quality foods*.
3 Beach Hut's altruistic values are directly connected to its *low taxes / good image / healthy margins*.
4 The company's green image helps them find new *customers / shareholders / employees*.

Listen again and complete the summary.

Beach Hut helps to protect Argentina's (1) ________________ by giving staff time off work to run educational programmes for (2) ________________. The company's image has been boosted by winning several (3) ________________ for environmentally friendly businesses; using these green logos on its (4) ________________ and (5) ________________ reinforces the message. In this way, Beach Hut has built a (6) ________________ customer-base despite a very (7) ________________ business environment. Customers value the fact that Beach Hut has a (8) ________________ strategy of building (9) ________________ businesses, not just looking for quick profits from a (10) ________________ model.

Discussion

6 With a partner, discuss your reactions to these quotes from the interview: take turns playing opposing roles as 'the capitalist' and 'the altruist'.

'Are profit and social responsibility really compatible?' 'Absolutely.'
'We've always felt that our employees should come first.'
'We work with local businesses as much as possible … it makes good business sense.'
'Taking care of the environment and the local community is very good P.R.'
'Our customers are very loyal because they know we share the same values.'
'The short-term model just doesn't work – not for business, and not for society.'

Glossary PAGE 156

altruism
biodegradable
credo
hybrid
sustainable
virtuous circle

6 Company and community

- meetings expressions
- adjectives for talking about ethics
- CSR collocations

6.2 Vocabulary Meetings, ethical behaviour and social performance

Meetings

1 Match up the beginnings of phrases you might use in a meeting 1–12 with the endings a–l.

1 I have received two
2 Has everybody received
3 If we can't agree, I think we should take
4 It's getting late, so I propose we close
5 I think this would be a good time to break
6 We have lots to discuss, so let's stick to

a) a copy of the agenda?
b) the meeting.
c) apologies for absence.
d) the agenda.
e) a vote.
f) for lunch.

7 It's five past nine, so I'd better open
8 Can we start by approving
9 We seem to have reached
10 That's interesting, but I think we're getting
11 I'll just give out this
12 Before we finish, we need to deal with

g) side-tracked.
h) any other business.
i) handout.
j) the meeting.
k) a unanimous decision.
l) the minutes of the last meeting?

2 Which phrases would you probably use:

1 at the beginning of a meeting?
2 at the end of a meeting?

Adjectives

3 Match the adjectives in bold in the article with the definitions below, as in the example.

ELASTIC ETHICS

It was Groucho Marx who said that if people didn't like his principles, he had others.

And unfortunately, business people and companies are not always as **reliable** or as **trustworthy** as we would like. Product descriptions are frequently not as **accurate** as they could be, for example when listing ingredients used in foodstuffs. Service is not always as **prompt** as we expect, even in so-called fast-food restaurants. But it is perhaps in the world of advertising where ethical standards seem to be the most elastic. Advertisements are frequently **deceptive** and often **confusing** or deliberately **misleading**, sometimes making extravagant promises. No doubt advertisers are neither more **dishonest** nor any less **altruistic** than the rest of us; they do not often make obviously **false** claims. It's just that, like Groucho, they sometimes seem a little too economical with the truth.

1 immediate or quick *prompt*
2 willing to do things which are not honest ______
3 intended to make someone believe something that is not true ______
4 appearing different from the way it really is ______
5 able to be trusted as honest ______
6 dependable ______
7 complicated, not easy to understand ______
8 not true ______
9 having a selfless concern for others' well-being ______
10 correct or true in every detail ______

Homework

"We could advertise it as 100% salt free."

Collocations

4 **Finish these extracts from a guide to corporate social responsibility by completing each one with verbs from the box that collocate with the words in bold.**

contribute identify with think supporting

PRO-ACTIVE SOCIAL PERFORMANCE

For most companies, rather than (1) supporting a different **charity** each year on an ad hoc basis, it is preferable to (2) think **long-term**. It can be very valuable for a company to (3) identify with **an issue** which is related to its business, and to (4) contribute **funds** regularly.

obey recognizing respecting uphold

ON-GOING SOCIAL PERFORMANCE

Obviously a fundamental of HR management is that companies should always (5) obey **the law**. But above and beyond that requirement, they have a moral duty to (6) uphold **standards** of common decency. This means for example (7) respecting **human dignity** when there are problems, and (8) recognizing **merit** when staff perform especially well.

~~acknowledge~~ ~~compensate~~ ~~limit~~ ~~negotiate~~

DAMAGE LIMITATION

The company's first duty in the case of an accident is to (9) limit the **impact** of the problem on its staff and on the community. It is then essential to (10) acknowledge **the problem**: nothing less than total transparency will do. After the crisis has passed, management should allow sufficient time to (11) negotiate **a settlement** which will satisfy all parties and (12) compensate **the victims** properly.

Internet research

Search for the keywords *ethical and unethical business practices* to find out about the kind of ethical issues many businesses face and the different ways of dealing with them. List the most important ones.

Discussion

5 **Work in pairs or small groups. If a company wants to be ethical and demonstrate corporate social responsibility, what specific practices and policies do you suggest this could involve in the following departments and areas of the business?**

- R&D
- Production and Quality
- Marketing and Sales
- HR
- Purchasing
- Finance

Draw up a list of guidelines and present them to the class.

Glossary PAGE 156

damage limitation
extravagant
misleading
settlement

- passive structures
- reported speech

Refresh your memory

The passive

be + past participle

it does → *it is done*
it is doing → *it is being done*
it did → *it was done*, etc.

used when the person who does the action is obvious or unknown

▶ **Grammar and practice** page 132

Reported speech

I've finished!
He said he had finished.

direct → reported
present → past
past → past / past perfect
present perfect → past perfect
will → *would*

when you report what someone said, move the original tense back in time

▶ **Grammar and practice** page 133

6.3 Grammar The passive and reported speech

The passive

1 In small groups, role-play a meeting between angry stakeholders and a company spokesperson. Take turns to be the spokesperson.

Stakeholders: using the notes provided, remind the spokesperson of all the allegations about the company's lack of social responsibility. Use active verbs to specify who is responsible and give your accusations more impact.

1. Town's water-supply deliberately polluted.
   Your factory deliberately pollutes our town's water-supply!
2. Toxic products manufactured, risk to workers' health.
3. Salary increases promised, but still not paid.
4. Redundancies anticipated, plans for compensation?
5. Local suppliers paid very late, sometimes never paid.
6. Enormous salaries paid to managers, but no investment in local community.
7. Child labour used by suppliers.
8. Local company taxes not paid.
9. Pension fund used to buy Chinese competitor, nothing left to pay future retirees.
10. Factory could be relocated to Eastern Europe to cut costs.

Spokesperson: using the notes provided, acknowledge what is true in the allegations, but avoid taking responsibility. Use the passive to avoid saying who is responsible.

1. The factory's activity does affect the water-supply, but R&D is developing solutions.
   Unfortunately it's true that the water-supply is sometimes affected, but solutions are now being developed.
2. We do manufacture some restricted products, but we respect all government safety procedures.
3. The HR manager did discuss salary increases, but the CEO has not confirmed them yet.
4. We will have to make some redundancies, but we will compensate workers who lose their jobs.
5. We have occasionally delayed payments, but we have always paid our suppliers.
6. We have to offer top salaries to keep the best managers, they invest a lot of money in the local economy.
7. Our suppliers employ young adults, but they have not employed children since 2010.
8. We paid most of last year's tax bill, and the mayor has agreed to postpone payment of the rest.
9. We did buy a Chinese company last year, but the Board plan to sell it again soon at a profit.
10. We are discussing a possible relocation, but we won't take a decision until next year.

Reported speech

2 With your books closed, try to remember as much as possible of what the spokesperson said.

He/She said that the water-supply was sometimes affected, but that solutions were being developed.

Internet research

Read the business pages of an online newspaper to find interesting comments and quotes from people and companies in the news. Tell a partner what was said.

3 **Read the three extracts from newspaper reports. Then say who made the 12 statements below and explain how you know this. What phrases helped you?**

CEO KLAAS ROOS announced an end to manufacturing in Europe, informing shareholders that labour costs could not be justified, and explaining that Asian textile imports could no longer be matched for price.

Speaking to our reporter on the spot, Ms Gronko explained that all villagers forced to leave their homes by the new road would be compensated. Asked to what level, she replied that she was unable to give a figure, but added that discussions were being held with local representatives.

Journalists are reported to have been refused entry to Plazachem's Tashkent plant after leakages of toxic chemicals were described by workers. Employees claimed that health and safety regulations had not been applied for the last five years, and that several fatal accidents had occurred. Plazachem management declined to comment. Asked how the company intended to compensate the victims of the accident, Mr Sanchez answered that no decision had yet been reached. Emphasizing the complexity of the legal situation, he suggested negotiations may be protracted.

1 'It's just too expensive.'
2 'It's dangerous: people have died.'
3 'We're still talking.'
4 'It could take years.'
5 'I don't know.'
6 'It's really not simple.'
7 'It's too early to say.'
8 'They will be paid.'
9 'We are closing down.'
10 'Your request has been denied.'
11 'We can't compete.'
12 'I'm afraid he's unavailable.'

6.3 Grammar

Listening and reporting

4 2:31–2:36 **A manufacturing plant in Kassra, a small city in Libya, has just made 500 people redundant. Listen to six extracts from a conversation between Geoffrey Bullard, the Plant Manager, and Leila Belabed, a member of the mayor's staff. For each extract, decide how Leila reported to the mayor, using appropriate verbs, as in the example.**

1 *I complained that 500 people had been made redundant and I reminded Mr Bullard that he had promised to create jobs for our city.*

5 **Explain these formal announcements to a foreign visitor in informal language.**

1 Protective glasses must be worn beyond this point.
You have to wear special protective glasses from this point onwards.
2 Visitors are requested to use the stairs while the lift is under repair.
3 Customers are advised that no refunds will be made without a receipt.
4 Deposits will only be refunded after the return of all equipment to reception.
5 All meetings are transferred to the training centre during redecoration of the conference room.
6 Only expenses which have been approved by a manager will be reimbursed.

Glossary PAGE 156

leakage
protracted
stakeholder

- expressions for meetings
- disagreeing tactfully
- roleplaying meetings

6.4 Speaking Meetings – teamwork

Discussion

1 Discuss how acceptable you find the following gifts from a seller to a corporate buyer.

a case of champagne   a corporate pen   a free sample of the product
a free weekend 'seminar' on a yacht   cash   employing a relative
lunch in a good restaurant

Listening

2 2:37 Listen to an extract from a management meeting about an ethical problem and answer the questions.

1 What did Mr Vieri do wrong?
2 What is the purpose of the discussion?
3 What do Stan and Jon disagree about?
4 What does Anna decide?

3 2:37 With a partner, find suitable words to complete the useful expressions for meetings in the checklist. Then listen again and check your answers.

Useful expressions: Managing meetings

Asking for opinions

What's your ________?
Would you ________?
Do you have any ________ on ...?

Giving an opinion

I ________ to think that...
In my ________, ...
It ________ to me that ...
I ________ strongly that ...

Disagreeing tactfully

I see your ________, but ...
I agree up to a ________, but ...
I'm ________ I can't agree.

Interrupting

Sorry to ________, but ...
Could I just ________ in here?

Asking for clarification

Sorry, I don't see what you ________.
So are you ________ that ...?
When you say ..., do you ________ ...?

Persuading

Don't you ________ that ...?
Wouldn't you ________ that ...?

Managing the discussion

Do we all ________ on that, then?
The next ________ on the agenda is ...
Can we ________ to the agenda?
Perhaps we should ________ for coffee.
Could we ________ back to this later?

Internet research

What are the essentials of a successful meeting? Search for the keywords *golden rules of meetings* to find out.

4 **With a partner, hold short meetings on the four issues below. Follow the structure provided. Take turns being A and B.**

1 A vodka manufacturer offers to sponsor your end-of-year party. Do you accept?
2 One of your suppliers uses child labour in Vietnam. What should you do?
3 Advertisements for your product show only slim, beautiful people. Is that OK?
4 Ethnic minorities and the disabled are under-represented in your firm. What can you do?

Student A		Student B
Give an opinion.		
↓		
Ask B's opinion.	→	Disagree.
	↙	
Interrupt.	→	Ask for clarification.
	↙	
Persuade.	→	Manage the discussion.

eWorkbook
Now watch the video for this unit.

Glossary PAGE 156

civil servant
disabled
ethnic minority
misconduct

5 **Work in small groups. Hold a management meeting to decide what to do in the following cases of employee misconduct in your company. For each case, discuss the following.**

- what action to take
- what corporate policy to adopt (if any)
- how you will implement your decisions

Case 1

Mike Ho, a buyer in your purchasing department, accepted cash from suppliers. In return, he ordered extra stock at higher than average prices.

Case 2

Marieta Myska, a sales manager, obtained confidential information about government contracts by having a relationship with a civil servant.

Case 3

Joseph Fisher, a project manager, used company resources and equipment to run a club for disabled children at weekends.

- the structure of reports and minutes
- linking words and expressions
- writing minutes

6.5 Writing Reports and minutes

Discussion

1 **Why should companies invest time and money in community projects?**

Model

2 **Mirratec Industries, a subsidiary of a multinational manufacturer of compressors for refrigerators and air-conditioning units, has a plant in the small Polish town of Bychawa. Read the report which Mirratec sent to Head Office, and the minutes of a management committee meeting at Head Office, and answer the questions.**

1 What are the arguments for and against involvement in the community centre project?
2 What did a) Head Office and b) Mirratec decide?

Bychawa Community Centre project

Earlier this year Mirratec was asked to invest in a project to build a Community Centre in Bychawa. As a rule, group policy is to give encouragement but only limited financial support to such community projects. However, in this case it was thought that the benefits to the company's image justified more active and extensive support, in particular after the recent difficult negotiations with the local authorities over the access road to the new workshop. Moreover, it was felt that employee involvement in the project would bring substantial benefits in terms of motivation and job satisfaction. It is therefore recommended that the company should contribute 50% of the funding; in addition, selected employees should manage key areas of the project during work time, such as design, fund-raising and construction.

Naturally, the project will require a high level of commitment from our staff in order to complete all stages on time, and it is hoped that department managers will be able to reduce staff workloads for the duration of the project.

In conclusion, it is believed that the community and the company will derive numerous benefits from the project and that overall, the company's image within the community will be greatly improved. It is expected that an ongoing close relationship with the community will have a positive effect on two strategic areas of our development, namely expansion of our manufacturing facilities and recruitment of our workforce locally.

Minutes of the Management Committee meeting, 15 April
Attendees: Jan Navratil, MD; Ines Caba, Production; Christopher Taberley, Finance

1. Bychawa Community Centre. JN reported that the plan had been favourably received at head office. Even so, there were concerns about the size of the investment and the project's impact on productivity. But he stressed that group management were aware of the need for good relations with local communities, and would support Mirratec's decision. Consequently, JN felt that they should go ahead.

   IC agreed that it was important to improve public relations, but emphasised the risks involved for production, for example, absenteeism and quality issues. She claimed that the project could become an excuse to take time off work, especially during the construction phase in the summer.

   CT reminded the meeting that only a small number of employees would be concerned. Obviously department managers would organize cover for any absences. In other words, production should not be affected. Furthermore, managers of other departments were very happy with the project on the whole. In brief, he suggested that the benefits in developing team spirit were clearly far greater than any potential risk to productivity. Finally, it was agreed that the project should be approved.

Internet research

Search for the keywords *email ethics* and make notes about ethical practice in electronic communication. Write a short report on your findings, using some of the linking words you studied in this module.

Analysis

3 Read the quotes below and answer the questions:

1 'It was thought that the benefits to the company's image justified more active and extensive support.' Identify five more impersonal reporting structures in the report in Exercise 2.
2 'JN reported that the plan had been favourably received at Head Office.' Identify seven more reporting verbs in the minutes in Exercise 2.
3 Why are impersonal reporting structures used in the report, whereas active reporting verbs are preferred in the minutes?

Language focus

4 Read the report and the minutes again. Underline the linking words and complete the table.

Function	Linking words
Addition	besides, mo________, in ad________, fur________
Conclusion	lastly, in c________, f________
Consequence	so, therefore, c________
Contrast	but, h________, e________ s________
Equivalence	that is to say, n________, in o________ w________
Example	for instance, s________ as, f________ e________
Generalization	in most cases, as a________, on the w________
Highlighting	mainly, chiefly, in p________, es________
Stating the obvious	of course, n________, ob________, cl________
Summary	to sum up, o________, in b________

5 Replace the inappropriate linking words in bold with a better choice from Exercise 4.

Josiah Wedgwood was a pioneer in social responsibility, building a village for his workforce in 1769. **For instance**, his products combined technology with classical culture. More than a century later, George Cadbury developed social housing for his chocolate factory workers. **As a rule**, Cadbury's® became one of Britain's most respected companies. Both men were pioneers of corporate social responsibility. **Overall**, they were also accused of paternalism.

Today, sustainable development policies aim to manage the effects of business on employees, the community, and, **on the whole**, on the environment. Multinationals like Shell are focusing on the idea of being good neighbours, **naturally**, by consulting local stakeholders before beginning new projects which may affect them.

Glossary PAGE 156

derive
greenfield site
paternalism
positive discrimination

Output

6 2.38 Listen to a later extract from the Mirratec Management Committee meeting as they move on to discuss the issue of diversity in Mirratec's workforce. Take notes. Then, with a partner, write a short summary of the discussion and decisions made. Use the minutes format on the opposite page.

- discussing corporate image
- roleplaying a decision-making meeting
- writing a report on a meeting

6.6 Case study Phoenix

Discussion

1 Would you like to have a recycling centre near your home? Why (not)?

Reading

2 Read the Internet page about Phoenix and answer the questions.

1 What kind of corporate image does the company try to project?
2 What do you imagine working at Phoenix is like?

INTERNET

PHOENIX Australia's leading independent vehicle recycling specialist

- Home
- Spare parts
- Recycling
- Jobs with Phoenix
- About us
- Contact

Every year almost a million of Australia's ten million cars reach the end of their useful lives. Phoenix provides a valuable community service by recycling over 75% of each vehicle.

Phoenix's mission is to protect and preserve Australia's unique ecology. We take special care to ensure that hazardous materials and toxic substances are processed safely and securely with minimum risk to the environment or the population.

At all our recycling centres across Australia, we believe in being good neighbours. We believe it is our duty to treat customers, employees and suppliers fairly, to respect the local environment and to be involved in community causes.

Internet research

Search for the keywords *automobile recycling contamination* to find out more about the risks and perspectives in this industry.

Roleplay preparation

Divide into three groups: Port Katherine Planning Department, Port Katherine Residents' Association, and Phoenix. Use the Exercises opposite (3, 4 and 5) to gather information for your group, in preparation for a public meeting (Exercise 6) to discuss the choice of site for a new recycling centre in Port Katherine. You will need to make a presentation at the meeting summarizing your views, stating which site you prefer and why, and explaining why the other sites are not appropriate. You should also be prepared to ask the other groups questions, and argue against their proposals if they conflict with your interests.

Listening

3 2:39 **Listen to part of a meeting at Phoenix's head office in Sydney and answer the questions.**

1 Why is Port Katherine a good choice for Phoenix's new site? Give four reasons.
2 What are the pros and cons of sites A, B and C from your group's point of view?
3 What do you think 'Operation Charm and Diplomacy' is?

Reading and discussion

4 **In your groups, prepare for the public meeting by reading a message and answering some questions.**

Group A – Port Katherine Planning Department: turn to page 116.
Group B – Port Katherine Residents' Association: turn to page 118.
Group C – Phoenix: turn to page 121.

5 **Read the agenda. Then, in your groups, prepare your presentation and strategy for the public meeting.**

Roleplay

6 **Roleplay the public meeting using the agenda above.**

Writing

7 **Write a short report on the meeting.**

Port Katherine Planning Department: write to Duncan Gillespie at the Lord Mayor's Office.
Port Katherine Residents' Association: write to your members.
Phoenix: write to your head office in Sydney.

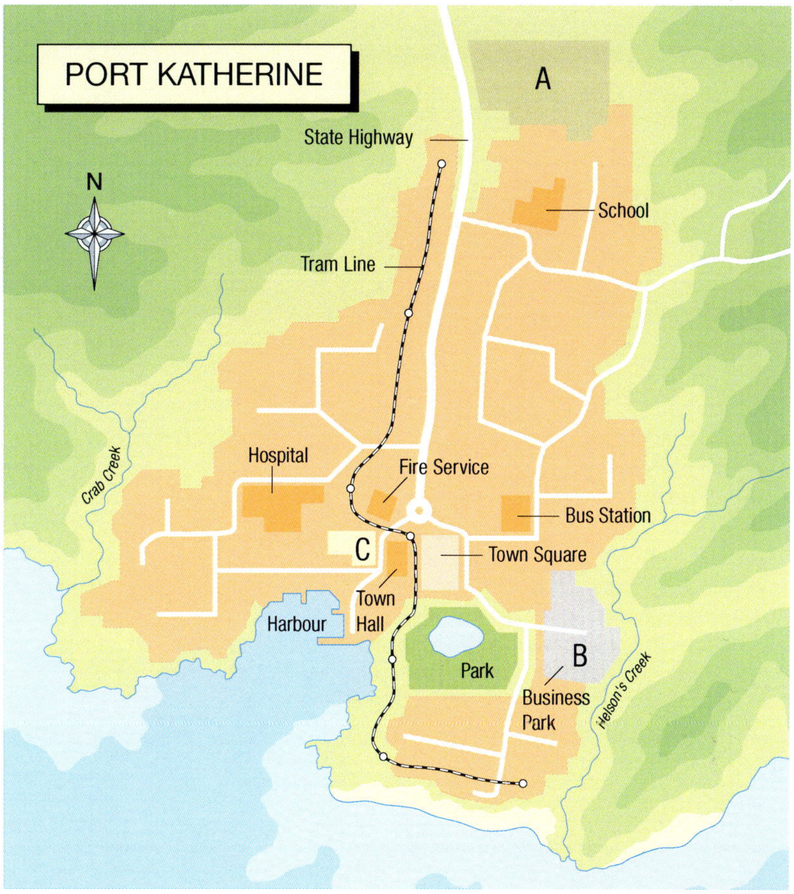

Agenda

1 Welcome and introductions
2 Opening presentations
  • Phoenix
  • Port Katherine Planning Department
  • Port Katherine Residents' Association
3 Questions and discussion of the three possible sites
4 Summary and conclusion

Glossary PAGE 156

hazardous
resident
resistance

Review 5

Making deals

1 Complete these paragraphs about e-tailing using the words in the box.

approach browsers databank expectation eyeballs merchandising purchase search ads website web chats

A Most visitors to a (1) _____ don't actually buy anything, so simply having lots of (2) '_____' doesn't mean there will be lots of sales. In fact, if the site attracts visitors through paid (3) _____ on Google or Yahoo!®, then bringing them actually costs money.

B Customer service reps answer customer questions via live (4) _____ on the site. When a customer engages in live chat with a sales rep, the average (5) _____ doubles in value.

C But instead of real customer service reps, many smaller e-tailers use animated characters that draw on a (6) _____ of answers to commonly asked questions. E-tailers hope that the animated characters will turn (7) _____ into buyers.

D When someone is shopping at home, they have an (8) _____ of privacy. Ted Martin, senior vice-president for (9) _____ and operations at Overstock.com, said: 'We're taking the conservative (10) _____ right now, we don't want to be intrusive.'

2 Complete this sentence about e-tailing using these words: *consent, privacy, tracking, violation*.

Research shows that most online shoppers consider (1) _____ their navigation of a site without their (2) _____ to be a (3) _____ of their (4) _____.

3 In each set of four below, match a verb on the left with a noun on the right to make collocations about an e-tail transaction.

1 look up a) on a link to get to the seller's site
2 pay b) the product you want in a cart
3 place c) a product on a search engine
4 click d) by credit card

5 browse e) the customer's credit card
6 debit f) the product from the warehouse
7 send back g) the site to find any interesting products
8 ship h) a faulty product under guarantee

4 The collocations below are useful in negotiating. Cross out the one verb in each group that does *not* collocate with the noun.

1 *fill / offer / place / take* an order
2 *ask for / be entitled to / find / offer* a discount
3 *discuss / go over / put on / sort out* the details
4 *make / put forward / put back / reject* a proposal
5 *extend / meet / miss / take* a deadline
6 *look for / meet / seek / reach* a compromise

5 Complete each sentence with a collocation from Exercise 4.

1 If you fail to do something by the agreed time, you _____ the _____.
2 If you tell a retailer you want to buy something from them, you _____ an _____.
3 If you finally get agreement after both sides had different starting points, you _____ a _____.
4 If you automatically have the right to a lower price, for example because of the quantity you are ordering, then you _____ a _____.

6 Look at the seven options below. Cross out the three that can never be used.

If we *increase / increased / will increase / would increase* our order, *do you give / will you give / would you give* us a discount?

7 Which version of the sentence in Exercise 6 is appropriate if you want to show you are unsure about increasing your order (it's just a possibility)? Write the whole sentence.

8 Which version of the sentence in Exercise 6 is the most common – you are just asking a simple question?

9 Complete the bargaining phrases in this dialogue using the pairs of words in the box.

providing + agree if + increased unless + guaranteed

Supplier: I might consider reducing the price (1) _____ you _____ your order.
Customer: It would be difficult for me to increase my order, (2) _____ you _____ the price for two years.
Supplier: I might be able to guarantee the price, (3) _____ you _____ to a five-year contract.

10 Choose the correct option.

1 What do you *recommend to me / recommend me*?
2 What do you *advise to do / advise me to do*?
3 I *suggest you / suggest* ordering 500 pieces initially, and then perhaps more later.
4 I *advise that you / advise you to* order 500 pieces initially.
5 I *suggested him / suggested to him* that he should order 500 pieces initially.

11 Complete the extracts from a business proposal using the words in the box.

agreed available below charges lowest replacement require should unlikely wish

1 As _____, please find _____ a proposal to install a series of photocopiers.
2 _____ you require on site support, our engineers are _____ seven days a week.
3 In the _____ event of a breakdown, we would provide a _____.
4 Our _____ are amongst the _____ on the market.
5 If you _____ to place an order, we _____ a deposit of 25%.

Review 6

Company and community

The company should …

- enhance shareholder value.
- recognize employees' merit.
- give fair and adequate compensation.
- provide clean and safe working conditions.
- provide new equipment and new facilities.
- carry on research and develop innovation.
- encourage civic improvements.
- support good works and charities.
- protect the environment and natural resources.
- avoid exploiting developing countries.
- build a sustainable business.

And employees need to …

- have a sense of security in their job.
- have equal opportunity for jobs and development.
- feel free to make suggestions and complaints.
- feel they can align themselves with the company's goals.

1 Read the corporate social responsibility declaration above. Complete the definitions 1–10 with words from the declaration.

1 the profit that a company makes for its investors ________ ________
2 money paid because someone is injured or has lost their job ________
3 rooms and equipment that are provided for a particular purpose ________
4 organizations that give help to people who need it ________
5 the land, water and air that people live in ________
6 treating someone unfairly in order to get a benefit for yourself ________
7 capable of continuing for a long time ________
8 a situation in which people have the same chances as everyone else ________ ________
9 things you say or write when you are not happy ______
10 agree with and support publicly (________ yourself with): ________

2 Complete the sentences about ethical behaviour using the phrases a–h.

The company should …
1 acknowledge any problem ___.
2 act with integrity ___.
3 compensate victims ___.
4 limit the impact of ___.
5 negotiate settlements ___.
6 obey the law or ___.
7 recognize merit when ___.
8 uphold standards of ___.

a) common decency
b) any problem
c) that exists
d) which satisfy everyone
e) for any damage caused
f) staff perform well
g) towards employees
h) face a lawsuit or fine

3 Complete the remarks of a chairperson at various stages of a meeting. Use the phrases in the box.

any other business	apology for absence
approving the minutes	break for coffee
close the meeting	come back to this
getting side-tracked	have any views
introduce the first item	see your point
stick to the agenda	take a vote
unanimous decision	wouldn't you agree

Beginning
Good morning, ladies and gentlemen. Is everyone here? I have received just one (1) ______ from Celia. OK, I think we can begin. Let's start by (2) ______ of the last meeting. Any comments? They're quite straightforward, I think. Good. Now, there is a lot to discuss today, so let's try to (3) ______. OK, who is going to (4) ______?

Middle
That's interesting, but I think we're (5) ______. Could we (6) ______ later? OK. Now, Antonio, we haven't heard from you. Do you (7) ______ on this issue? …
Thank you, Antonio. I (8) ______, but you have to consider the impact on our budget. (9) ______ that there will be substantial costs if we do as you suggest? …
OK, there seems to be a consensus, so we don't need to (10) ______. This would be a good time to (11) ______.

End
Good, I think we've reached a (12) ______ on this. Before we finish we need to deal with (13) ______. Does anyone have any other issue that we haven't discussed? OK, I think we can (14) ______.

4 Put each verb in brackets into the correct form, active or passive. The first two are present simple and the last four are past simple.

'The company (1) ________ (try) to limit its impact on the environment, but sometimes mistakes (2) ________ (make). It is true that some radioactive waste (3) ________ (lose) in transit last week. However, I am pleased to report that we (4) ________ (take) action immediately. The driver of the truck (5) ________ (find), and we (6) ________ (dismiss) him after completing our enquiries. Press reports that he had been drinking are completely exaggerated.'

5 Find pairs of linking words/phrases with the same meaning.

as a rule	clearly	consequently	especially
finally	in addition	in particular	in brief
in conclusion	in other words	moreover	obviously
on the whole	that is to say	therefore	to sum up

6 Which two words/phrases from Exercise 5 would you use to:

1 add a second point to support your argument? ________
2 highlight one fact or point? ________
3 make a generalization? ________

7 Mergers and acquisitions

- the risks of M&A
- pros and cons of taking over a business

Internet research

Search for the keywords *surviving a merger* to read about people who have experienced takeovers and the advice they give.

7.1 About business Risks and opportunities in M&A

Discussion

1 **In financial terms, what are the benefits and risks when two people decide to get married? Think about living costs, purchasing power, employment, tax, investment, entertainment, etc.**

How do you think the situation is similar or different when two companies merge?

Skim reading

2 **Read the article opposite and answer the questions.**

1 Who are the students and why do they want M&A classes?
2 What lessons do they learn?
3 What are good reasons for mergers and acquisitions?
4 What are the wrong reasons?

Reading for detail

3 **Read the article again. With a partner, discuss why these statements are *T* (true) or *F* (false).**

1 Every year over 500 mergers and acquisitions in the US fail to deliver increased value.
2 American executives are keen to get a share in multi-billion dollar takeovers.
3 Executives wishing to attend M&A courses have to have an MBA.
4 Experienced managers tell attendees about typical mistakes they have made.
5 Because of the risks, business school professors do not recommend mergers.
6 Shareholders can often only judge the success of their CEO's acquisitions policy several years after a takeover.
7 Austin says that empire-building, diversification and increasing debt are the wrong reasons for a merger.
8 According to Austin, many CEOs embark on mergers and acquisitions for irrational, emotional reasons.

Listening for gist

4 2:40 **Listen to an interview with Bernard Degoulange, an M&A specialist at Banque de Reims, who talks about choosing targets for acquisition. What are the five Gs?**

Listening for detail

5 2:40 **Listen again and answer the questions.**

1 According to Bernard Degoulange, what is the best reason for a merger?
2 Explain how he uses the example of champagne and whisky to show why external growth is necessary.
3 Explain each of the points summarized by the five Gs.
4 What opportunity does a merger offer the competition, and why is it possible?
5 Why is a merger a traumatic period according to Bernard Degoulange?
6 How does he say companies should help people get through this trauma?

Glossary PAGE 156

due diligence
gene
homogenize
open enrolment
prestigious
susceptible
takeover bid
turmoil

Discussion

6 **You are the owners of Bradburgers, a hamburger restaurant in your town. With your five employees, you have established a reputation for fast, good quality food, and the business is making a good profit. One of your competitors in the next street is Kadri's Kebabs, which sells takeaways and delivers kebabs to homes and offices. There are 15 employees. Kadri and his two brothers are excellent cooks, but poor managers; their kebab house is losing money, and is up for sale. What are the pros and cons of taking over the business? Think about the five Gs in particular.**

Lessons in M&A

SOME 1,500 TO 2,000 mergers and acquisitions are completed per year worldwide, of which around half are in the US. With deals worth astronomical sums, ($25bn for HP® Compaq, $35bn for Daimler-Chrysler, and $77bn for Exxon-Mobil,) it comes as no surprise that American executives are queuing up to go back to school for M&A classes. And although it's true that improving earnings and asset growth are not the only goals in takeovers, the fact that many mergers result in a net loss of value suggests that schooling is sorely needed!

Every year hundreds of executives attend M&A courses at prestigious institutions from New York to L.A. In these 'open enrolment' classes, the only condition of attendance is your, or rather your company's, ability to pay the fees: as much as $1,000 per day. At least that seems to demonstrate that the B-schools know something about improving earnings!

So what do you learn in a week with America's top finance professors? 'We aim to equip participants with techniques based on best practice in the key areas of merger activity performance,' says Ted Austin from the Delaney School of Business. 'We cover all aspects of the conception, planning, due diligence, negotiation and integration stages.' Austin also draws on case studies and guest speakers to illustrate some of the most common acquirer errors: over-valuation, over-confidence, 'under-communicating', and underestimating the value of your newest assets – the people in the company you've just bought. In the turmoil of integration, your best engineers and managers may be more susceptible to attractive offers from the competition.

There is no doubt that M&A is a risky business. With a 70% plus failure-rate, you might think that B-school professors would do well to discourage their students from launching takeover bids. But you'd be wrong. Austin describes some of the other (good) reasons for mergers and acquisitions: 'I suppose the most popular reasons mentioned in CEOs' messages to shareholders are developing synergies and making economies of scale – these are sometimes conveniently long-term goals! Other objectives may be increasing market share; cross-selling, when for example a bank can sell insurance to its existing clients; diversification, if a company is perceived to be too dependent on a niche market; or quite simply taking on debt, the so-called poison pill, in order to make itself a less attractive target for would-be buyers.'

The bankers, brokers and lawyers will be pleased to know there are still many good reasons to merge. But what about the wrong reasons? 'They mainly involve excessive pride or arrogance on the part of management,' says Austin. 'Wanting to build too big an empire, too quickly, and overextending the financial, commercial and human capacity of the organization. These courses aim to help executives bring their CEOs back down to earth: learning to follow your head rather than your heart is the key lesson in avoiding very expensive mistakes.'

'A risky business with a 70% plus failure-rate.'

- financial information
- describing charts and graphs
- describing results and consequences

7.2 Vocabulary Business performance

Discussion

1 Match these newspaper headlines with the extracts they belong to. Decide why the headlines are good or bad news.

1. **Titanic Enterprises go under**
2. Air New Zealand in the black
3. **OLDIES RECORDS COVER COSTS**
4. **LIVERPOOL F.C. IN THE RED**
5. BRIZAL COFFEE BREAK EVEN
6. Predictions Inc. make a profit

a. After a series of expensive transfer deals the club has failed to meet financial goals.

b. The music firm was a hit with investors as record revenues matched expenses.

c. South American shareholders were optimistic as the news filtered through of a probable return to profitability.

d. The futurology specialists will report a miraculous return on investment at tomorrow's AGM.

e. Profitability rose as sales of flights to rugby internationals took off.

f. As the company's stock sank to rock-bottom, chairman Leonard Caprio described it as 'only the tip of the iceberg'.

Giving financial information

2 Read sentences 1–6 and a–f from a financial report. Mark each sentence to show whether the words in **bold** indicate an increase ↗, a decrease ↘ or stability →. Which phrase means something else?

1 Last year our billings **rose** by 90%.
2 Variable costs **are falling**.
3 We expect fixed costs **to stabilize**.
4 In 2001 our stock **slid** to a record low.
5 Production costs **fluctuate** over the year.
6 Liabilities **reach a high** when business is slow in August.

a) Our overheads should **level off**.
b) Our shares **slumped** during the crash.
c) Our turnover almost **doubled**.
d) Cost of sales **varies** from month to month.
e) Our debt **peaks** at the end of summer.
f) Our operating costs **are dropping**.

3 Match each sentence 1–6 with a sentence a–f with a similar meaning.

4 Choose the correct label, a or b, for each graph below.

1
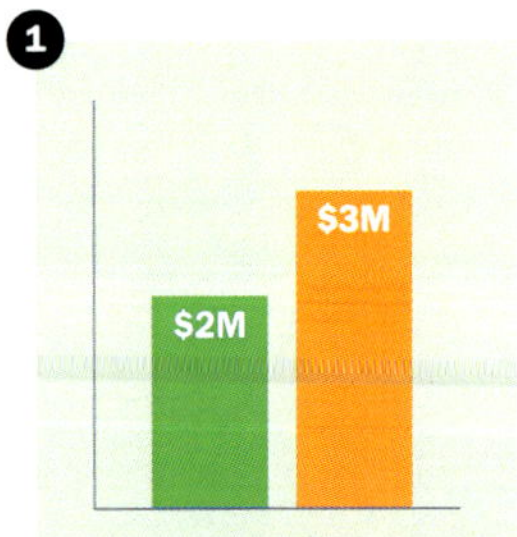

a) Sales increased by $3M.
b) Sales increased to $3M.

2
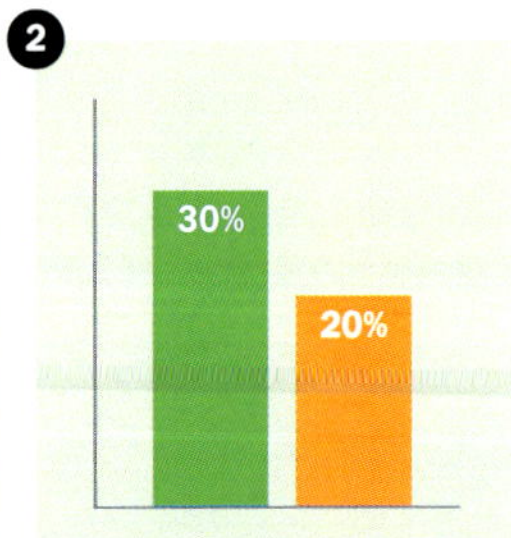

a) There was a decrease of 10%.
b) There was a decrease to 10%.

3
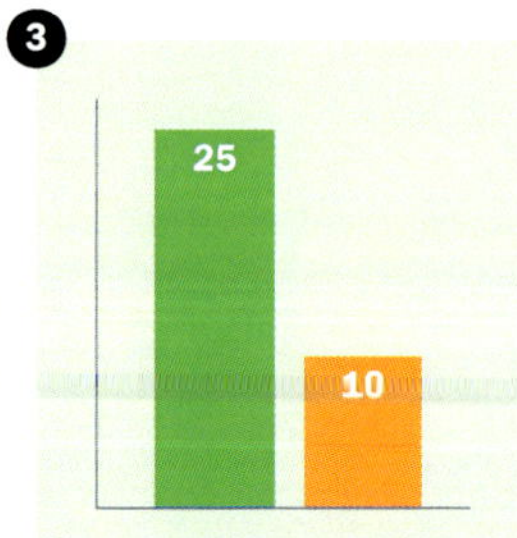

a) Prices fell by €15.
b) Prices fell to €15.

4
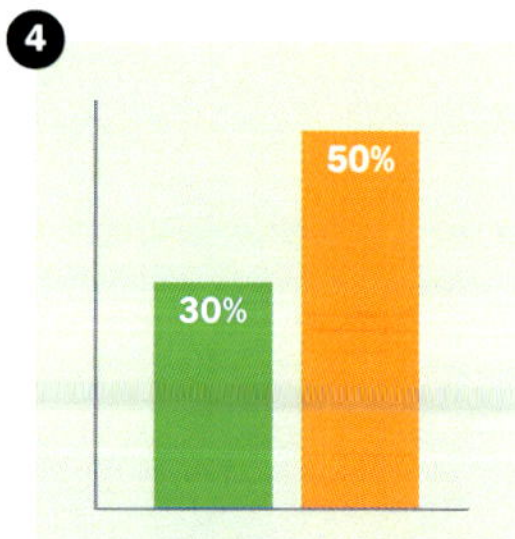

a) There was a rise of 30%.
b) There was a rise from 30%.

Internet research

Search for the keywords *bulls* and *bears* to find out about two types of stock market investors. What other 'animals' can you find on the stock markets?

5 **Match the causes 1–8 with the effects a–h in each set of four below.**

1 There was a **considerable improvement** in the company's image
2 We plan to acquire new technology;
3 As a result of its strategic alliances,
4 A wave of corporate raids resulted in

a) as a result, debt will **grow slightly**.
b) the company enjoyed moderate growth.
c) a **sudden surge** in redundancies.
d) thanks to a joint venture with a prestigious American corporation.

5 After the merger, our profitability will **improve significantly**
6 Due to lower labour costs,
7 They saw **a slight increase** in sales
8 Share prices often **go up sharply**

e) profits will **shoot up dramatically**.
f) as a consequence of their diversification into new markets.
g) because of rumours of hostile takeovers.
h) as a result of economies of scale.

6 **The phrases in bold in Exercise 5 describe different degrees of change. Put them in order from smallest (1) to largest (4).**

	1	2	3	4
Verb + adverb	*grow slightly*			
Adjective + noun	-			

7 **Complete the sentences below using phrases in the box. Sometimes there is more than one possible answer.**

as a result   as a result of   resulted in   thanks to   due to
as a consequence   as a consequence of   because of

1 The FTSE 100 fell again ________ increasing economic uncertainty.
2 Rumours of a merger ________ Tenzin Pharma gaining 6%.
3 Nidden PLC has successfully resisted a raid; ________ its price has levelled off.
4 Henry Halen climbed quickly ________ excellent third quarter results.
5 Profit warnings from several computer companies ________ significant drops in price.
6 JTL Holdings' Brazilian subsidiary went bankrupt. ________ its stock fell to £22.

Which phrases explain causes? Which introduce effects?

Listening for detail

8 2:41 **Listen to a stock market report and complete the graph of Fraxis Corp's share-price history.**

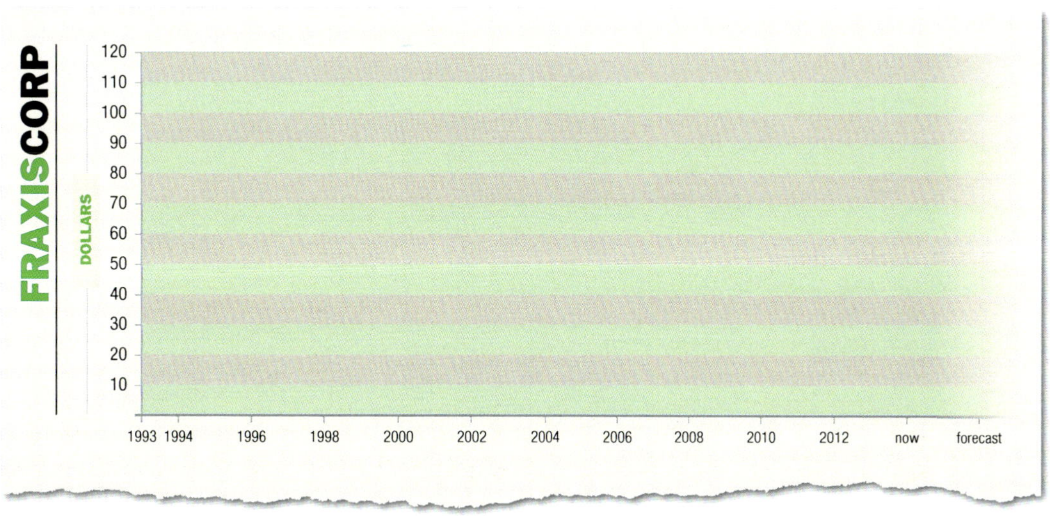

Presenting

9 **With a partner, practise describing the information in a graph.**

Student A: turn to page 116.
Student B: turn to page 120.

Glossary PAGE 156

be in the black
bid
filter through
flotation
FTSE 100
rumour

7 Mergers and acquisitions

- *will* and *going to*
- present continuous
- *could, may, might, be likely/unlikely, be bound to*

7.3 Grammar Future forms and expressing likelihood

Refresh your memory

Future forms
***will* + do**
I'll open the window.
instant decisions, predictions, future facts
***going to* + do**
It's going to rain.
plans & intentions, prediction based on present situation
is/are doing
I'm seeing the doctor at 10.30.
fixed arrangements for the future

▶ **Grammar and practice** page 134

Expressing likelihood

▶ **Grammar and practice** page 135

Arrangements, plans and contingencies

1 **With a partner, look at Tom's diary. Talk about his arrangements, plans, and intentions for next week. Be careful to use appropriate future forms.**

On Monday, he's not working, so he'll probably sleep late. He might have breakfast at Starbucks™, and then he's going to clean his flat.

◀ | ▶ | + | E-DIARY | ↺

	am	pm
Monday	Day off work! Sleep late, breakfast at Starbucks? Must clean flat!!	Eye doctor 3.45. Go swimming later? Big match on TV; order pizza, invite Martin?
Tuesday	Drive car to garage for service. Bus to work? or walk if sunny.	Marketing Presentation 2.00 (don't forget to ask Kate for help with PPT) Pick up car 6.30.
Wednesday	No meetings. Paperwork, prepare for Thurs, etc.	Dinner with Ashley. Book nice restaurant, buy flowers!
Thursday	Customer visit. Train 7.30, arrive 9.30. Taxi to office, meeting 10.00	Lunch at The Tree (table booked) Ask customer about needs for next year. Home late.
Friday	Best day to ask boss about holidays? NB if Thursday successful.	Finish early. Call Ashley if dinner went well.
Saturday	My birthday! 23 – that's really old! Buy food for tonight	Birthday party at Tom's house. Let's dance! If Ashley can't come, invite Kelly.
Sunday	Sleep? or play squash? Read newspapers Must phone Mum!	Help Tom clean up. Go for walk with Ashley (or Kelly?) if no rain. If rain, cinema?

2 **Tell your partner what's in your own diary/PDA/smartphone/head for next week.**

Expressing likelihood

3 **In small groups, take turns to make predictions about the things below. Use expressions from the table opposite to evaluate the probability of your predictions actually happening.**

1 a sports event
2 the economy in your country
3 your next exam/test/evaluation
4 the weather
5 the job market
6 the next election
7 next season's fashions
8 your own predictions

A: *I think Brazil will win the World Cup.*
B: *No, it's unlikely.*
C: *There's no way! Spain are much stronger!*

B: *I think there's a good chance that the economy is going to continue getting worse before it gets better.*
A: *Definitely. There's no doubt that the recession is going to carry on for some time yet.*
C: *I'm not so sure. I think we could see things starting to improve soon.*

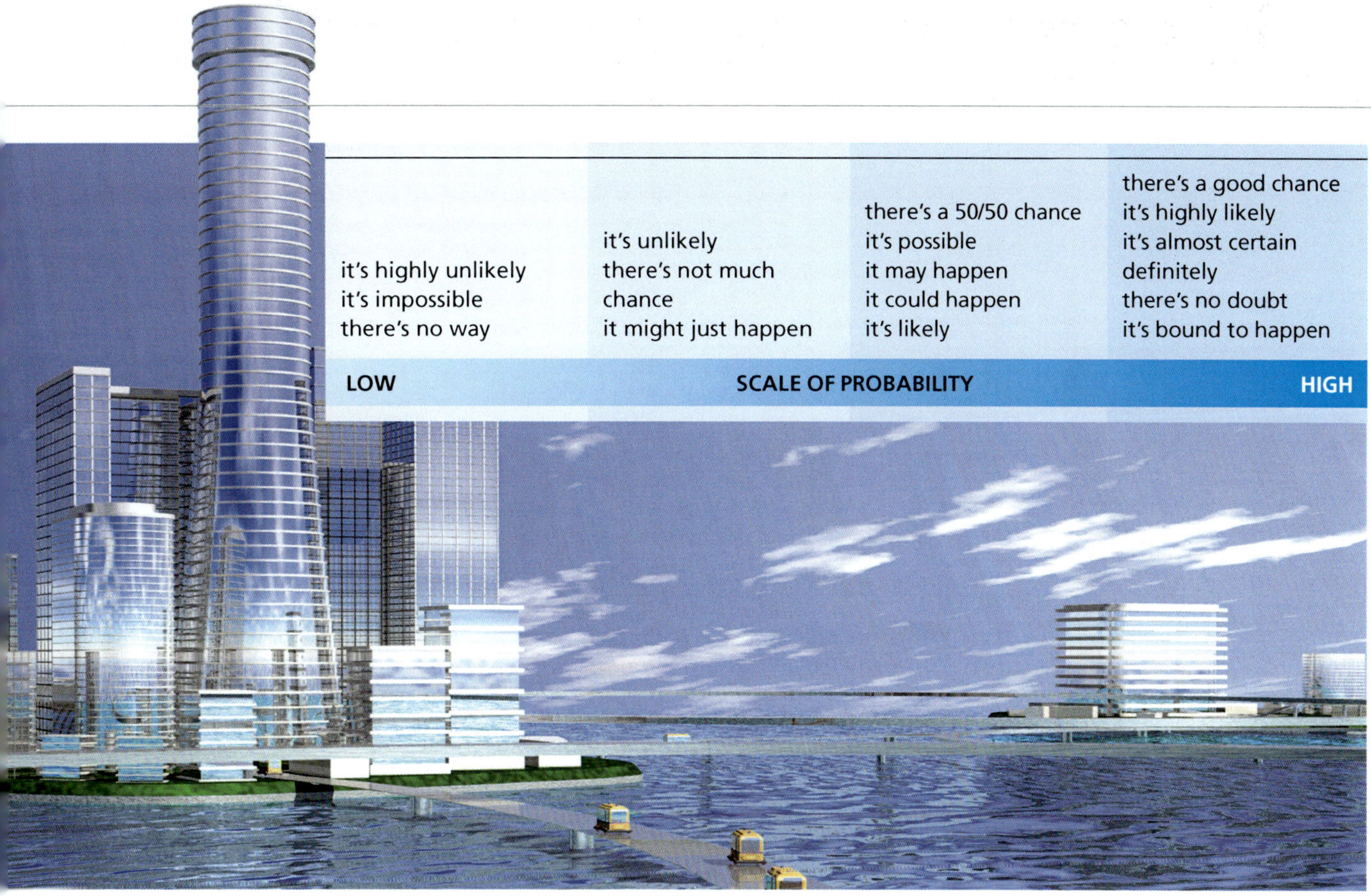

LOW			HIGH
it's highly unlikely it's impossible there's no way	it's unlikely there's not much chance it might just happen	there's a 50/50 chance it's possible it may happen it could happen it's likely	there's a good chance it's highly likely it's almost certain definitely there's no doubt it's bound to happen

SCALE OF PROBABILITY

Discussion

4 Work in groups of three. You are futurists. Choose a column each, A, B or C. Prepare a one-minute presentation discussing the likelihood of each event happening by 2050. Using the expressions from Exercise 3 again and take turns to present your views, answer questions and defend your ideas.

A	B	C
Everyone will work from home.	Everyone will go back to university every ten years.	Nobody will work more than three days a week.
There will be a single world currency.	Mobile cities will be built on the oceans.	Virtual offices will be accessible from anywhere in the world.
There will be hotels and conference centres on the moon.	The majority of senior managers will be women.	Chinese will be the language of business.

Internet research

Search for the keywords *Alvin Toffler* to find out about this leading futurist and his company's work.

Listening

5 2:42 Listen to a conversation between two friends at a party, and mark the future events in the box *U* (unlikely) or *P* (planned).

☐ go freelance ☐ start evening classes ☐ stay at Artip ☐ find a new job
☐ Artip take-over ☐ read the job ads ☐ give up smoking and drinking
☐ retrain as a marketing assistant

Which arrangement has Ashley forgotten to mention?

Discussion

6 With a partner, discuss your plans, intentions and hopes for the future. Talk about:

- the rest of the day
- this evening
- tomorrow
- the weekend
- next week
- next month
- next holidays
- next term
- next year
- your next job
- the next 25 years
- your retirement. (It's never too soon to plan ahead!)

- different visual aids
- expressions for describing visuals
- giving a presentation

7.4 Speaking Presentations – visuals

Discussion

1 **Mark these presentation tools *E* (essential) or *N* (non-essential) to a good presentation, then compare with a partner and explain your choices.**

☐ a laptop ☐ a video projector ☐ a DVD player and TV ☐ a laser pointer
☐ a flip chart and pens ☐ a blackboard and chalk ☐ an interactive whiteboard (IWB)
☐ a set of handouts ☐ a 35-mm slide projector ☐ presentation software

Listening for gist

2 2:43–2:46 **Listen to four presenters. What mistakes are they making? Match extracts 1–4 with the tips for effective presentations a–d below.**

a) Don't put too much data on slides: no more than six lines of text, and no more than six words per line. ☐
b) Too many visuals confuse the audience: don't overload them with slides. ☐
c) Don't be too technical: adapt to the target audience, and don't read out text on slides. ☐
d) Help the audience to understand by introducing, highlighting and explaining the most important information. ☐

Listening for detail

3 2:47 **Listen to a better presentation. Which of the three slides a, b, or c below is the presenter describing?**

A
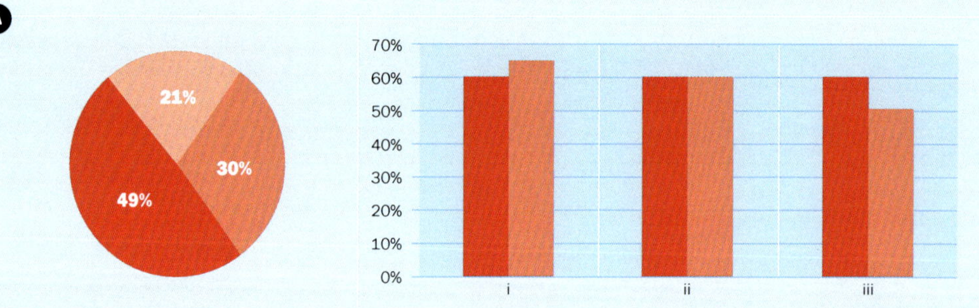

B
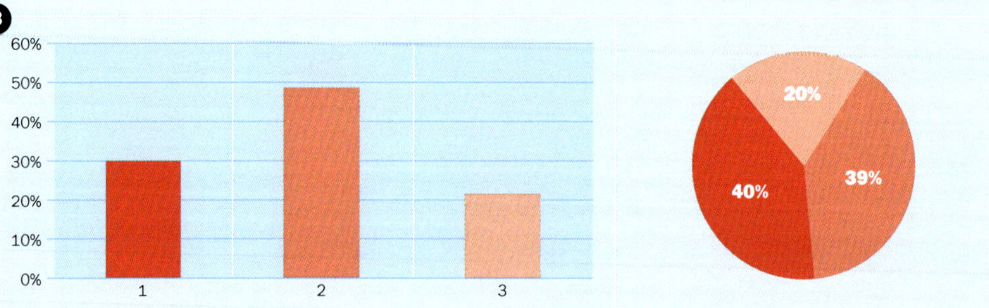

C
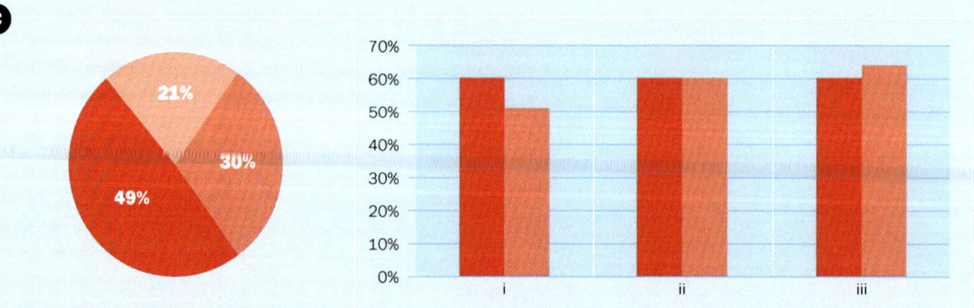

Internet research

What do the terms vertical and horizontal integration mean? Find out about current trends in vertical integration in the music, drinks or TV industries.

4 2:47 **With a partner, choose the correct option in the checklist of useful expressions for presenting visuals. Then listen again and check your answers.**

Useful expressions: Presenting visuals

Introducing a slide or visual

I'd like you to look at this slide.
My next slide *presents / shows / contains* two charts …
Let's *look / see / show* at the second chart.

Highlighting

As the graph shows , …
As you will *mark / notice / remark* in the pie-chart , …
As you can *perceive / see / look*, after a merger …

Contrasting

in contrast to …
compared *with / regarding / in relation to* almost half who said …
moreover / notwithstanding / whereas it remains about the same in …

Explaining and interpreting

The figures seem to *recommend / suggest / explain* that …
This is *because / resulting / due to* a perceived drop …
The results *involve / indicate / interpret* that retailers …
as *contrary / opposite / opposed* to manufacturers …
This is the *result / reason / record* of improved product quality …

Presenting visuals

5 **The pie-chart shows how typical Americans spend their income.**

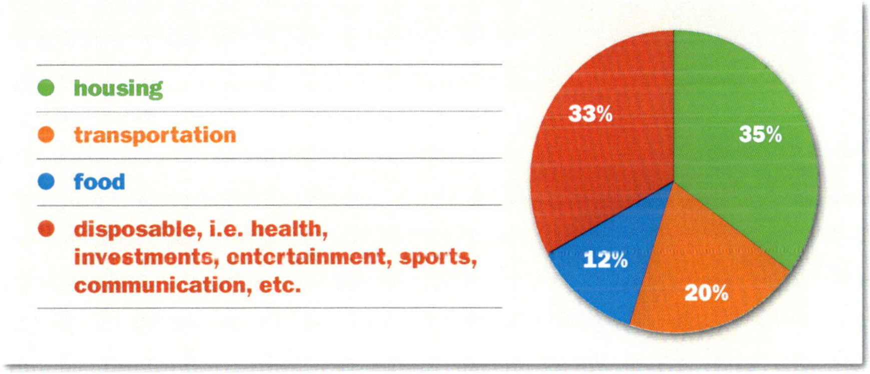

Draw two pie-charts, showing how you use your income today, and how you think you might use it in 20 years from now. In small groups, present your charts using the framework below.

1 Introduce the first chart.
2 Highlight points of interest.
3 Explain anything unusual.
4 Interpret what your chart says about you and your lifestyle.
5 Repeat points 1–4 for your second chart, and contrast the second chart with the first.

Presentation

6 **Work in groups of three. Your company, which manufactures tennis racquets, is looking for a suitable takeover target in order to diversify and accelerate growth. Each person will present one company: decide together which is the best candidate for acquisition.**

Student A: turn to page 115.
Student B: turn to page 117.
Student C: turn to page 121.

Glossary PAGE 157

crucial
deteriorate
disposable income
highlight
overload

7 Mergers and acquisitions

- format of slides
- being brief and concise
- writing presentation slides

7.5 Writing Presentation slides

Discussion

1 Decide which two of the following you would not expect to find in a presentation slide. Why not?

backgrounds bold text bullet points different fonts
footnotes italics logos paragraphs photos sound effects

Model

2 Read the three PowerPoint slides. Which is the best way of presenting the information, and why?

A

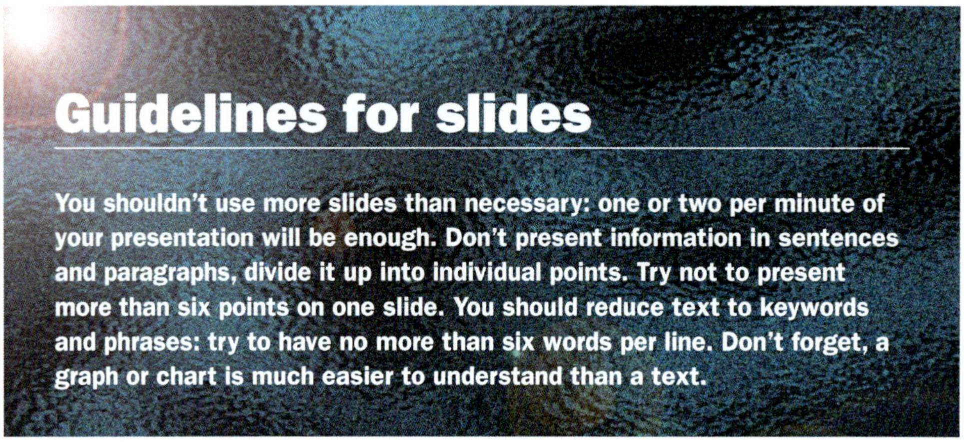

B

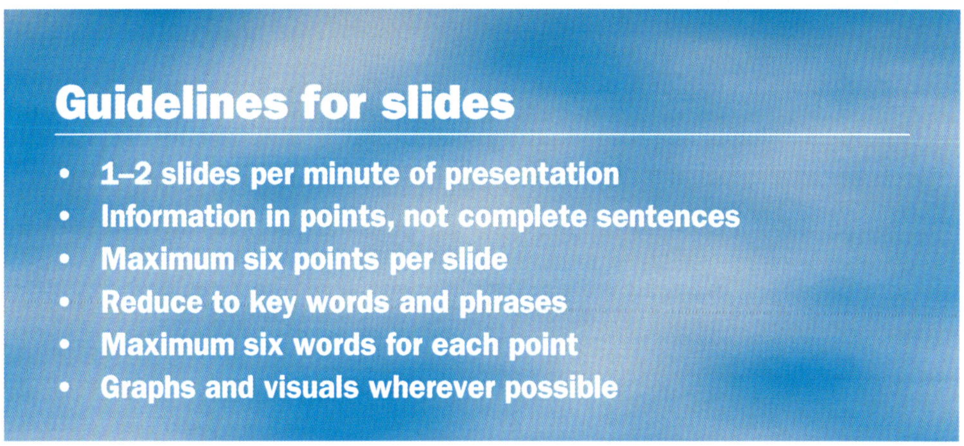

C

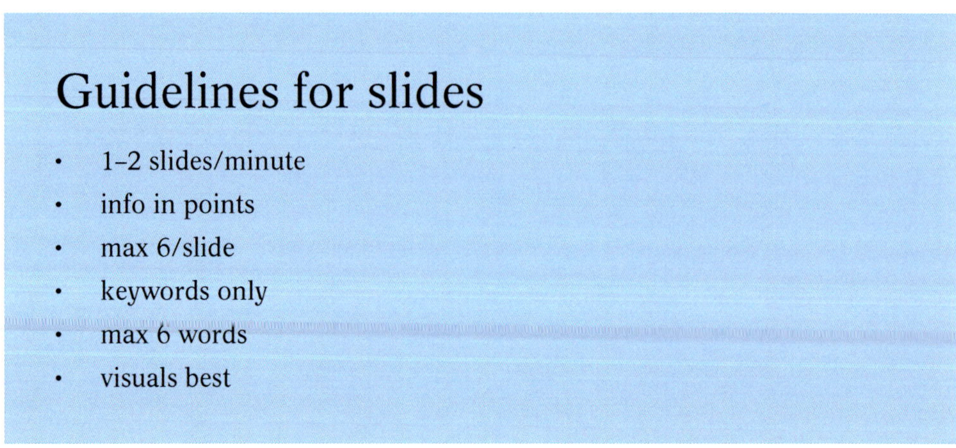

Internet research

Search for the keywords *Death by PowerPoint* to find out more about the pros and cons of multimedia presentations.

Analysis

3 Compare slides A and B. Which words have been retained and what kind of words have been deleted in slide B?

Language focus

4 Underline the key words in each extract to include on a slide about writing presentations. Then reduce each point to six to eight words.

1 One of the most challenging aspects of writing a presentation is the need to organize the information in a logical way.
2 Choose attractive background and text colours that are comfortable for the audience to read.
3 Presentation software can be fun to use. Be creative, but do not include too many effects which may distract your audience from your content.
4 Make sure the text is large enough that the audience can read it easily from the back of the room. Also, use a standard font that is not too complicated or distracting.
5 Use positive statements like 'The figures show …' rather than vague language like 'The data could possibly suggest …'

5 Reduce this presentation extract to five points on one slide.

'I'm here this morning to present the three possible scenarios which, in our discussions with the bank and our consultants, we have identified as the three most realistic futures for our company. Our first option is to do nothing: we know that the market is becoming more and more competitive, but if we are careful, we can continue to survive – at least for some years. Our second option is to borrow money to invest in new technologies in order, hopefully, to develop new, high-margin products for our existing customers, and for new markets. The third and final scenario is to launch a takeover bid to acquire Iticom, who already have the technology we need to enter those new markets immediately. Ladies and gentlemen, after carefully considering all the options, it is this third scenario which I intend to recommend. It is, of course, a high-risk scenario, but it is a scenario which holds enormous potential for our company.'

Output

6 2:48 Listen to a presentation about Galway Software. Take notes on the strengths, weaknesses, opportunities and threats the speaker has identified, and his proposal. Then write slides to illustrate the presentation.

Writing slides

7 Plan a short presentation on a subject of your choice and write a maximum of six slides. Exchange slides with a partner and give each other feedback.

Glossary PAGE 157

bullet points
distracting
font
vague

- comparing financial information
- analysis of the viability of a merger

7.6 Case study Calisto

Discussion

1 **Calisto, IMM and Reysonido sell musical instruments in Central America. Look at the figures and compare the three businesses.**

	FY	FY -1	FY -2
IMM	(M$)	(M$)	(M$)
Sales	21	20	25
Cost of Sales	10.5	10	12.5
Total Operating Expenses	8	9	10
EBIT	2.5	1	2.5
CALISTO	(M$)	(M$)	(M$)
Sales	15	18	20
Cost of Sales	7.5	9	10
Total Operating Expenses	9	9	9
EBIT	(1.5)	0	1
REYSONIDO	(M$)	(M$)	(M$)
Sales	10	11	12
Cost of Sales	4	4.4	4.8
Total Operating Expenses	6	6	6
EBIT	0	0.6	1.2

(EBIT = earnings before interest and tax)

Reading

2 **Read the newspaper article and answer the questions.**

1 How has Dylan achieved its impressive growth?
2 What effect has it had on the market?
3 Which company has adapted best to the new market leader?

Dylan rocks instrument market

New figures yesterday confirmed the meteoric rise of Dylan Instruments to number one in Central America's musical instrument market (see charts). Panama-based newcomers Dylan, who have modelled their business on PC direct sales giant Dell, have pushed former market leader Instrumentos Musicales Mejicanos (IMM) into second place. Under the charismatic leadership of CEO Abejundio Dylan, the firm has used slick marketing and aggressive discounting to capture market share from all its competitors. 'We aim to have 50% of the local market in two years' time,' trumpets Dylan. Competitors like IMM, Calisto and Reysonido are considering alliances to ensure their survival; several smaller players have already gone out of business.

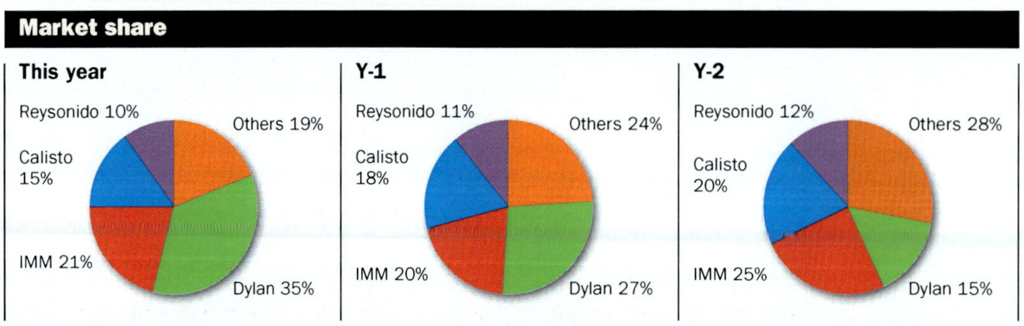

Internet research

How can smaller companies compete with a dominant market leader? Search for the keywords *Avis: We Try Harder* to read about how Avis™ took on a giant.

Listening for gist

3 2:49 **Listen to a presentation by Calisto's President to the Board of Directors and list the company's six options in Column 1 of the table.**

Options	Notes
1 Cut jobs	- same strategy as ______ - would reduce operating expenses by ______ %
2 ______	- same strategy as ______ - would reduce production costs by ______ % - would increase operating expenses by ______ per year
3 ______	- next year's sales: ______ - cost of sales would increase to ______
4 ______	- price: ______ - advantages: ______ - disadvantages: ______
5 ______	- price: ______ - bonus: ______ - repayments: ______ - combined sales: ______
6 ______	- sell off our ______

Glossary PAGE 157

charismatic
meteoric
ruthless
slick
trumpet

Listening for detail

4 2:49 **Listen again and complete the notes on Calisto's six options in Column 2 of the table above.**

Discussion and presentation

5 **In small groups, meet as consultants to Calisto's Board of Directors.**

1 Review Calisto's six options, as well as your own ideas, and decide what strategy you will recommend.
2 Prepare a presentation outlining your recommendations to the Board, using slides to structure and support your arguments.
3 Give your presentation. Yours will be in competition with those of other groups. As Calisto's Board of Directors, the class should ask questions and vote for the best presentation.

eWorkbook
Now watch the video for this unit.

8 International trade

- issues in sales mistakes
- credit agencies and insurance

Internet research

Fluctuations in the exchange rate between currencies can be an important issue in exporting. Search for the keywords *Big Mac Index* to find out a fun way of measuring these.

8.1 About business Export sales and payment

Discussion

1 How can selling your product in other countries be more difficult than at home? With a partner, list four aspects of export sales where there may not be a level playing field.

Scan reading

2 Read the article opposite from a trade magazine. Which four export mistakes did Eisenhart Games make?

Reading for detail

3 Read the article again. Which eight lessons does Vincenti say exporters have to learn?

Listening for detail

4 2:50 Listen to an interview with James Sullivan, a sales manager with Nehling and Hynes, an American credit agency, and answer the questions.

1 Which two kinds of service do credit agencies provide?
2 How large is Nehling and Hynes' database, and why is this important?
3 How are credit ratings useful?
4 What proportion of European and US firms purchase credit insurance?
5 Which advantage does credit insurance give Daryl Vincenti in Saudi Arabia?
6 On average, how much does international credit insurance cost?

Reading for detail

5 Read this extract from a guide to methods of payment in international trade. Put the methods in order from the safest (1) to the riskiest (4) from the exporter's point of view.

☐ **Open account**
Goods are shipped directly to the buyer, with a request for payment.

☐ **Advance payment**
Payment is expected by the exporter, in full, before goods are shipped.

☐ **Bills for collection**
A bill of exchange is sent from the exporter's bank to the buyer's bank. When the buyer agrees to pay on a certain date, they sign the draft. The documents and goods are released to the buyer against this acceptance.

☐ **Letters of credit (L/Cs), also known as documentary credits (DCs)**
Documentary credit is a bank-to-bank commitment of payment: the buyer's bank guarantees that payment will be made when the shipping documents are found to be in compliance with terms set by the buyer.

Discussion

6 As the exporter, decide what methods of payment in Exercise 5 you would require from these customers.

1 The buyer is a well-known company in a large country in western Europe. This is a first order but you hope the buyer will become a regular customer.
2 The buyer is in a country where currency exchange is controlled by the government. Requests for foreign currency payments must be justified by supporting documents.
3 The buyer is a new customer in a country with a fragile economy and a poor credit rating.
4 The buyer is a large North American company with a reputation for slow payment.
5 The buyer is one of your suppliers in a neighbouring country.
6 The buyer represents a small company in a developing country and is a personal friend.

7 You and a friend design and sell your own line of T-shirts at rock concerts. You have been very successful in your own country, and now several contacts in other countries have expressed interest in your product. What problems do you anticipate if you start to export, and what solutions can you suggest?

Glossary PAGE 157

chase
creditworthiness
level playing field
take on board
think outside the box
without a trace
wizard

Pinball wizard learns from mistakes

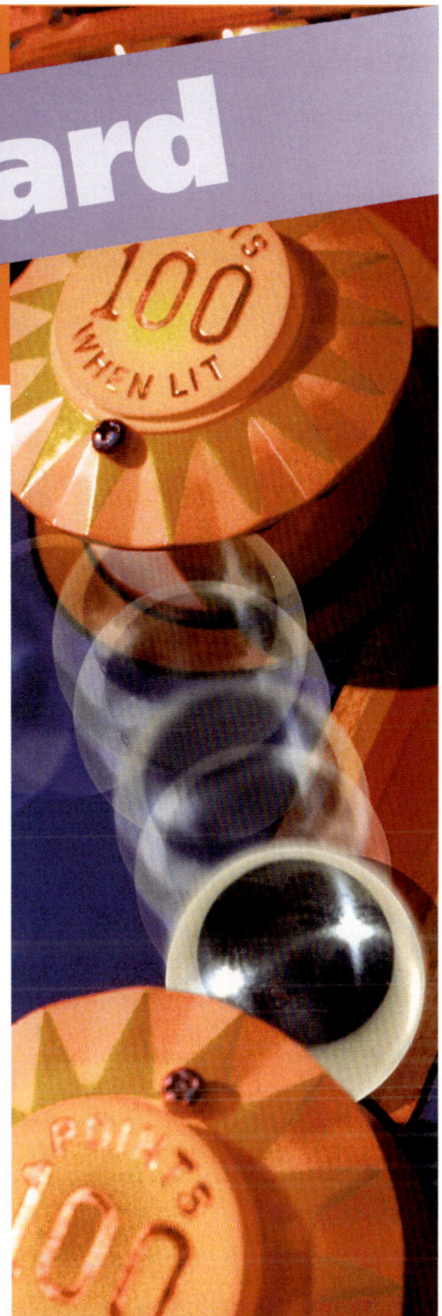

AT CHICAGO-BASED EISENHART GAMES, Daryl Vincenti is known as the 'export wizard'. Over the last three years, the pinball machine manufacturer has developed a profitable new market in the Middle East. 'Times are hard for pinball in the US,' says Vincenti. 'Competition from video games and computers has hit small manufacturers like us really hard, so we have to find new markets.' Eisenhart now has some 35% of a growing Middle East market, but it hasn't been easy. 'We made a lot of mistakes at the beginning,' confesses Vincenti, 'but we learned fast. We're now starting to work in S E Asia, and things are much easier because we've taken important lessons on board in the Middle East.'

Vincenti puts using a good credit agency at the top of his lessons learned list. 'When you've invested time, effort and money in making an export sale, you want to get paid! After wasting a lot of time chasing payments, a friend introduced me to Nehling and Hynes. We learned that by using a credit agency to check out your customer's creditworthiness and to insure against non-payment, you can make export virtually risk-free.'

Other lessons learned centred on adaptability. 'Be flexible: you have to learn to think outside the box,' says Vincenti. 'And don't assume that what works well in your domestic market will automatically go down well in another. You should also be prepared to modify your product specifications to meet local conditions, and to focus on different aspects of the marketing mix. In the Middle East, for example, price is not everything. We started out trying to sell on price: we soon learned that over there, image, quality and service are all more important.'

'You don't succeed in export markets by giving them a couple of hours a week when things are slow at home.'

Vincenti also stresses that would-be exporters should make a firm commitment to export, but focus on one market, rather than trying to sell all over the world. 'You don't succeed in export markets by giving them a couple of hours a week when things are slow at home. You have to put in a lot of time, get out there and meet your customers, and manage your local distributors proactively – if you don't, it's "game over". Eisenhart learned the hard way when they signed an exclusive deal with an agent in the Gulf; at the end of the first year, sales were zero, and the agent had disappeared without trace.

A final lesson is to remember that appearances can be deceptive, warns Vincenti: 'One day we received a 15-word fax in approximate English from what seemed to be one man and a camel somewhere out in the desert. We thought it was a joke, but a week later we decided we should answer it anyway. They're now our biggest customer.'

8 International trade

- collocations for making and processing payments
- credit and insurance
- exports

8.2 Vocabulary International deals and payments

Collocations

1 **Complete the collocations for talking about payment by choosing the correct noun in the box for each group of verbs.**

an application a deal an invoice a payment conditions goods

issue		provide		submit	
settle	1 ________	load	2 ________	vet	3 ________
query		ship		approve	

state		negotiate		make	
meet	4 ________	reach	5 ________	miss	6 ________
comply with		sign		chase	

Decide whether the buyer or the seller carries out the actions above.

Phrasal verbs

2 **Put the words in these guidelines for exporters in the correct order. Each sentence contains a phrasal verb.**

1 check / customer's / your / on / creditworthiness / up / new
2 doubts / insurance / if / you / take / about / getting / have / out / paid
3 behind / their / customers / do / not / get / payments / with / let
4 as / invoices / soon / become / they / chase / as / overdue / up
5 act / getting / your / difficulties / quickly / if / customer / is / into

3 **Match definitions a–e with the correct phrasal verb from Exercise 2.**

a) get something officially from a specialist organization ☐
b) moving towards a particular condition or situation ☐
c) find out information about something or someone discreetly ☐
d) find out what is being done about something ☐
e) fail to do something at the right time ☐

Internet research

What is a thesaurus and when is it useful? Search for the keyword *thesaurus*. Then, in an online thesaurus, search for the nouns *credit*, *cash* and *trade*. For each noun, find synonyms, antonyms and common collocations.

Listening

4 2:51–2:55 **Listen to five conversations about export issues. Use verb–noun collocations from Exercises 1 and 2 to say what is happening in each.**

1 A Slovakian company has <u>*submitted*</u> an application for credit.
Bruno asks his colleague to ________ on their ________.
2 The company is going to ________ ________ on a shipment.
They need to do this to ________ with the conditions in the contract.
3 Francesca's boss ask her to ________ up an invoice.
She doesn't want Kawasaki to get ________ with their payments.
4 Mr Takahashi ________ the ________. He asks for more time to pay. The company seems to be ________ into difficulties.
5 The companies talk about how the goods will be ________. In the end, they ________ a deal.

Collocations

5 How many two-word collocations can you make by combining the words *credit*, *insurance* and *customer* with the nouns in the box?

card claim credit insurance line loyalty
period policy portfolio sales terms

6 Use collocations from Exercise 5 to complete these sentences.

1 Frequent-flyer schemes, free gifts and credit are all ways of developing ________.
2 To avoid cash-flow problems, sales teams need to be given a clear ________.
3 An ________ provides cover in case of an accident.
4 Because old customers leave, a sales person must constantly be looking to add to their ______.
5 ________ reduces the risk of default on export payments.
6 After the fire, the company filed a ________ for compensation.

Defining words

7 With a partner, practise defining words relating to business transactions.

Student A: use the information below.
Student B: turn to page 121.

Give Student B definitions for 1, 2, 4, 6, 7 and 9 across. Student B will give you definitions for 1, 3, 5 and 8 down and 10 and 11 across to help you complete the crossword.

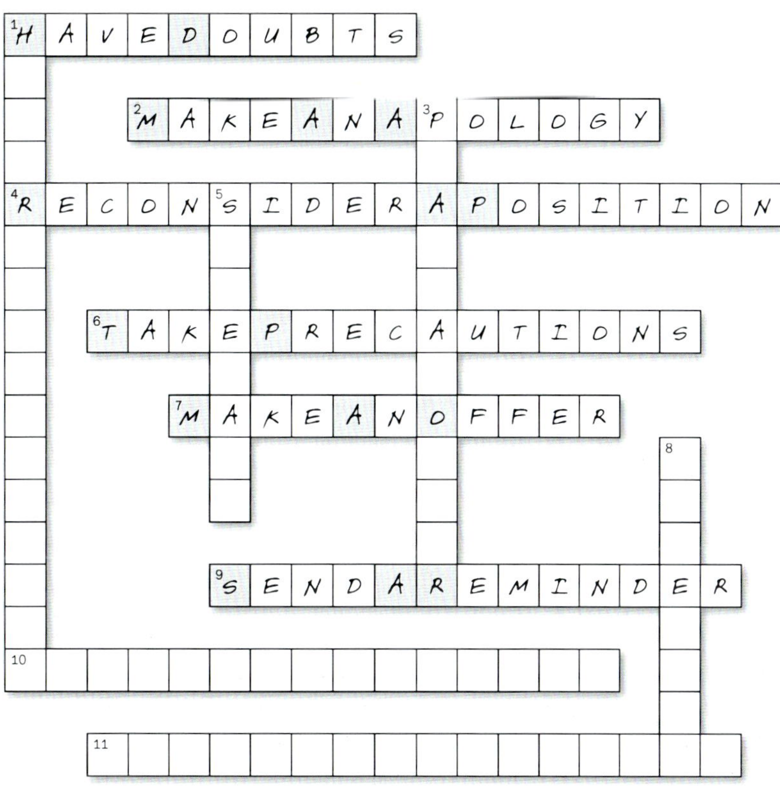

Glossary PAGE 157

file a claim
forwarder
frequent-flyer schemes
get behind with

8.2 Vocabulary

8 International trade

- time expressions with *in*, *on* and *at*
- *ago, last, next, yesterday* and *tomorrow*
- dependent prepositions

Refresh your memory

in
periods
the morning, July, the winter, 2007, the 80s

on
days and dates
Monday, the 17th, New Year's Day

at
times and special times
3pm, breakfast, the weekend, Christmas

ø
expressions with *last, next, ago, yesterday, tomorrow*

▶ **Grammar and practice** page 136

8.3 Grammar Prepositions

Prepositions of time

1 With a partner, ask and answer the questions about your country using the appropriate preposition.

1 When do most people start and finish work?
2 When do students usually do most of their work?
3 When does the New Year begin?
4 When are the school holidays?
5 What other times are popular for holidays?
6 When is the best time for tourists to visit?
7 What time do people usually eat breakfast, lunch and dinner?
8 When is it impolite to telephone people?
9 When are you allowed to make a lot of noise?
10 When are salaries usually paid?
11 How quickly do companies usually pay their bills?
12 When are the sales?

Dependent prepositions

2 Find the verb in each group that does not have the same dependent preposition as the other three. Write the preposition in the space provided.

against for from to in of on ~~to~~ with for

1	listen	(let)	consent	refer	(*to*)
2	comply	sympathise	resort	associate	(______)
3	pay	wait	vote	object	(______)
4	depend	rely	insist	attend	(______)
5	result	invest	borrow	succeed	(______)
6	suffer	emerge	hear	account	(______)
7	discuss	apply	look	apologize	(______)
8	consist	react	approve	think	(______)
9	listen	belong	leave	relate	(______)
10	fight	insure	protect	ask	(______)

Listening for gist

3 2:56–2:65 **Listen to ten short dialogues and use a word from the box to describe what the people are discussing. Be careful to use the right preposition.**

access apologizing aptitude complying damage
dependence hearing insuring investing satisfaction

1 They are discussing _________ _________ property.
2 She is talking about _________ _________ what she said to her.
3 She is lucky that there isn't much _________ _________ her car.
4 They are admiring her _________ _________ languages.
5 They are worrying about their company's _________ _________ one big firm.
6 _________ _________ the American Food and Drug Administration is essential if they want to sell the product in the States.
7 She is explaining the company policy of _________ _________ non-payment.
8 They are expressing their _________ _________ this year's results.
9 They are worried about not _________ _________ Taiwan.
10 There is as system failure, so they don't have _________ _________ data.

Speaking

4 With a partner, or in groups of four, play prepositions tennis. Student A 'serves' by saying a verb from the list in Exercise 2. Student B 'returns' by saying a short sentence with the verb and correct preposition (without looking at the list!). Student B then says another verb from the list which Student A 'returns' with the correct preposition and another verb, etc. Score a point each time your opponent answers incorrectly.

A: rely
B You can rely on me to get the right answer. agree
A: I don't agree with that at all! react

Listening for detail

5 2:66 Listen to the conversation between Paul, a manager, and his assistant, Jenny. Complete the schedule with the times or time periods, using the appropriate prepositions.

1 Jenny is picking up tickets *this evening, before 6.00.*
2 Jenny is dropping tickets off at office ______
3 Paul's flight leaves ______
4 Check-in opens ______
5 Finance meeting finishes ______
6 Paul's kids go to bed ______
7 Paul is staying in the States ______
8 Paul is attending six meetings ______
9 Paul's return flight leaves ______
10 Paul is preparing the Merosom pitch ______
11 Merosom announce their decision ______
12 Paul will read files for New York meetings ______

Internet research

Search for the keywords *how to become a millionaire*. As you read, make a list of five words followed by a dependent preposition, which you feel are useful to learn.

Glossary PAGE 158

drop off
jet-lagged
pitch

Speaking

6 Work in groups of three. You are going to hold a conversation about one of the subjects below.

- how to become a millionaire
- how to persuade a bank to lend you money
- how to get promotion
- how to find and keep customers
- how to manage professional stress
- how to manage your boss

Student A: turn to page 117.
Student B: turn to page 119.
Student C: turn to page 120.

- expressions for checking understanding
- correcting and reformulating
- roleplaying a negotiation

8.4 Speaking Negotiations – diplomacy

Discussion

1 **Read the information in the box. With a partner, discuss whether you think the countries and regions below are *L* (low-context) or *H* (high-context) cultures.**

	Low-context cultures	High-context cultures
Focus of negotiations	problem-solving, deadlines are important	relationship-building, time is flexible
Communication style	direct, verbal, few non-verbal signals	indirect, dislike conflict, avoid saying no
Business organization	individuals more important than the group	group more important than individuals

☐ China ☐ USA ☐ Australia ☐ N Europe
☐ Middle East ☐ Latin America ☐ UK ☐ Japan

What does this mean for international negotiators?

Listening for gist

2 2:67–2:69 **Listen to three negotiation extracts. What went wrong in each case? Think about high- and low-context cultures, as well as the actual phrases used.**

3 2:70–2:72 **Listen to alternative versions of the three negotiations. How do the negotiators avoid misunderstandings?**

4 2:70–2:72 **With a partner, choose the correct options in the checklist of useful expressions for being diplomatic. Then listen again and check your answers.**

Useful expressions: Diplomatic negotiations

Checking understanding

Correct me if I'm *impolite / wrong / inappropriate*, but you seem to be saying that …
Have I *got / seen / caught* this right?
Would I be *true / fair / right* in saying that …?
If I've understood *just / correctly / really* …

Correcting misunderstandings

I'm afraid there seems to be a slight *misunderstanding / mistake / mishap*.
I'm sorry, that isn't quite what I *want / meant / expected*.
Perhaps I haven't made myself *sense / right / clear*.

Reformulating

Let me put it another *angle / way / time*.
What I was trying to *say / mean / tell* was …
Allow me to *repeat / rephrase / reform* that.
What I *meant / told / expressed* was …

Diplomatic language

5 **Match the direct remarks 1–4 with diplomatic forms that were used in Exercise 3.**

Direct	Diplomatic
1 I'm not ready to make a decision.	a) Perhaps we should talk again in a few days?
2 This project is totally unrealistic.	b) I think we might need more time to explore all the implications.
3 Let's finish the meeting now.	c) We would be very happy to give you the same terms as Auckland, if you were in a position to order the same volume.
4 We won't pay for shipping unless you give us a bigger order.	d) I'm afraid we feel there are still quite a large number of difficulties to face in this project.

Internet research

Search for the keywords *high low context* *polychronic culture* to find out more about Edward T Hall's work on culture and communication.

6 **Complete the summary. Diplomatic language often uses:**

- modal verbs like *could*, ________, ________, ________
- softening adverbs like *maybe* or ________
- qualifiers like *a bit*, *rather*, *a little* or ________
- introductory warnings like *I'm sorry*, *actually*, ________
- (negative) questions rather than statements.

7 **'Translate' the direct remarks into diplomatic language, and vice versa.**

Direct	Diplomatic
1	Wouldn't it be easier for everybody if we held the meeting here rather than in Colombia?
2 If you don't want to do business, just say so!	
3	Actually, I was wondering whether you might reconsider your position on that particular issue?
4 So you don't want to sell us your products?	
5	Couldn't we perhaps start a little earlier than 11am tomorrow? We might find we would make a bit more progress.
6 That's not true. I never said that!	
7	To be honest, I'm inclined to think that business trips aren't quite as useful as everybody says they are.
8 So you don't trust us to pay?	

Negotiating

8 **With a partner, take turns to choose a subject and hold short negotiations following the chart below. Be diplomatic!**

1 buying worldwide rights to your partner's movie script
2 buying advertising space on your partner's car
3 buying worldwide rights to using your partner's name
4 buying equity in your partner's business

Student A	Student B
1 Make an offer.	
	2 Check understanding.
3 Correct misunderstanding, if necessary, reformulate offer.	
	4 Make a counter offer, or go to 5.
5 Accept offer, or go to 2.	

Glossary PAGE 158

consensus
implication
quit

eWorkbook
Now watch the video for this unit.

8.4 Speaking

- payment requests
- sounding polite
- writing requests and reminders

8.5 Writing Requests and reminders

Discussion

1 Answer the questions below. Then compare your answers with a partner.

1 What is your philosophy on credit?
a) never borrow money b) use credit in moderation c) get as much credit as you can
2 If you have to ask someone to repay money they owe you, how do you feel?
a) embarrassed b) angry c) nothing, it's only money
3 What would you write to remind someone they owe you money? Why?
a) a text message b) an email c) a letter

Model

2 Read the emails below. Which email 1–4 is:

a request? ☐ a reminder? ☐ a refusal? ☐ a final demand? ☐

Highlight the phrases which helped you to decide.

1 INBOX | REPLY | FORWARD

According to our records, our invoice number 061704 for €15,789 is now overdue. If, however, this invoice has already been settled, please disregard this email.

2 INBOX | REPLY | FORWARD

In answer to your enquiry of 2 September about trading on open account, we regret to inform you that we are unable to agree to your request due to your insufficient credit rating. We hope you will understand the reasons for this decision, and we trust that we can continue to do business together as in the past.

3 INBOX | REPLY | FORWARD

Further to our email of 23 May, we have still not received payment for the outstanding sum of €15,789. We regret to inform you that we are suspending all shipments until this outstanding balance has been settled.

4 INBOX | REPLY | FORWARD

As we now intend to place regular orders with your company, we would appreciate being able to trade on open account. We are confident this arrangement will be to our mutual benefit, and we look forward to an early reply.

Analysis

3 Make complete sentences by using one phrase from each column. The first one has been done for you.

1 I am writing to enquire	agree to	which is still outstanding.
2 I am afraid group policy	the sum of €21,552	to extend credit terms of 60 days.
3 We are pleased to	whether you would be able	of this outstanding balance.
4 May I remind you that	your early settlement	the terms you propose.
5 We wrote to you on 4 November	does not allow us	to our legal department.
6 Would you let us	regarding the balance of €12,650	is still outstanding?
7 We would appreciate	but to pass the matter on	as soon as possible?
8 We shall have no alternative	know your decision	to give more than 30 days' credit.

Which sentences are used in:

a request? ☐ a reminder? ☐ a refusal? ☐ an agreement? ☐ a final demand? ☐

Internet research

If your customers are slow payers, one way to improve cash-flow is factoring. Search for the keywords *factoring receivables* to find out how factoring works, and its advantages and disadvantages.

Language focus

4 Which is the most polite form, a or b?

1 a) In view of the increase in our volume of business, …
b) Considering how much more business we're giving you, …
2 a) About the longer credit you asked for, …
b) With regard to your request for improved credit terms, …
3 a) Re: your letter dated 31/1, …
b) Further to your letter of 31 January, …
4 a) We look forward to receiving your order.
b) We expect you to order quickly.
5 a) We're giving you a week to pay, …
b) Unless we receive payment within seven days, …
6 a) We would like to apologize for the delay in sending the enclosed cheque.
b) We are sorry we took so long to send the enclosed cheque.
7 a) This was an unfortunate oversight due to circumstances beyond our control.
b) We forgot, but it wasn't our fault.
8 a) We can assure you that it will not recur.
b) Don't worry, it will never happen again.

5 Complete the emails using vocabulary from Exercises 2, 3 and 4.

1 INBOX | REPLY | FORWARD

In ______ of the increase in our volume of ______, I am writing to ______ whether you would be prepared to ______ credit terms of 60 days.
Would you let us ______ your decision as soon as ______?

2 INBOX | REPLY | FORWARD

With ______ to your request for improved credit ______, I am afraid that group ______ does not ______ us to extend more than 30 days' credit.

3 INBOX | REPLY | FORWARD

______ to your email of 17 July, we are pleased to agree to the ______ you propose, and we look ______ to receiving your order.

4 INBOX | REPLY | FORWARD

May I ______ you that the sum of €101,000 is still ______ on your account?
We would appreciate your early ______ of this outstanding ______.

5 INBOX | REPLY | FORWARD

We would like to ______ for the delay in sending the ______ cheque. This was an unfortunate ______ due to circumstances beyond our ______, and we can assure you that it will not ______.

6 INBOX | REPLY | FORWARD

We wrote to you on 11 April ______ the balance of €15,550 which is still ______.
Unless we receive payment ______ seven days, we shall have no ______ but to pass the matter on to our ______ department.

Which email is:

a request? ☐ a reminder? ☐ a refusal? ☐
a final demand? ☐ an apology? ☐ an agreement? ☐

Glossary PAGE 157

disregard
extend
factoring
outstanding
overdue
oversight
settle

Writing

6 Work in groups of three to write and reply to requests and reminders.

Student A: turn to page 117.
Student B: turn to page 119.
Student C: turn to page 120.

- managing customer credit
- finding a solution for improving cash flow

Internet research

Search for the key words *collecting debt* to find out how small businesses can recover payments more quickly.

8.6 Case study Jeddah Royal Beach Resort

Discussion

1 Brainstorm a list of services which large hotels can charge for in addition to accommodation.

Reading for detail

2 Read the extract from a business magazine and answer the questions.

1 How does giving credit increase room revenues and attract more clients?
2 Why do luxury hotels prefer to issue their own credit cards rather than be paid by VISA, MasterCard®, American Express®, etc.?
3 What are the advantages for the customer of a 'cashless resort'?
4 Who is Riaz Hussain and what are his responsibilities?

THE JEDDAH ROYAL BEACH RESORT

THE JEDDAH Royal Beach Resort is one of Saudi Arabia's newest and most luxurious hotels. In a fiercely competitive market where foreign corporations provide 75% of revenues, every hotel from the five-star palace to the one-star motel needs to increase room revenues to be able to invest in new facilities to attract new clients. One of the major incentives in the armoury of modern hotel marketing is credit. The Royal Beach, like many of its competitors, has its own credit manager, whose job is to manage the credit which the hotel uses to encourage customers to spend freely on additional services.

One of Riaz Hussain's first innovations as Credit Manager was to introduce an in-house credit card to the Royal Beach. Such credit cards are increasingly popular, allowing hotels to develop customer loyalty as well as to avoid paying commission to credit card companies. The Royal Beach advertises itself as a 'cashless resort': customers are able to use their electronic membership card to make reservations via the Internet, to speed up check-in and check-out, and to pay for a host of services including accommodation, telephone and fax, restaurant and bar bills, leisure activities, limousines, airline tickets and even cash advances with no exchange problems. With its own boutiques, nightclub, beach, water sports and golf course, it's easy for guests from all over the world to spend several days in the sun (and perhaps several weeks' salary!) with nothing more than their plastic smart card in their pocket.

Riaz Hussain's responsibilities include vetting corporate and individual applications for credit, following clients who reach or exceed their credit limits, and organizing debt recovery from indelicate guests, or their corporate sponsors, who 'forget' to settle their bills.

Listening for detail

3 2:73 **Listen to a conversation between Riaz Hussain and Frederick, the front office manager at the Jeddah Royal Beach Resort, and complete the customer database entries.**

Customer: Ms Koepple	**Customer:** Mr Kobayashi	**Customer:** Mrs Saman
Company:	**Company:**	**Company:**
Company credit rating: good / average / poor / unknown	**Company credit rating:** good / average / poor / unknown	**Company credit rating:** good / average / poor / unknown
Current credit limit: 0	**Current credit limit:**	**Current credit limit:**
Credit limit requested:	**Credit limit requested:**	**Credit limit requested:**
Notes:	**Notes:**	**Notes:**

4 2:73 **Listen again and answer the questions.**

1 Why doesn't Riaz like having rock groups in the hotel?
2 If Ms Koepple leaves today without paying, how much will the hotel lose?
3 How much credit is Riaz prepared to allow her?
4 Why does Frederick think Mr Kobayashi is a difficult customer?
5 Why is Frederick suspicious of him?
6 What happened with Mrs Saman's company last year?
7 Why are Mrs Saman and her brother important for the hotel?

Discussion

5 **Look at the chart showing the Jeddah Royal Beach Resort's customer payments. Describe the trends for:**

1 cash payments 2 short credit periods 3 longer credit periods 4 uncollectibles.

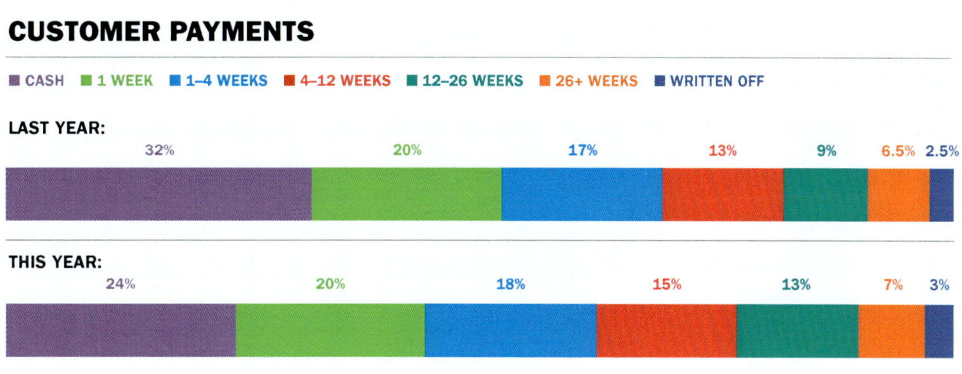

6 **With a partner, talk about these questions. Then change partners, compare and explain your decisions.**

1 How can the trends in payments be explained?
2 How can the hotel improve its cash flow?
3 How should Riaz Hussain deal with each of the three customer applications in Exercise 3?

Glossary PAGE 158

armoury
loyalty
uncollectible
vulgar
word of mouth

Writing

7 **Write a short letter to each customer explaining your decision.**

Review 7

Mergers and acquisitions

1 Match each word or phrase about finance in the box with its definition below.

acquisition   assets   due diligence
economies of scale   fixed costs   liabilities
liquidity   merger   turnover   variable costs

1 full investigation of a company's activities and finances ________
2 the amount of money that a company owes ________
3 the process of combining two companies to form a bigger one ________
4 something that someone buys (especially a company that has been bought by another company) ________
5 costs that alter directly when the business alters its level of output (e.g. raw materials, components, labour costs for factory workers) ________
6 costs that do not alter when the business alters its level of output (e.g. rent, marketing, management salaries) ________
7 things such as money, buildings or equipment that a person or company owns ________
8 measure of a company's ability to quickly convert assets into cash ________
9 reductions in the cost of producing a unit of a product that occur as the output increases ________
10 total amount of money coming into a company from sales (usually given as an annual figure) ________

2 Find words or phrases from the box in Exercise 1 that have the same or similar meaning to the following.

1 cost of sales/direct costs ________
2 overheads/indirect costs ________
3 cash-flow ________
4 debts ________
5 revenue/income ________

3 Match the words in the box with their definitions (and extra information).

climb   dip   deteriorate   fluctuate   jump
peak   rise   slide   soar   stabilize

1 become higher (literally: to move up using your hands and feet) ________
2 become less (literally: to put something into a liquid and quickly lift it out again) ________
3 change frequently, especially from a high level to a low one and back again ________
4 stop changing and become steady ________
5 get worse (opposite: improve) ________
6 get worse gradually (literally: to move smoothly and quickly across a surface) ________
7 increase (opposite: fall) ________
8 increase quickly to a high level (literally: to fly high in the sky) ________
9 increase suddenly and by a large amount (literally: push your body off the ground using your legs) ______
10 reach the highest point before becoming lower (the noun means 'the top of a mountain') ________

4 Read this sentence:

There was a ______ increase in sales.

Make adjectives that can go in the empty space using the letters and meanings given.

(Clue: the letter in bold is always the first letter.)

1 ________ a**b**cdeeilnors (large)
2 ________ aac**d**imrt (sudden and surprising)
3 ________ adee**m**ort (neither big nor small)
4 ________ ahpr**s** (sudden)
5 ________ acfgiiinn**s**t (large or noticeable)
6 ________ ghil**s**t (small in size)
7 ________ dden**s**u (quick and unexpected)

5 Look at one way to show 'cause & effect':

The new technology we bought last year ***resulted in*** *a significant increase in productivity.*

Now show 'effect & cause' using these words to complete the gaps: *a, as, because, due, of, of, result, thanks, to, to.*

The increase in productivity last year was
(1) ________ /
(2) ________ /
(3) ________ /
(4) ________ the new technology we bought.

6 Complete the sentences using the most appropriate form: *will, be going to* or the present continuous. Use contractions (*I'll, I'm*) where possible.

1 (describing your plans) Next year ________ (we/enter) the Croatian market by buying a small local firm.
2 (making a promise) Don't worry, ________ (you/have) the goods by the end of the week.
3 (giving details of a fixed arrangement) ________ (I/meet) Barbara from 9:00 to 10:00 at her office, and I should be back around 10:30.
4 (making an instant decision) Is that my mobile phone ringing? I'm sorry, ________ (I/turn) it off.

7 Complete this presentation extract using the words and phrases in the box.

as a result of   however   let's move on
next slide shows   notice from the chart
resulted in   seem to suggest   whereas

... OK, (1) ________.
My (2) ________ our administration costs one year after the merger. You will (3) ________ that the figures (4) ________ no noticeable impact on costs (5) ________ the merger. But this hides the real situation. Initially, the merger (6) ________ many large compensation payments for managerial staff who lost their jobs, and this increased costs. (7) ________, over the longer term salary costs are coming down as a result of the cuts. Next year we expect administration costs to be 2.3M, (8) ________ this year they will be about 2.9M.

Review 8

International trade

1 In each set of four below, match a verb on the left with a noun on the right to make phrases about export sales.

1 Don't sell	a) proactive with local distributors.
2 Be	b) a firm commitment to export.
3 Make	c) outside the box.
4 Think	d) on price rather than quality.
5 Trade	e) an exclusive deal.
6 Sign	f) time, effort and money.
7 Be prepared	g) on open account.
8 Invest	h) to modify product specifications.
9 Ask	i) payments can be done by the credit agency.
10 Chasing	j) a credit agency about a customer's creditworthiness.
11 Focus on	k) that what works in your domestic market will also work abroad.
12 Don't assume	l) one market, rather than trying to sell all over the world.

2 Find two words in Exercise 1 that match with these definitions.

1 the ability of a company to repay debts _________
2 trying hard to get something you want _________

3 The collocations below are used in international business transactions. Cross out the one verb in each group that does *not* collocate with the noun.

1 *issue / reach / settle / query* an invoice
2 *assume / provide / load / ship* goods
3 *chase / comply with / state / meet* conditions
4 *negotiate / reach / sign / state* a deal
5 *check in / check out / check up on* a customer's creditworthiness
6 *fall behind / get behind / move behind* with payments

4 The words in bold below are all in the wrong places. Put them in the correct places.

After the exporter and foreign customer finally (1) **check up on** a deal, the exporter will (2) **comply with** the goods and (3) **reach** an invoice. The exporter must (4) **issue** all the conditions in the contract, and if they do they can expect to be paid on time. It is a waste of time if they have to (5) **ship** customers who (6) **chase** payments. If there is a problem with payment, the exporter can use a credit agency to (7) **get behind with** a customer's creditworthiness.

5 Complete the text with these time prepositions: *at, during, from, in, until, within.*

(1) _________ the 90s we worked with a series of different local agents. (2) _________ 2002 we started using APL, and they have been our exclusive agent (3) _________ that time (4) _________ now. They are very good at collecting payment from local customers, and we give them the discretion to ask for payment (5) _________ either 60 or 90 days. They forward to us all payments they have collected, after taking their commission, and we receive money from them (6) _________ the end of every month.

6 Put the words in the diplomatic sentences into the correct order.

1 Direct: *I'll explain it again if you want.*
Diplomatic: it / let / me / way / another / put.
2 Direct: *You are not convinced.*
Diplomatic: wrong / me / if / you / correct / but / I'm / saying / that / seem / to / be / you / are / not / convinced.
3 Direct: *You are wrong!*
Diplomatic: I'm / a / slight / misunderstanding / there / seems / to / be / afraid.
4 Direct: *You don't understand!*
Diplomatic: I / clear / myself / haven't / made / perhaps.
5 Direct: *You want to withdraw from the project, right?*
Diplomatic: you / would / be / saying / I / right / in / that / want / to / withdraw / from / the / project?

7 Use the words in brackets to make the direct sentences more diplomatic.

1 We need more time. (I think/might)
____
2 There are still many difficulties. (I'm afraid/quite a large number)
____
3 We must renegotiate parts of the contract. (perhaps/should/one or two)
____
4 That will be very expensive. (won't/rather)
____

8 Complete this email sequence using the words and phrases in the box.

according to	early settlement	further to
have no alternative	now overdue	
outstanding balance	pass this matter	
regret to inform		

Email 1 (Reminder)

(1) _________ our records, our invoice number KL788 is (2) _________. The total sum is €25,600. We would appreciate your (3) _________ of this (4) _________.

Email 2 (Final demand)

(5) _________ our email of 14 June re invoice KL788, we have still not received payment for the outstanding sum of €25,600. We (6) _________ you that we (7) _________ but to (8) _________ to our legal department.

9 Match the words *outstanding* and *overdue* with their definitions.

1 not paid when expected; late _________
2 not yet paid _________

10 Which of the two words from Exercise 9 has a second meaning of 'excellent and impressive'?

Additional material

1.2 Vocabulary Work organization and responsibility

Defining words (page 13, exercise 8)

Student A

Give Student B definitions for 1, 3, 5, 7 and 9. Student B will give you definitions for 2, 4, 6, 8 and 10 to help you complete the crossword.

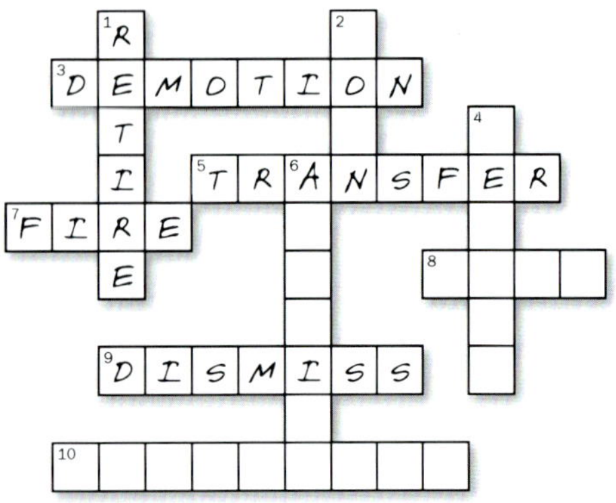

1.3 Grammar Past tenses and advice structures

Giving advice (page 15, Exercise 9)

Student A

1 **You have recently started work with a well-known firm of management consultants. Ask your partner for advice about the problems below, and react to their suggestions. Use the expressions in the box to help you.**

1 You work from 8am to 7pm every day but you can never finish your work.
2 You find it difficult to set goals.
3 Your clients don't take you seriously: they think you're too young for the job.
4 Every time you call a friend, your colleagues give you black looks.
5 You have lots of ideas to share in meetings, but your boss keeps interrupting you.

> I'm having problems with … Can you give me any advice?
> Do you have any ideas about how to …?
> What do you suggest I do about …? I just can't seem to …
> What would you do? I see what you mean, (but …)
> You've got a point, (but …) You may be right, (but …)
> OK, point taken. Yes, you're quite right.

2 **Your partner will tell you about their problems. Suggest two or three alternatives for each problem. Use the expressions in the box to help you.**

> Have you tried –ing …? Have you considered –ing …?
> How about –ing …? Have you thought of –ing …?
> You could … Why don't you …? You might want to …

1.4 Speaking Meetings one-to-one

Roleplay (page 17, Exercise 7)

Student A

1 You are a new employee at the R&D laboratory of a Finnish electronics company. You come from Brazil. You find the atmosphere in the company miserable: people work alone, mostly in silence, so you try to make them happy by being friendly, sharing sweets and biscuits, and singing songs. You have a lot of work: because you work best in the evening, you stay late to finish it. You think the centre would be more productive if everyone relaxed and enjoyed their work. Your supervisor, Student B, has asked you to attend an informal meeting: this is an opportunity for you to explain your ideas and give Student B some helpful advice.

2 You are Student B's supervisor at a large travel agency in Australia. You are worried about Student B because he/she refuses to communicate with other members of staff and hardly speaks in staff meetings. You have given Student B a lot of responsibility because you feel he/she has excellent potential, but he/she is not sharing the work with the team. The travel business has a reputation for extreme stress, and you are concerned that Student B is trying to do too much. Australians value teamwork and consider sports and social events an integral part of corporate life. Hold an informal meeting with Student B to advise him/her on how to relate to colleagues and achieve a better work-life balance.
Start the meeting by asking Student B if he/she is enjoying the job.

1.6 Case study Counselling

Roleplay (page 21, Exercise 6)

Problem holder A: Tokyo

You are experiencing culture shock in Tokyo. After two months in the marketing department of a large electronics company, you feel that you have achieved nothing. Your job description is very general; you spend most of your time processing answers to long market survey questionnaires. You are a very creative person, but when you suggest new ideas at meetings, they are usually met with silence. One colleague was very upset because you drew attention to a mistake in his presentation.

Your apartment is very small and your journey to work takes 90 minutes each way. After a long day at work, your colleagues do not understand that you do not have time to go to the restaurant with them. You would like to learn Japanese to communicate better, but when you meet Japanese people socially, they always want to speak English. You feel you are wasting your time and learning nothing.

2.1 About business Call centres

Roleplay (page 22, Exercise 6)

Role A

You are going to take part in a debate. Try to convince the others in your group of the benefits of setting up your call centres in a low-cost country like India or the Philippines. As well as your own ideas, refer to the following:

Outsourcing enables companies to
- reduce costs
- be more competitive by offering customers lower prices and better service
- preserve jobs in production
- benefit from more competent and more motivated staff
- bring new technology to developing countries
- help developing countries to improve their economies.

Locating the call centre in your own country would be too expensive and using cloud-based technology could make the company over-dependent on technology you don't have in-house expertise to manage.

2.4 Speaking Dealing with problems by telephone

Giving instructions (page 28, Exercise 1)

Student A

Without saying what it represents, give Student B instructions to draw the symbol in Grid 1. Student B will then give you instructions to draw another symbol in Grid 2.

1

	13				30				14
40				15				50	
			16				60		
		17				70			
	18				80				19
90				99				88	
			77				66		
		55				44			
	33				22				11
10				9				8	

2

A				B				C	
	D				E				F
		G				H			
			I				J		
K				L				M	
	N				O				P
		Q				R			
			S				T		
U				V				W	
	X				Y				Z

2.4 Speaking Dealing with problems by telephone

Improving a conversation (page 28, Exercise 4)

Read this conversation aloud with your partner, then decide how the conversation could be improved and practise your improved version.

Helpline: Yes?
Customer: Oh, hello. Is that Autosales?
Helpline: Yes.
Customer: Oh, good. Well, I'm calling about the new car I bought last week. It won't start.
Helpline: Oh.
Customer: Well, can you do something about it?
Helpline: I'm new here. I don't know much about cars, actually.
Customer: Well, could you put me through to someone who does?
Helpline: No.
Customer: What do you mean, 'no'?
Helpline: I mean, no, I can't. There's nobody else here.
Customer: Well, can I leave a message?
Helpline: Yes, all right. What's your name?
Customer: It's McCready. Alistair McCready.
Helpline: Er, McWhat?
Customer: No, McCready. That's M-C-C-R-E-A-D-Y.
Helpline: Got it.
Customer: All right. Well, I'll be expecting your call. Goodbye.
Helpline: Don't hold your breath!

2.5 Writing Formal and informal correspondence

Output (page 31, Exercise 5)

Student A
You work in the Accounts Department at Relopharma, a medium-sized pharmaceuticals company. Compose and send business email 1 below, using appropriate style. When you receive an email from another student, read it, then answer it following the instructions in Exercise 2. Continue in this way until you have written and sent four emails.

1 You have a problem with the accounts payable database – some entries are disappearing. It looks like some kind of virus, but your anti-virus software hasn't detected any problems. Write an email to your colleague, Student B, in Information Systems, explaining the problem and asking for help.

2 You have received an email about an invoice from Student C at Nakisoft, a software supplier. You have no records of this invoice in your database. Write an email to Student B asking them to confirm the purchase and, if appropriate, to obtain a duplicate invoice.

3 You have received another email from Nakisoft about software training. Write to Student B to complain: the week in question is impossible because you have to close the accounts.

4 You have received an email from Nakisoft about a patch. Write a reply to Student C explaining that the link on their website doesn't work.

3.3 Grammar Articles, relative clauses and noun combinations

Definitions game (page 41, Exercise 9)

As
Help the other team guess the noun combinations below by giving definitions using a relative clause. If you want to make it more difficult, use synonyms instead of the exact terms in the noun combinations.

1 vertical writing languages
2 a management consultancy firm
3 a customer satisfaction survey
4 pilfer-proof packaging
5 stress-raising automation
6 a sandwich degree course

4.3 Grammar Present tenses

Asking questions (page 53, Exercise 6)

Student A

1 **You are interviewing Student B for a job at your sports club. Ask Student B the right questions to obtain the answers below. Score one point for each correct answer you receive.**

1 At weekends.
2 Since I was at school.
3 Several years ago.
4 During the holidays.
5 No, only a few weeks.
6 The Economist.
7 For two years.
8 No, not yet.
9 In the next six months.
10 No, I haven't.

2 **You are being interviewed for a job at Student B's community arts centre. Answer the questions they ask.**

5.6 Case study St John's Beach Club

Negotiating (page 73, Exercise 5)

Student A (travel agent)
Negotiate the best deal possible with the buyer (Student B). Your standard price is $150 per person per night. This includes all meals, drinks, snacks, activities and sports (except golf). Remember you are in competition with other travel agents for the same product.
Score points as indicated for each item below.

Item	Points
Cost per person per night	
• more than $140	2
• $120 – $140	0
• less than $120	-5
Upgrade to executive suite, per person, per night	
• $50	2
• $25	1
• $10	-2
Number of participants	
• 22	1
• 24	2
• 26	3
Number of nights	
• 7	1
• 8	2
• 9 or more	3
Free access to golf course	-1

7.4 Speaking Presentations – visuals

Presentation (page 95, Exercise 6)

Student A
Present the three slides on Ultraxport and explain why this company would be a good acquisition.

1

2

3
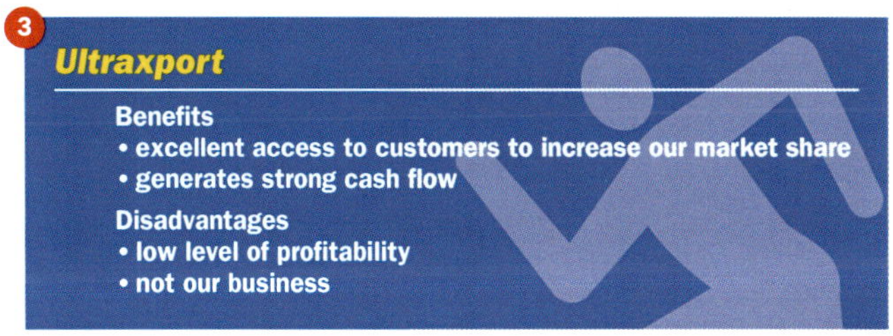

2.5 Writing Formal and informal correspondence

Output (page 31, Exercise 5)

Student B

You work in the Information Systems Department at Relopharma, a medium-sized pharmaceuticals company. Compose and send business email 1 below, using appropriate style. When you receive an email from another student, read it, then answer it following the instructions in Exercise 2. Continue in this way until you have written and sent four emails.

1 You want your software supplier, Nakisoft, to organize training on a new software tool for your Accounts Department as soon as possible. Write an email to Student C at Nakisoft asking them to contact Student A in your Accounts Department with dates for the training.

2 You have received an email from your colleague, Student A, in Accounts, about a software problem. You think it could be a virus. Write an email to Nakisoft explaining the problem and asking them to contact Student A directly to resolve the problem.

3 You have received another email from Student A about an invoice. Write an email to Student C at Nakisoft apologizing for the delay and asking them to send you a duplicate invoice.

4 You have received another email from Student A about training. Reply to Student A explaining that there is no alternative.

6.6 Case study Phoenix

Reading and discussion (page 85, Exercise 4)

Group A – Port Katherine Planning Department

Read the email you have received and answer the questions.

INBOX | REPLY | FORWARD

Hi,
The Mayor has just received a letter from the Residents' Association about the Phoenix project. They're very unhappy about site A. They're concerned about the risks of large trucks passing close to the school, as well as the noise and dust, etc. As you know, the elections are coming up soon, so we don't want to upset these people. However, Port Katherine desperately needs new jobs and investment, so we can't afford to lose Phoenix. They've also promised to get involved in community projects, although we don't know yet exactly what that means. The Mayor would like the Planning Department to set up and chair a meeting with the Residents' Association and Phoenix to talk things over and try to find an agreement. Could you arrange that for us? A few words about the other sites: we've invested a lot of money in the business park, site B, but for the moment it's still costing us money. If Phoenix buy land on the business park, we'll recover part of our investment, the residents will be reasonably happy, and we'll benefit from higher tax rates than on sites A or C. There's plenty of space for expansion (more jobs!) and there's no access problem. We can make some concessions on the price of the land if necessary. There are good reasons for choosing site C, near the harbour. However, the big problem is access. We'd have to build a new access road, which would be very expensive.
Let me know how the meeting goes. Thanks a lot,
Duncan
Duncan Gillespie, Lord Mayor's Office, Port Katherine

1 Who is the email from?
2 What is your role at the meeting?
3 Why is it important to keep the residents happy?
4 Why is the Phoenix project important for the town?
5 Which is the best site from your point of view?

7.2 Vocabulary Business performance

Presenting (page 91, Exercise 9)

Student A

1 Present Chanco's stock market history using the information from the graph, explaining causes and effects.

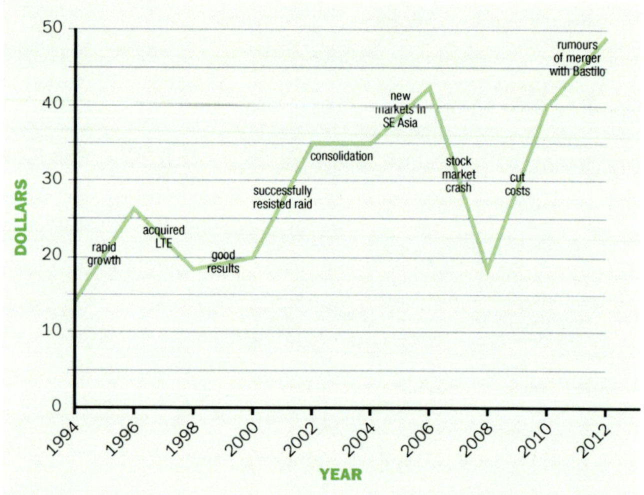

2 Listen to Student B's presentation of Bastilo Corp. and complete the graph.

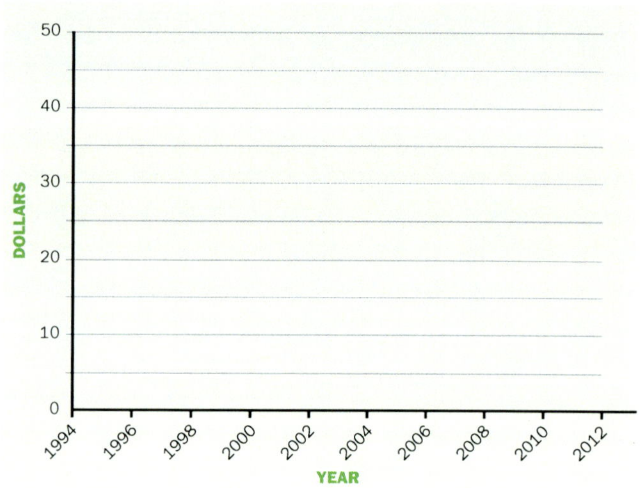

4.3 Grammar Present tenses

Present perfect and past simple (page 52, Exercise 3)

Student B

You and your partner work for an international recruitment agency. Your clients are looking for:

1 a Spanish-speaking science graduate
2 an undergraduate with marketing experience
3 a graduate accountant, to be a future finance director
4 a French-speaking graduate in business
5 an arts undergraduate with experience in the Far East
6 a Portuguese-speaking graduate with experience in sales.

You have each interviewed and tested five candidates. Exchange information with your partner to complete the tables and decide together which candidates are most suitable for each request.

Candidate	Graduation	Work experience	Management potential test
Mr Salmon			
Ms Bianco	last October, Maths	car sales in Argentina and Brazil	A+
Mrs Grey			
Miss Rose	next summer, Languages	marketing in Australia and Japan	A
Mr Da Silva			
Mr Green	last November, Physics	call centres in California and Florida	B+
Mr Schwartz			
Miss Plum	last September, Business	financial services in Mexico and Quebec	B
Ms Violeta			
Mr Braun	last September, Finance	computing and accounts in China	C-

2.1 About business Call centres

Roleplay (page 22, Exercise 6)

Role C

You are going to take part in a debate. Try to convince the others group of the benefits of using a cloud-based approach for your new call centre where agents work from home, wherever they live. As well as your own ideas, refer to the following:

A cloud based approach would allow your company to:

- radically reduce costs – you won't need to pay for the maintenance and running of business premises
- be more competitive by offering customers lower prices and better service
- preserve jobs in production
- hire the best staff because you won't be limited by where they are located
- offer a local service globally
- offer more flexibility in terms of hours and working conditions.

7.4 Speaking Presentations – visuals

Presentation (page 95, Exercise 6)

Student B

Present the three slides on Piezoteknik labs and explain why this company would be a good acquisition.

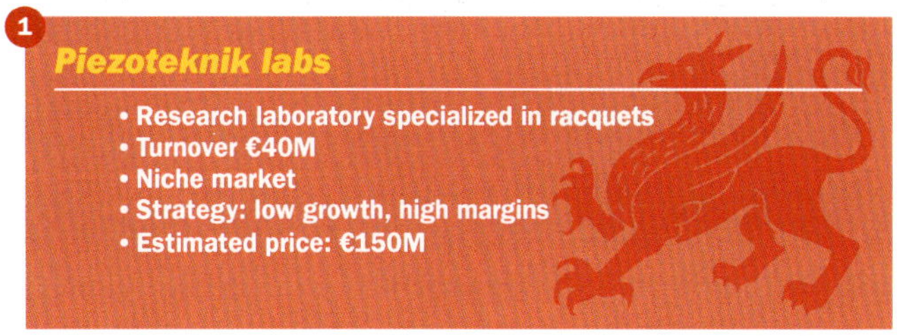

8.3 Grammar Prepositions

Speaking (page 105, Exercise 6)

Student A

Choose six words from the list below and write them on separate small pieces of paper. Hold a conversation with Students B and C on one of the topics listed on page 105. The goal is to use all six words in the conversation. The first person to use all their words (with the correct preposition) is the winner.

hear (v) conform (v) rely (v) look forward (v) respect (n)
responsibility (n) dealings (n) substitute (n) object (v) depend (v)

8.5 Writing Requests and reminders

Writing (page 109, Exercise 6)

Student A

You work at Red Sea Products Inc, a manufacturing company in Saudi Arabia. Compose and send business email 1 below, using appropriate style. When you receive an email from another student, read it, then answer it following the instructions in Exercise 2. Continue in this way until you have written and sent four emails.

1 You have worked for several years with Beefeater Shipping Corp (Student B), who ship your products all over the world. You currently pay them at 60 days, and you almost never pay late. However, your own customers are paying more and more slowly. Write to Beefeater asking them to increase your credit period to 90 days.

2 You have received an email from Canada Import Co (Student C), one of your best customers. Reply, agreeing to their request, but reminding them politely that they haven't paid a bill from last quarter.

3 You have received a reply from Beefeater to your request in Exercise 1. Send a cheque and an apology, or ask for more time, explaining why you can't pay for the moment.

4 You have received a reply from Canada Import to your reminder in Exercise 2. If they sent a cheque, send a friendly reply, thanking them for the payment and reminding them that your payment terms for open account trading are strictly 30 days and no more. If they didn't send a cheque, send a final demand threatening legal action, and suspending the decision to trade on open account.

1.2 Vocabulary Work organization and responsibility

Defining words (page 13, Exercise 8)

Student B

Student A will give you definitions for 1, 3, 5, 7 and 9 to help you complete the crossword. Give Student A definitions for 2, 4, 6, 8 and 10.

1.3 Grammar Past tenses and advice structures

Giving advice (page 15, Exercise 9)

Student B

1 Your partner will tell you about their problems. Suggest two or three alternatives for each problem. Use the expressions in the box to help you.

> Have you tried -ing ...? Have you considered -ing ...?
> How about -ing ...? Have you thought of -ing ...?
> You could ... Why don't you ...? You might want to ...

2 You have recently started work in a government department. Ask your partner for advice about the problems below, and react to their suggestions. Use the expressions in the box to help you.

1 Your boss doesn't trust you: she checks every document you write and always manages to find something wrong.
2 You are frustrated by all the procedures you have to respect: even the simplest tasks seem to take a long time.
3 The atmosphere in the office is very sombre: your colleagues are all much older than you.
4 You find it difficult to sleep at night because your job is so stressful.
5 You hate writing reports, but it's an important part of your job.

> I'm having problems with ... Can you give me any advice?
> Do you have any ideas about how to ...?
> What do you suggest I do about ...? I just can't seem to ...
> What would you do? I see what you mean, (but ...)
> You've got a point, (but ...) You may be right, (but ...)
> OK, point taken. Yes, you're quite right.

4.3 Grammar Present tenses

Asking questions (page 53, Exercise 6)

Student B

1 You are being interviewed for a job at Student A's sports club. Answer the questions they ask.

2 You are interviewing Student A for a job at your community arts centre. Ask Student A the right questions to obtain the answers below. Score one point for each correct answer you receive.

1 Yes, I am.
2 By bus.
3 Three times a day.
4 Business English.
5 A long time ago.
6 Yes, almost.
7 Tomorrow morning.
8 Yes, several times.
9 No, not at the moment.
10 Since the beginning of the year.

1.6 Case study Counselling

Roleplay (page 21, Exercise 6)

Problem holder B: Birmingham

You were hoping that the UK would be an exciting centre of popular culture, but after two months in Birmingham, you are not enjoying life. You live several miles from the city centre, and seem to spend a lot of your time on dirty, uncomfortable buses. The weather is depressing; cold, grey and wet, and the food is bland and fatty with few fresh vegetables. You caught a cold soon after you arrived and it seems impossible to get rid of it. People at work are friendly, but the local accent is really difficult to understand. You are finding it difficult to make friends with English people, mainly because their idea of having a good time is going to a noisy pub and drinking as much as possible, or watching football, which you hate. You are starting to feel lonely and depressed; you are seriously thinking of giving up and going home.

2.1 About business Call centres

Roleplay (page 22, Exercise 6)

Role B

You are going to take part in a debate. Try to convince the others in your group of the advantages of setting up a call centre in your own country and the disadvantages of other solutions. As well as you own ideas, refer to the following:

Setting up your call centre in such a location would allow your company to:
- offer the best possible service, tailored to local needs
- create jobs and help the local economy
- ensure local success and acceptance of your business.

Outsourcing makes customers angry due to:
- language and cultural problems
- operators not having sufficient local knowledge.

Outsourcing is responsible for:
- job losses in industrialized countries
- exploitation of desperate workers in developing countries
- emphasizing inequalities between North and South/East and West
- encouraging unrealistic expectations in the developing world.

Using cloud-based technology where everyone works from home means there is no sense of team or company spirit, it is more complicated to monitor and product knowledge development and training are more difficult.

6.6 Case study Phoenix

Reading and discussion (page 85, Exercise 4)

Group B – Port Katherine Residents' Association

Read part of a letter your association has sent to the Mayor, and answer the questions.

> ... deeply concerned about plans to build a recycling centre on a site close to our school and a quiet residential area. The idea of monster trucks on a narrow road used by small children to walk to school is frankly terrifying and completely irresponsible.
>
> Moreover, the risks and nuisance to the school and the surrounding residents from noise, smoke, fumes and dust are totally unacceptable, not to mention the fire hazard and risk of soil contamination from so many flammable and toxic materials. The residents are prepared to take whatever measures are necessary to resist the choice of site A.
>
> If the recycling centre must be built in Port Katherine (surely Perth, as a large industrial city, would be better for business?), site C is clearly a far more logical and environmentally rational choice. This site is in an industrial environment, on land which is currently derelict and worthless, with the appropriate fire and emergency services close by, and offers the added advantage of convenient transport by sea as an ecological and economical alternative to monster trucks. As for the choice of site B, surely it would make the business park less attractive to other, less industrial, companies?
>
> As the elections approach, we, the residents of Port Katherine, trust that you will take the necessary measures to ensure that ...

1 How do the members of your association feel about the environment?
2 What does your association have in mind when it says 'whatever measures are necessary to resist the choice of site A'?
3 Why do you think the Mayor and the Planning Department have to take your association seriously?
4 Which is the best site from your point of view?
5 What are your objectives at the meeting?

2.4 Speaking Dealing with problems by telephone

Giving instructions (page 28, Exercise 1)

Student B

Student A will give you instructions to draw a symbol in Grid 1. Without saying what it represents, give Student A instructions to draw the symbol in Grid 2.

1

	13				30				14
40				15				50	
			16				60		
		17				70			
	18				80				19
90				99				88	
			77				66		
		55				44			
	33				22				11
10				9				8	

2

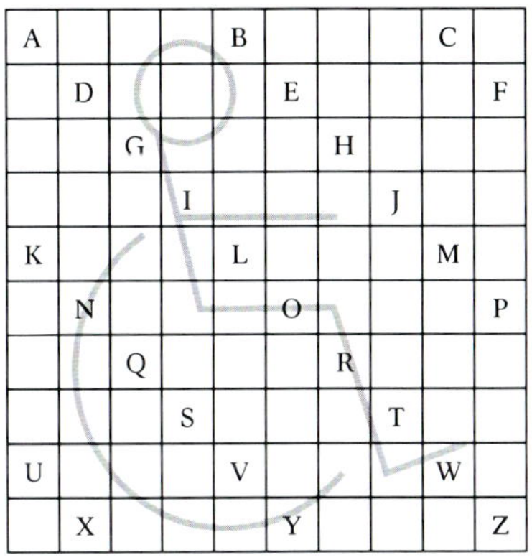

A				B				C	
	D				E				F
		G				H			
			I				J		
K				L				M	
	N				O				P
		Q				R			
			S				T		
U				V				W	
	X				Y				Z

2.5 Writing Formal and informal correspondence

Output (page 31, Exercise 5)

Student C

You work at Nakisoft, a small company specializing in accountancy software. Relopharma is your biggest customer. Compose and send business email 1 below, using appropriate style. When you receive an email from another student, read it, then answer it following the instructions in Exercise 2. Continue in this way until you have written and sent four emails.

1 You have not received payment for your invoice 6695 KF for software you supplied four months ago. Write a polite email to Student A in Relopharma's Accounts Department asking if there is a problem.

2 You have received an email from your customer, Student B, in Relopharma's Information Systems Department. Write an email to Student A telling them that, as requested by Student B, you have set up the training for week 52.

3 You have received another email from your customer, Student B. The problem is caused by a Trojan which is undetected by anti-virus software. The solution is to download a patch from your website and install it on each PC. Write an email to Student A explaining what to do.

4 You have received an email from Student B about an invoice. Write a reply to Student B attaching the document requested.

5.6 Case study St John's Beach Club

Negotiating (page 73, Exercise 5)

Student B (buyer)

Negotiate the best deal possible with the travel agent (Student A). Remember you cannot exceed a global budget of $28,000. Score points as indicated for each item below.

Item	Points
Cost per person per night	
• more than $140	0
• $120 – $140	2
• less than $120	4
Upgrade to executive suite, per person, per night	
• $50	0
• $25	1
• $10	3
Number of participants	
• 22	0
• 24	2
• 26	3
Number of nights	
• 7	0
• 8	1
• 9 or more	3
Free access to golf course	1

8.3 Grammar Prepositions

Speaking (page 105, Exercise 6)

Student B

Choose six words from the list below and write them on separate small pieces of paper. Hold a conversation with Students A and C on one of the topics listed on page 105. The goal is to use all six words in the conversation. The first person to use all their words (with the correct preposition) is the winner.

insist (v) comment (v) complain (v) apologize (v) effect (n)
involvement (n) access (n) demand (v) attend (v) result (v)

8.5 Writing Requests and reminders

Writing (page 109, Exercise 6)

Student B

You work at Beefeater Shipping Corp, an international freight forwarding company. Compose and send business email 1 below, using appropriate style. When you receive an email from another student, read it, then answer it following the instructions in Exercise 2. Continue in this way until you have written and sent four emails.

1 You have recently shipped several containers of goods bought by Canada Import Co (Student C) from your customer Red Sea Products Inc (Student A) to your warehouse in New York. Canada Import were supposed to collect the containers two months ago, but they are still in your warehouse. Write to Canada Import, reminding them about the containers and offering to ship them to Canada for $1.20 per mile per container, payment at 30 days.

2 You have received an email from Red Sea Products. Reply, agreeing to their request, but reminding them politely of an invoice for $10,000 which is overdue.

3 You have received a reply from Canada Import to your email in Exercise 1. Write a reply, either agreeing to or refusing their request, and reminding them that the space their containers are occupying in your warehouse is costing you money, so you need a quick decision on your offer to ship them to Canada.

4 You have received a reply from Red Sea Products to your reminder in Exercise 2. If they sent a cheque, send a friendly reply, thanking them for the payment and reminding them that the new terms of 90 days mean strictly 90 days and no more. If they didn't send a cheque, send a final demand threatening legal action, and suspending the decision to increase the credit period to 90 days.

1.4 Speaking Meetings one-to-one

Roleplay (page 17, Exercise 7)

Student B

1 You are Student A's supervisor at the R&D laboratory of a Finnish electronics company. In Finland, people like to concentrate hard on their work so that they can finish early and go home to enjoy sports and leisure activities. You have called Student A to an informal meeting because some members of your team have complained about him/her: they say that they can't organize the work efficiently because Student A always arrives late. He/She disturbs their concentration by talking loudly to friends on the phone, singing and whistling. He/She eats and drinks in the lab, which is against company rules, takes long breaks and wears unsuitable clothes. Hold an informal meeting with Student A to advise him/her on how to adapt to the local work culture.
Start the meeting by asking Student A if he/she is enjoying the job.

2 You are a new employee at a large travel agency in Australia. You come from Vietnam, where modesty and discretion are highly valued. You feel that some of your Australian colleagues have no respect for management: they are always giving their personal opinions in meetings, they call everybody by their first names, even managers, and spend more time talking about rugby or cricket than working. Your supervisor, Student A, is a demanding manager who has set your department ambitious objectives; you are trying to do your best to compensate for your colleagues' inefficiency, so you work late in the evenings and at weekends. Consequently, you have no time to socialize with other people in the company. You are not sleeping enough, so you have to drink a lot of coffee to stay awake, and you feel very stressed. Take the opportunity of the meeting your supervisor has asked for to suggest, respectfully, that your colleagues should take their work more seriously.

1.6 Case study Counselling

Roleplay (page 21, Exercise 6)

Problem holder C: Chicago
After two months in Chicago you feel miserable and exhausted. You come from a small, quiet town in the country. The noise and the speed of life in Chicago are driving you crazy. You work in an enormous open-space office in a large insurance company, where you are constantly disturbed and find it impossible to concentrate. Your manager is not satisfied with the quantity of work you are producing and told you very directly that you weren't working hard enough. You feel stressed out and are suffering more and more from severe headaches. You would like to go and walk in a park to relax after work, but it's too dangerous to walk the streets at night. You live at the YMCA. Your neighbours and colleagues are very friendly, and they are always inviting you out in the evenings and at weekends, but they want to go dancing or play sports and you just need to rest and relax.

8.3 Grammar Prepositions

Speaking (page 105, Exercise 6)

Student C
Choose six words from the list below and write them on separate small pieces of paper. Hold a conversation with Students A and B on one of the topics listed on page 105. The goal is to use all six words in the conversation. The first person to use all their words (with the correct preposition) is the winner.

succeed (v)	consent (v)	wait (v)	sympathize (v)	tax (n)
solution (n)	comment (v)	damage (n)	invest (v)	consist (v)

7.2 Vocabulary Business performance

Presenting (page 91, Exercise 9)

Student B

1 Listen to Student A's presentation of Chanco and complete the graph.

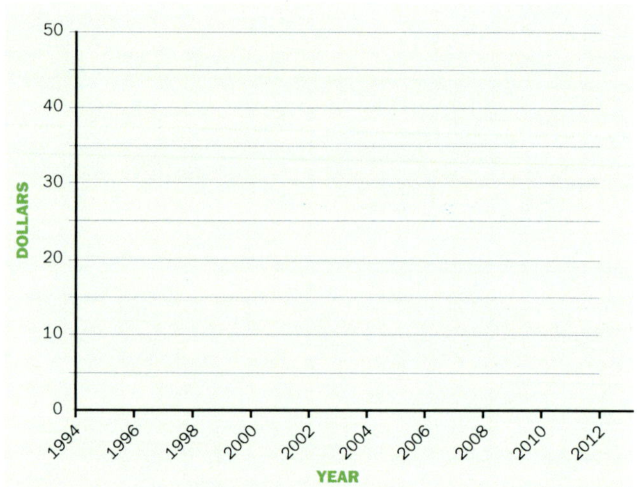

2 Present Bastilo's stock market history using the information from the graph, explaining causes and effects.

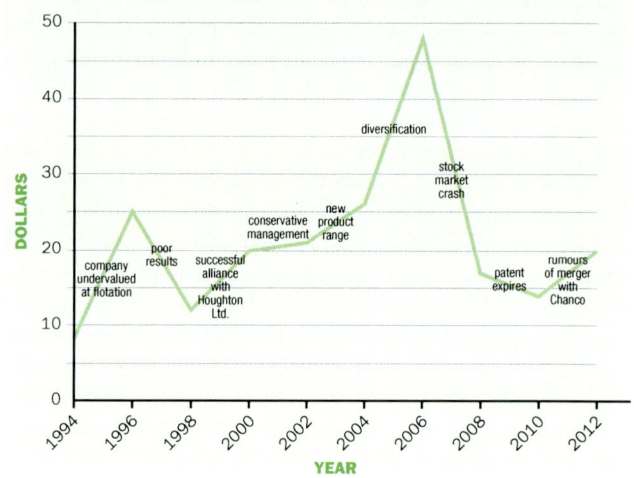

8.5 Writing Requests and reminders

Writing (page 109, Exercise 6)

Student C
You work at Canada Import Co, a company which imports goods from all over the world to North America. Compose and send business email 1 below, using appropriate style. When you receive an email from another student, read it, then answer it following the instructions in Exercise 2. Continue in this way until you have written and sent four emails.

1 You have worked with Red Sea Products Inc (Student A) for more than two years and you are one of their best customers. Until now you have paid by Bill of Exchange at 60 days, but you would prefer to trade on open account in order to have more flexibility. Write to Red Sea Products requesting this change.

2 You have received an email from Beefeater Shipping Corp (Student B) offering to ship your containers from New York to Canada. Your current forwarding company charges $1.10 per mile per container and allows you to pay at 60 days. Write to Beefeater enquiring if they can improve their offer.

3 You have received a reply from Red Sea Products to your request in Exercise 1. Send a cheque and an apology, or ask for more time, explaining why you can't pay for the moment.

4 You have received a reply from Beefeater to your enquiry in Exercise 2. If their terms are now satisfactory, write an email confirming the order for shipping your containers to Canada. If the terms are not satisfactory, write an email rejecting their offer, apologizing for the delay in collecting your containers and promising to have them collected by next week.

3.3 Grammar Articles, relative clauses and noun combinations

Definitions game (page 41, Exercise 9)

Bs

Help the other team guess the noun combinations below by giving definitions using a relative clause. If you want to make it more difficult, use synonyms instead of the exact terms in the noun combinations.

1 a dead-end job
2 brand-building packaging
3 material-saving carton
4 call centre wages
5 newly empowered advisers
6 email risk policy

5.4 Speaking Negotiations – bargaining

Negotiating (page 69, Exercise 9)

Student B

Harry Petersen's application service provider, Holman Multimedia, has gone out of business, taking with it Harry's site which was turning over a thousand dollars per day. Harry needs to hire a new provider. This time he is determined to negotiate a contract which will protect his business if there are problems. You represent Easytail, a new supplier. Your boss has given you a list of points to negotiate below. Try to negotiate more 'Ideals' than 'Unacceptables'.

	Ideal	Acceptable	Unacceptable
Set-up time	> 2 weeks	2 weeks	< 2 weeks
Cost	15% more than Holman	same as Holman	less than Holman
Payment terms	< 30 days	30 days	> 30 days
Contract	> 18 months	12–18 months	< 12 months
Penalties if site is offline	no penalties	20–30% of average turnover	> 30% of average turnover
Penalties if contract is broken	no penalties	20% of turnover for 1 month	> 20% of turnover for 1 month

6.6 Case study Phoenix

Reading and discussion (page 85, Exercise 4)

Group C – Phoenix

Read the email from Head Office in Sydney and answer the questions.

INBOX | REPLY | FORWARD

Hi,
Just a few words about the meeting in Port Katherine. We want you to represent Phoenix in the best possible light – 'Operation Charm and Diplomacy', remember? We need to make friends and to sell the benefits of having a Phoenix recycling centre in their town: protect the environment, new jobs, investment, growth, higher profile for the town, taxes, involvement in community projects, etc. By the way, on the subject of community projects, find out what they're interested in, but try not to make any expensive commitments, OK?
Port Katherine will be our centre for most of Western Australia. In the long term, it could become the largest recycling centre on the continent, so it's pretty important for us. It's a good site for us, but they need us more than we need them. If things get difficult, we can go somewhere else.
Site A has the best access, but there's the problem of the school. Site B is expensive, and it's not flat, which means that limiting the risk of contamination by fluids is more difficult. Site C has poor access, unless the town builds a new access road. And I don't think they've really understood what having a recycling centre in the middle of the town would mean. Obviously, as we have our own trucking division, transport by sea is not an option for us. Anyway, I know you'll do a good job. Let me know how the meeting goes.
Justin

1 What are your objectives at the meeting?
2 What sort of community projects do you think Phoenix could support?
3 What are Phoenix's plans for Port Katherine's future?
4 Which is the best site for Phoenix?
5 What arguments can you use against choosing the other sites?

7.4 Speaking Presentations – visuals

Presentation (page 95, Exercise 6)

Student C

Present the three slides on Yarax Sports and explain why this company would be a good acquisition.

1
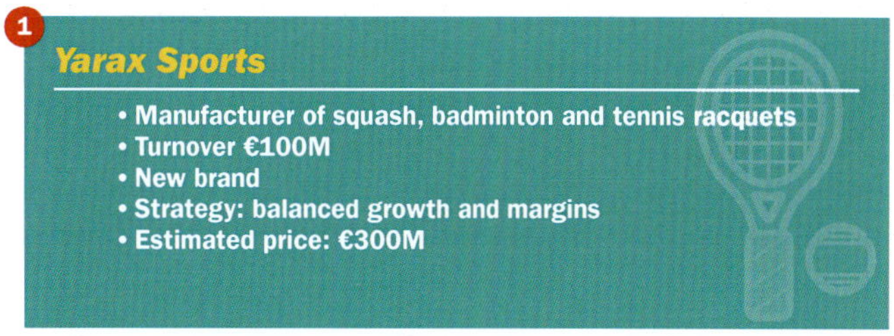

2

3
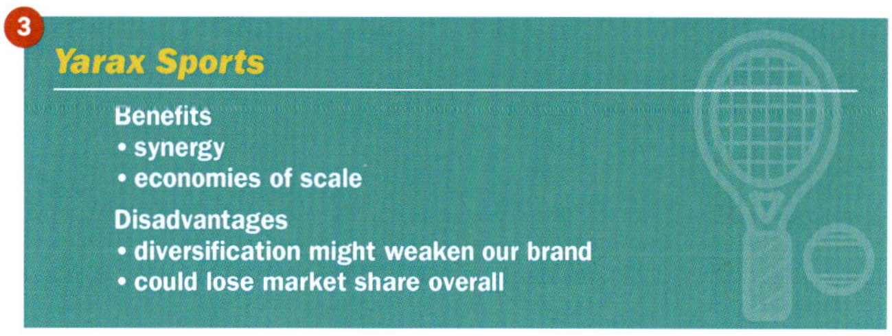

8.2 Vocabulary International deals and payments

Defining words (page 103, Exercise 7)

Student B

Student A will give you definitions for 1, 2, 4, 6, 7 and 9 across to help you complete the crossword. Give Student A definitions for 1, 3, 5 and 8 down and 10 and 11 across.

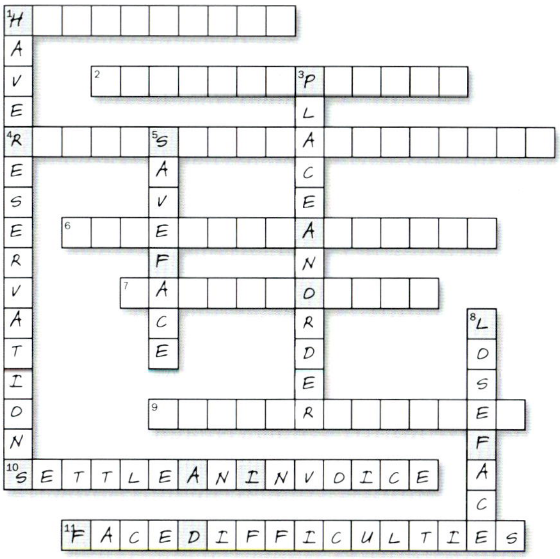

Grammar and practice

1 Corporate culture

Past tenses

1 **Read a diary entry written by Joelle, a student on a work placement. Of the verbs in bold, identify which are examples of the:**

- past simple
- past continuous
- past perfect.

I **was doing** my work placement in a large bank near to where I live. I **was working** in the back office (I **had asked** to do something where I could deal directly with clients, but they **said** no). Anyway, one day something really awful **happened**. My supervisor **had given** me some client information to enter into a database, and I **was filling in** the various fields on the screen. While I **was entering** the information, I suddenly **saw** a name I **recognized** – it **was** a friend from school called Sylvie. It seems that she **had applied for** a loan to have some cosmetic surgery! Of course, the bank **had** strict confidentiality rules and the next time I **saw** Sylvie I **didn't mention** anything. But, even so, I wish that I **hadn't found out** about it.

2 **Complete the summaries of the main use of each tense in Exercise 1 by writing the correct tense name in each gap.**

- You use the _________ to show that one event happened before another.
- You use the _________ to describe an activity in progress that gives the background to the main events.
- You use the _________ to describe the main events of the story.

3 **Put one verb into the past simple and one into the past continuous in each sentence.**

1 I _________ (revise) for my Economics exam when you _________ (call).
2 I'm sorry, I _________ (not/hear) what you said. I _________ (read) this article about Johnny Depp.
3 I _________ (see) Eva yesterday. She _________ (talk) to some friends outside the library.
4 While I _________ (work) in the bar last summer I _________ (meet) this guy called Fabio.

4 **Look at the sentences in Exercise 3 again. In general, does the activity in progress (past continuous):**

1 stop when the main event happens? *or*
2 continue after the main event happens? *or*
3 either 1 or 2 – we only know by the context.

5 **Put one verb into the past simple and one into the past perfect in each sentence.**

1 Before I _________ (get) my full-time job at the bank, I _________ (already/work) there for several months as an intern.
2 It's OK, don't worry, I _________ (just/finish) revising for my exam when you _________ (call).
3 It _________ (be) so nice to talk to Eva yesterday. I _________ (not/see) her for ages.
4 I _________ (not/meet) a man like Fabio before. He really _________ (listen) to me.

6 **It may not be necessary to use the past perfect if you use *before* or *after* to make the time sequence clear. Both underlined forms are correct:**

Before *I arranged the doctor's appointment, I* ***<u>spoke / had spoken</u>*** *to my supervisor.*

<u>Underline</u> the correct forms in bold. Sometimes both are correct, sometimes only one.

1 I understood the marketing part of the course much better after my internship **finished** / **had finished**.
2 The traffic was terrible, and when I got there the meeting **already started** / **had already started**.
3 Before I was promoted to Sales Director, I **was** / **had been** a sales consultant in our main city-centre branch.
4 By the end of the course I realized that I **bought** / **had bought** over a dozen books.

7 **Match the time expressions on the left with the tense they are often used with on the right.**

1 while	a) past simple
2 already, by the end of	b) past continuous
3 last year, two months ago	c) past perfect

Telling a story

8 **When you tell a story, you can use the word *anyway* to:**

1 change the subject *or*
2 return to a previous subject.

Find the word *anyway* in Exercise 1 and say how it is used.

9 **When you tell a story, you can use the words in the box. Find pairs with the same meaning.**

actually after that apparently eventually
in fact in the end it seems that obviously
of course the next thing that happened was

10 **Read a story written by Janek, a student who had a holiday job. Put the verbs into the correct form: past simple (x7), past continuous (x3) and past perfect (x4).**

One day last summer I (1) _________ (work) in a bar on the beach. I (2) _________ (just/leave) school and I was young and naive. Anyway, on that day I (3) _________ (serve) the drinks by myself – my other colleagues (4) _________ (not/ arrive) for work yet. A man (5) _________ (come) up to the counter and (6) _________ (ask for) 'a whisky on the rocks'. I (7) _________ (want) to be helpful, so I filled a glass with whisky, (8) _________ (take) it over to where he (9) _________ (sit) with his friends and (10) _________ (place) it on the rocks next to him. The next thing that happened was they all started laughing and laughing. I (11) _________ (never/be) so embarrassed in my life. Of course, when I realized my mistake I (12) _________ (see) the funny side as well, and in the end everything (13) _________ (be) OK. In fact, by the end of the evening, I (14) _________ (become) friends with them all. But, even today, when I hear the phrase 'on the rocks' it reminds me of that day.

11 **A story is often told in four stages:**

1 Background situation
2 Problem
3 Solution/resolution
4 Comment

In Joelle's diary entry in Exercise 1, the four stages are:

1 from *I was doing* … to … *said no*.
2 from *Anyway*, … to … *surgery*!
3 from *Of course* … to … *anything*.
4 from *But even so* … to … *about it*.

Identify the four stages in Janek's story in Exercise 10.

1 from _______________ to _______________
2 from _______________ to _______________
3 from _______________ to _______________
4 from _______________ to _______________

12 **Write a short story about something that happened to you while you were at work, for example:**

- while you were doing a holiday job
- while you were doing an internship
- while you were helping a family member.

Before you begin, look again at the diary entry in 1 and the story in Exercise 10. Also, use the vocabulary in Exercise 8 and Exercise 9 to help you.

Advice structures

13 **Correct the mistake in each sentence.**

1 You should to do it today.
2 You ought do it today.
3 He shoulds do it today.
4 Do I should do it today?

14 **You can give advice using both *must* and *should*:**

You ***must*** speak to your supervisor.
You ***should*** speak to your supervisor.

1 Which sentence means: 'It's a good idea to speak to your supervisor'?
2 Which sentence means: 'It's necessary to speak to your supervisor'?

15 **Complete the sentences by using the verb *apply* in its correct form (*apply*, *to apply* or *applying*).**

1 Why don't you _________ for that job?
2 How about _________ for that job?
3 You ought _________ for that job.
4 You should _________ for that job.

16 **Grade these replies from 1 (agreement) to 4 (disagreement).**

☐ No, that's not a good idea.
☐ That might be worth trying.
☐ I'm not sure about that because …
☐ That sounds like a good idea.

Should and *must* are examples of **modal verbs**. Other modal verbs are: *can*, *could*, *will*, *would*, *may*, *might* and *shall*. Modal verbs have special characteristics:

- They are 'auxiliary verbs'. This means they are used with another main verb.
  You should learn to set goals.
- Two modal verbs cannot be used together.
  NOT ~~*I can will meet you.*~~
- They are followed by the infinitive without *to*.
  NOT ~~*I must to meet him.*~~
- They only have one form, so there is no third person *-s*, no *-ing* form and no *-ed* form.
- To make a question you put the modal verb in front of the subject.
  Should I …? *Can I …?*
- To make a negative you put *not* after the modal verb (often shortened to *-n't*)
  You shouldn't … *You can't …*

Modal verbs are used to express ideas such as advice, ability, obligation, probability. The same modal verb can have different meanings.

2 Customer support

Yes/No questions

1 Complete the table with these auxiliary verbs: *are, did, did, do, does, had, had, has, have, is, was, were, would.*

Present simple	________ you work there? ________ she work there?
Present continuous	________ you working there now? ________ he working there now?
Past simple	________ you work there before? ________ she work there before?
Past continuous	________ you working there then? ________ he working there then?
Present perfect	________ you ever worked there? ________ she ever worked there?
Past perfect	________ you already worked there? ________ she already worked there?
Modals	________ you work here next year?

Now complete the rule using these words: *subject, main verb, auxiliary verb.*

You form *yes/no* questions using:
__________ + __________ + __________.

2 Read Frank's answers in the telephone conversation, then write Geeta's questions using the same tense.

Geeta: (1) __________ this software from us?
Frank: Yes, I bought it from you.
Geeta: (2) __________ a guarantee?
Frank: Yes, I have a two-year guarantee.
Geeta: (3) __________ restarting the computer?
Frank: Yes, I've tried doing that.
Geeta: (4) __________ at your computer right now?
Frank: Yes, I'm sitting at my desk.
Geeta: (5) __________ the software again, please?
Frank: No, I won't reinstall it again! I thought you were a helpline, but you're not being very helpful.

3 Underline the correct short answers.

1 Do you work in customer support?
Yes, I work. / Yes, I am. / Yes, I do.
2 Are you working in customer support now?
Yes, I work. / Yes, I am. / Yes, I do.
3 Did you work in customer support before?
No, I didn't work. / No, I didn't.
4 Have you ever worked in customer support?
No, I never worked. / No, I haven't.

Wh- questions

4 You make questions beginning with *Wh-* or *How* to ask for more information. Complete the text using *two* of the following items in *each* gap.

How   how far   How much   What   Why
are   do   does   will   will

Providing back office functions for global business is vital for India's economy. (1) ________ India earn from this per year? About $2 billion. (2) ________ so many companies outsourcing to India? The answer is simple: it's cheaper. But (3) ________ this process go? Surprisingly, not much further, at least as far as India is concerned. The problems are poor infrastructure, labour shortages and, in particular, wage inflation. (4) ________ we know there will be a problem? Because the same thing happened before: to Ireland in the 90s. So (5) ________ companies do? They will simply outsource their business processes to other countries, such as the Philippines, Malaysia, Vietnam and Eastern European nations.

5 Compare how *What* and *Which* are used. Then complete the sentences below using *What* or *Which*.

***What* + noun**	***Which* + noun**
• things • wide choice	• people and organizations • limited choice

1 ________ type of car do you drive?
2 ________ university do you go to?
3 ________ day would be best for you: Saturday or Sunday?
4 ________ time shall we meet? I'm free all day.

Sometimes *who, what* or *which* is the subject of the sentence. In this case, you don't use an auxiliary verb.

Who told you? NOT ~~*Who did tell you?*~~
What happened? NOT ~~*What did happen?*~~

6 Match the questions with the answers.

1 Who called?
2 Who did you call?
3 Who got the job?
4 Which job did he get?

a) The one he wanted.
b) Pete got it.
c) I called Mary.
d) Alice called.

7 Write the questions for the answers given.

1 ______________ at the station?
I met Sue.
2 ______________ at the station?
Sue met me.
3 ______________ at the training day?
Thierry spoke. It was really interesting.
4 ______________ about?
He spoke about how to set up a small business.

Making requests

8 **Saying *Help me with my bags!* or even *Help me with my bags, please!* can sound too direct. Instead, use:**

Polite request forms
Can/Could *you help me with my bags?*
Will/Would *you help me with my bags?*
Do you think you could *help me with my bags?*
I wonder if you could *help me with my bags.*
I was wondering if you could *help me with my bags.*

1 Add the word *possibly* in the correct place in this sentence:
I wonder if I could leave a few minutes early today?
2 Fill in the missing letters to make two more polite request forms.
a) I'd be really g_ _ _ _ _ _ l if you could help me.
b) I'd really a_ _ _ _ _ _ _ _ e it if you could help me.

9 **Read the contexts 1–4 then match each one with an appropriate request form a–d.**

1 asking for help from a friend who should be helping you, but isn't ☐
2 asking a small favour of your brother/sister ☐
3 asking a small favour of a colleague who is doing something else ☐
4 asking a big favour of a senior colleague who is doing something else ☐

a) Can you give me a hand?
b) Come on, give me a hand here!
c) I was wondering if you could possibly give me a hand.
d) Do you think you could give me a hand?

10 **When you agree to a request, 'OK' can sound too relaxed and informal. There are other more customer-friendly alternatives. Fill in the missing letters.**

Can you give me a hand?

1 Yes, _ _ c_ _ _ _ _.
2 Yes, c_ _ _ _ _ _ _ y.
3 Yes, s_ _ _.

11 **Match the first part of the phrase with the last part to make requests using *mind*.**

1 Do you mind if I …
2 Would you mind if I …
3 Would you mind …

a) closed the window?
b) closing the window?
c) close the window?

Requests with *mind* mean: 'Is it a problem for you?'
So answering 'no' means: 'no problem'.
Would you mind helping me with this software?
No, *not at all./****No,*** *of course not.*

12 **If you want to refuse any kind of request, you can say:**

A_ _ _ _ _ _ _ / To be h_ _ _ _ _, it's a bit inconvenient right now.

Giving instructions

13 **Match phrases 1–5 with a definition a–e.**

1 You can do it. ☐
2 You might have to do it. ☐
3 You don't have to do it. ☐
4 You mustn't do it. ☐
5 You have to do it. ☐

a) It's necessary to do it.
b) It's OK – you're allowed to do it.
c) It's not necessary to do it.
d) I'm telling you not to do it.
e) It's possible that some action is necessary.

14 **Choose the three phrases from the first group in Exercise 13 that mean the same as:**

1 Don't do it!
2 You need to do it.
3 You needn't do it.

- To say it is **necessary** to do something, use:
  You ***have to*** *do it./You****'ll have to*** *do it.*
  You ***need to*** *do it./You****'ll need to*** *do it.*
  (The forms with *'ll* are more informal.)
- To say it is **not necessary to do** something (i.e. there is a choice), use:
  You ***don't have to*** *do it.*
  You ***needn't*** *do it.*
- To say it is **necessary *not* to do** something, use:
  You ***mustn't*** *do it!*
  Don't *do it!*

15 **In the affirmative, *you have to* and *you must* are very similar. But notice from the box above that, in the negative, *you don't have to* and *you mustn't* are different.**

Complete the text below using *have to, don't have to* or *mustn't*.

You (1) _________ work in customer support but, if you do, then you will sometimes be faced with very angry callers. Luckily, there are some techniques to help you. First, you (2) _________ interrupt while the other person is speaking. They need to be able to express what they are feeling. Of course, if they're angry, then the message may get confused, so when they finish, you (3) _________ ask short, simple questions to establish the facts. Most companies insist that during this first call you (4) _________ accept any legal responsibility for the problems, but that's OK – you (5) _________. You can, however, still be sympathetic and try to help. Above all, your attitude is important – you (6) _________ be calm and patient at all times.

Articles

1 Complete the sentences using *the*, *an* or no article.

1 I have ___ idea. Let's develop ___ completely new model with extra features – we could call it 'Premia'. Of course, it would sell at ___ much higher price.
2 When we launch ___ new 'Premia' model, we will have to redesign ___ packaging. We want to differentiate it from ___ standard model we sell now.
3 Anyone who works in ___ marketing will tell you – ___ packaging is very important – ___ products don't just sell themselves.

2 Complete the grammar rules using *the*, *a/an* or *no article*.

1 You use _________ when the listener doesn't know which person or thing you are talking about because:
- you are mentioning it for the first time or
- it is not specific.

2 You use _________ when it is clear which person or thing you are talking about because:
- it's clear from the context or
- there is only one or
- you have already mentioned it.

3 You use _________ when you are talking generally.

3 Fill in the gaps using *the* or *a/an*.

1 I've brought with me ___ mockup of our latest GPS device – ___ mockup shows how compact the new product will be.
2 I'd like to finish ___ presentation by telling you ___ story.
3 Have you heard about ___ MP-bunny? It's ___ electronic rabbit that dances and talks.
4 We've developed ___ great new product – ___ idea came from our R&D department.

4 Fill in the gaps using *the* where necessary.

1 People say that ___ money makes ___ world go round.
2 ___ money we spend on ___ market research is only a small part of our whole budget.
3 ___ football these days is much more commercialized than ___ football they played 20 years ago.
4 ___ plastic is often used as a packaging material, and ___ plastic we use is 100% biodegradable.

Defining relative clauses

5 Read how to join two short sentences.

Here is the package. We designed it last week.
→ *Here is the package* ***which/that*** *we designed last week*.
(NOT *Here is the package which we designed ~~it~~ last week.*)
Here is the CV of the Portuguese candidate. She got the job.
→ *Here is the CV of the Portuguese candidate* ***who/that*** *got the job*.
(NOT *Here is the CV of the Portuguese candidate who ~~she~~ got the job.*)
The underlined phrases are relative clauses.
The words in **bold** are relative pronouns. You use *which* for things, *who* for people and *that* for both things and people.
(In speech, *that* is more common for things, and *who* is more common for people.)

Join the sentences below. Write both relative pronouns.

1 FedEx® is an international company. It operates in the transportation business.

____

2 Charlie Wang is a dynamic man. He runs the New China Packaging Company.

____

Relative clauses without the relative pronoun

6 Look at the two joined sentences with the underlined relative clauses in the box in Exercise 5.

In one of the sentences you can leave out the relative pronoun. Write the whole sentence again, without any relative pronoun.

____

7 Underline the correct words in bold to make a rule. Think about your last answer and look again at the box above to help you.

- You can leave out *who*, *which* or *that* in a defining relative clause if they are followed immediately by **a verb / a pronoun / a noun**.
- You must keep *who*, *which* or *that* if they are followed immediately by **a verb / a pronoun / a noun**.

Relative clauses with *whose*

8 **The relative pronoun *whose* shows possession. Read the examples in the box.**

FedEx® is an international company. Its reputation is very good.
→ *FedEx is an international company* ***whose*** *reputation is very good.*
Charlie Wang is a dynamic man. His ideas about business are very interesting.
→ *Charlie Wang is a dynamic man* ***whose*** *ideas about business are very interesting.*

Combine these sentences using *whose*.

1 These are the views of the consultants. Their report was used by the government.
whose report
2 Look at this article about that German manufacturing company. Their production was outsourced to Slovakia.
whose

Prepositions in relative clauses

9 **Tick (✓) the two sentences that are in modern spoken English.**

1 Microsoft® is a company about which I know quite a lot.
2 Microsoft is a company which I know quite a lot about. ✓
3 The person to whom I spoke was called Sandra.
4 The person I spoke to was called Sandra. ✓

Normally you put a preposition at the end of the relative clause (although this may not be the end of the sentence).
The word *whom* following a preposition is rare in modern English. It sounds very formal.

Non-defining relative clauses

10 **Read the examples of non-defining relative clauses in the box.**

FedEx®, **which is one of America's largest companies,** has its head office in Memphis.
Charlie Wang, **who is President of New China Packaging,** has some interesting ideas about cross-functional teams.

Underline the correct words in bold to make rules.

- A non-defining relative clause **identifies exactly which person or thing we mean / simply adds extra information.**
- In a non-defining relative clause you **use / do not use** commas around the clause.
- In a non-defining relative clause you **can / cannot** leave out *who* or *which*.
- In a non-defining relative clause you **can / cannot** use *that*.

Noun combinations

11 **Read the information about noun combinations in the box.**

A **credit card** is a card used for getting credit.
A **company credit card** is a card used for getting credit that has been provided by a company.
An **insurance document** is a document that shows you have insurance.
A **travel insurance document** is a document that shows you have insurance for travel.

So, the main noun comes at the end, and any others describe it.

An adjective can come at the beginning. The examples below are all two-part adjectives.
a **long-lasting printer cartridge**
a **high-quality water treatment system**
a **six-month government training course**

Make two-word noun combinations from the words in each group.

1	rate	features	inflation	product
	inflation rate, product features			
2	force	focus	task	group
3	forecast	aid	hearing	sales
4	leader	stock	market	control
5	price	feedback	customer	range

12 **Make three-word noun combinations by putting the words in the correct order.**

1	product	team	design	______
2	hero	film	action	______
3	development	strategy	staff	______
4	engineer	computer	software	______
5	feedback	program	customer	______
6	construction	bridge	project	______

13 **Choose the best adjective to put at the beginning of each noun combination in Exercise 12. Find a solution that uses each adjective once only.**

~~hard-working~~ long-term nice-looking
over-budget self-employed web-based

1 a *hard-working product design team*
2 a ______
3 a ______
4 a ______
5 a ______
6 an ______

Present simple and present continuous

1 Match the verb forms in bold in the sentences below with their uses a–d below.

1 I **speak** English mainly in my English lessons, and sometimes when I'm on holiday.
2 I'm bilingual – I **speak** French and German, like many Swiss people.
3 Don't ask me now – can't you see I'**m speaking** on the phone?
4 I've had a terrible argument with another team member, although we'**re** still **speaking**.

a) Present continuous used for an action happening around now, but not at this exact moment. ☐
b) Present continuous used for an action happening right now. ☐
c) Present simple used for a fact or permanent situation. ☐
d) Present simple used for a habit or routine. ☐

2 In these mini-dialogues the tenses are correct, but there are four mistakes of form. Find and correct the mistakes.

1 A: You work on Saturdays?
B: No, luckily I not work on Saturdays.
2 C: You are going for an interview today?
D: No, I not going today – the interview is tomorrow.

3 Put one verb into the present simple and one into the present continuous in each sentence.

1 Have you met Freda? She _________ (come) from Berlin. Oh, there she is. She _________ (come) over here now.
2 Usually we _________ (have) just two hours of English a week. But this month I _________ (have) some private lessons to help me get a better grade in the exam.

4 The time expression can give a clue about which verb tense to use. Look at the time expression in bold then put the verb into the correct form.

1 **Right now** I _________ (do) two assignments, one for Economics and one for Quantitative Analysis.
2 **Every semester** we _________ (have) an exam on all the material we've studied.
3 **Once a day** I _________ (check) all my emails.
4 **This week** a friend from Ireland _________ (stay) with me.
5 **At the moment** I _________ (wait) to hear from an IT company who I sent my CV to.
6 **From time to time** I _________ (do) a bit of work in my father's company – usually during the summer.

5 Some verbs (called 'state' verbs) are not usually used in a continuous form. Tick (✓) the verb forms that are correct. Change the incorrect forms in bold into the present simple.

1 The soup **is tasting** delicious!
2 The soup **is boiling**.
3 Sorry, **I'm not following** you.
4 Sorry, **I'm not understanding** you.
5 What **are you saying**?
6 What **are you meaning**?
7 This book **is belonging** to me.
8 This book **is selling** for €15 on Amazon.
9 Please don't interrupt me – I'**m doing** a grammar exercise.
10 This grammar exercise is easy – I'**m knowing** all of the answers.

Common state verbs

be believe belong cost depend know
like mean measure need see seem taste
think understand want weigh

Present perfect

6 Match the verb forms in bold in the sentences below with their uses a–c.

1 **I've worked** here for nearly a year.
2 **I've worked** in several different bars and restaurants since leaving university.
3 I put my old camera for sale on eBay and **I've sold it**! With the money I'll be able to buy a better one.

a) Present situation caused by a past event. ☐
b) People's experiences up to now (*when* they happened is not important). ☐
c) Something that started in the past and continues up to the present. ☐

7 Complete the grammar explanations in the box with these words: *present simple, present continuous, present perfect*.

- The _________ has several uses, but it shows that the speaker is looking back from the present to the past.
- The _________ has several uses, but it shows that a present action or situation is temporary.
- The _________ has several uses, but it shows that a present action or situation is permanent.

Now look back at all the example sentences on this page and compare with the explanations.

8 Underline the correct words in **bold**.

1 I've been a student at this university **for / since** I was 19.
2 I've been a student at this university **for / since** three years.
3 I had a great time **for / during** my university days.
4 I had a great time **for / during** the first two years at university, but after that there was a lot of work.
5 I was a student at that university **since many years / many years ago.**

9 **Complete the rules in the box using these words:** ***ago, during, for, since.***

- _________: used with periods of time; used with the past simple and present perfect; answers the question 'how long?'
- _________: used with periods of time; used with the past simple; answers the question 'when?'
- _________: identifies the point an event began; used with the present perfect.
- _________: used to say how far back in the past something happened; used with the past simple.

10 **Complete the sentences with these words associated with the present perfect:** ***ever, never, already, just, yet.***

1 Erica? She's _________ left. If you go out to the car park, you'll catch her.
2 Erica? She's _________ left. In fact, she left several hours ago.
3 Erica? She hasn't left _________. If you go up to the second floor, you'll catch her.
4 Have you _________ been really late for an interview? What happened?
5 We've _________ received so many application forms for one job. It's amazing!

Present perfect and present perfect continuous

11 **Read sentences 1–8. A tick (✓) means correct, and a cross (✗) means incorrect.**

1 **I've lived** here since last summer. ☐
2 **I've been living** here since last summer. ☐
3 **She's been interviewing** since 8am – she must be tired. ☐
4 **She's interviewed** since 8am – she must be tired. ☐
5 **She's interviewed** James Matthews and **has offered** him the job. ☐
6 **She's been interviewing** James Matthews and **has been offering** him the job. ☐
7 **I've written** two assignments this week. ☐
8 **I've been writing** two assignments this week. ☐

Refer to the examples above to complete the grammar rules in the box. Write ***present perfect, present perfect continuous, present perfect*** **or** ***present perfect continuous.***

- When you talk about people's experiences up to now, you use the ____________ or ____________.
- When you focus on the action itself, not the result, you use the ____________.
- When you focus on the result, not the action, you use the ____________.
- When you say 'how many' you use the ____________.

12 **Put each verb into the correct form: present perfect simple or present perfect continuous. Some sentences may use the same form twice.**

1 I _________ (send off) job applications all summer but I still _________ (not/have) any luck.
2 I _________ (send off) about 20 job applications this summer – perhaps I _________ (apply) for the wrong kind of job.
3 Joanna looks really disappointed – she _________ (just/receive) her exam results and I'm sure she _________ (fail).

Choosing forms: more practice

13 **Put each verb into the correct form: present simple, present perfect or past simple.**

1 Sales _________ (go up) by 5% last year.
2 Sales _________ (go up) by 5% so far this year.
3 Sales _________ (go up) by 5% every time we have an advertising campaign.
4 I _________ (work) for Johnson & Johnson for two years. It's a good company, but now I think it's time for a change.
5 After university I _________ (work) for Johnson & Johnson for two years. Then I was invited to join Novartis.
6 I _________ (work) for Johnson & Johnson. There's a great atmosphere in my department.

14 **Complete the text by using each of these forms once: present simple, present continuous, present perfect, present perfect continuous, past simple.**

'I really (1) _________ (want) that job I (2) _________ (apply) for a few weeks ago. I (3) _________ (wait) for ages – I wonder if they (4) _________ (decide) anything? I (5) _________ (sleep) so badly at the moment.'

5 Making deals

Types of conditionals

1 Read sentences a–c below.

a) If I **use** Amazon, I **buy** more books than I really want, and then I **don't have** the time to read them afterwards!
b) If I **use** Amazon to find that book about marketing, **it'll arrive** within a week, and I **won't need** to go round all the bookshops looking for it.
c) If I **used** Amazon to find that book about marketing, **it'd be** cheaper, but of course I **wouldn't be** able to look at it first.

Now answer these questions by writing *a*, *b* or *c*.

1 Which sentence shows there is a high probability of one event happening? ☐
2 Which sentence shows I'm just imagining one event that is unlikely to happen? ☐
3 Which sentence is not about one specific event? ☐
4 In which sentence could *If* … be replaced with *Whenever* … or *Every time* …? ☐

2 Refer to sentences a–c in Exercise 1. Complete these statements by underlining the correct words in bold.

1 Sentence a) is called the **zero** / **first** / **second** conditional and the time reference is **past** / **present** / **future** / **general**.
2 Sentence b) is called the **zero** / **first** / **second** conditional and the time reference is **past** / **present** / **future** / **general**.
3 Sentence c) is called the **zero** / **first** / **second** conditional and the time reference is **past** / **present** / **future** / **general**.

First conditional

3 Correct the mistakes in these sentences. Think carefully about the word *will*.

1 If we will continue talking, I'm sure we find a compromise.
2 If I will agree to that price, can you sign today?

4 Match an *if* clause 1–3 with a main clause a–c.

1 If you bring down the price, ☐
2 If they're asking for a discount, ☐
3 If we've discussed all the details, ☐

a) can we finish the meeting?
b) we'll place an order.
c) tell them it's impossible.

5 Underline the correct words in bold to make a rule. Refer to Exercises 1–4 above to help you.

The first conditional refers to a **likely / unlikely** event in the future. In the *if* clause you use the **present simple / any present tense** (simple, continuous or perfect) and in the main clause you use *will* or other modals or the imperative.

6 Read the whole sentence then underline the phrase in bold that is best in the context.

1 If I get lost, **I'll / I might** call you on my mobile – there's nothing else I can do.
2 If you sign the contract today, **we'll be able to / we might be able to** deliver by the end of the month, but I can't promise anything because our factory is very busy at the moment.
3 If you give us a 5% discount, **I'll be able to / I should be able to** place an order, but I just need to check with my boss first.

Modals in conditionals have their normal meanings. So:
- *will* means 'the result is certain'.
- *should* means 'the result is probable'.
- *might/could* mean 'the result is possible'.

7 Compare these sentences with the similar ones in Exercises 3 and 4.

I'm sure we'll find a compromise if we continue talking.
We'll place an order if you bring down the price.

Now complete the rule:

When the *if* clause comes at the end, you leave out the __________ in writing.

if and *when*

8 In the sentences below you can use either *if* or *when*. Compare the two alternatives. If the meaning is the same, write *S*. If the meaning is different, write *D*.

1 **If / When** I use Amazon, I buy more books than I really want. ☐
2 **If / When** I use Amazon to find that book about Marketing, it'll arrive within a week. ☐

Now underline the correct answers in bold.

a) In Sentence 1, the word *if* suggests **certainty / uncertainty** about using Amazon.
b) In Sentence 2, the word *when* suggests **certainty / uncertainty** about using Amazon.

- In zero conditional sentences, *if* and *when* have the same meaning.
- In first conditional sentences, *if* and *when* do not have the same meaning. *If* shows uncertainty and *when* shows certainty.

if and *unless*

9 Underline the correct word in **bold**.

1 **If** / **Unless** business improves, I'll lose my job.
2 **If** / **Unless** business improves, we'll all get a pay rise.
3 **If** / **Unless** you put down a 10% deposit, we can accept your order.
4 **If** / **Unless** you put down a 10% deposit, we can't accept your order.

> *unless = if not*
> **Unless** business improves, I'll lose my job.
> = **If** business does**n't** improve, I'll lose my job.

10 Rewrite these sentences using *unless*.

1 If we don't leave now, we'll miss the start of the film.
_________________, we'll miss the start of the film.
2 If he doesn't agree to our terms, we should walk away from the negotiation.
_________________, we should walk away from the negotiation.

Second conditional

11 Read sentences 1–4 then match the forms in **bold** with their best explanations a–d below.

1 If we **increase** our order, **will** you give us a discount?
2 If we **increased** our order, **would** you give us a discount?
3 If we **increased** our order it **would** be very risky. We might never resell all the items to our customers.
4 If we **increased** our order it **would** be too risky. We would never resell all the items to our customers.

a) First conditional: there is a high probability of the event happening. ☐
b) Second conditional: there is no probability at all of the event happening – it is purely imaginary ☐
c) Second conditional: there is a low probability of the event happening, but it is not out of the question. ☐
d) Second conditional: there is no reference to probability, instead the speaker is using the past form to be indirect/tentative/diplomatic. It is easier for the other person to say 'no' without losing face. ☐

12 Correct the mistakes in these sentences. They should both be second conditionals.

1 If I would be the boss of this company, I will improve communications by having regular meetings.
2 If we would paid a 50% deposit now, you reduce the price to €25,000?

> The second conditional refers to an unlikely, impossible or imaginary event in the future. In the *if* clause you use the past simple and in the main clause you use *would/might/could*.
> The second conditional can also be used to make the speaker sound indirect/tentative.

providing (that)/as long as, etc.

13 Read the example sentence then underline the correct words in **bold** in the box to make a rule.

I might consider working abroad, providing (that)/provided (that)/as long as/so long as the money was good.

> The expressions *providing, provided, as long as* and *so long as* all mean *if and only if*. They emphasize the condition. They have a **first** / **second** conditional form, so they are followed by a verb in the **present** / **past** simple.

Verbs patterns with *recommend/suggest/advise*

14 Read the verb patterns in the box.

> *recommend/suggest* something
> *recommend/suggest* something *to* someone
> *recommend/suggest (not) doing* something
> *recommend/suggest (that)* someone *do* something
> *advise (not) doing* something
> *advise* someone *(not) to do* something
> *advise (not) doing* something
>
> NOT I recommend ~~you~~ this.
> NOT I recommend ~~you~~ doing this.
> NOT I recommend ~~it~~ that you do this.
> NOT I advise ~~you~~ doing this.
> NOT I advise ~~that~~ you to do this.

Now correct these sentences by deleting one word from each.

1 I suggest we to buy the cheaper model.
2 I recommend it that we have a short break.
3 I advise that you to look again at the figures.
4 What do you suggest me?
5 I recommend you not parking here.

6 Company and community

The passive

1 Compare sentences a and b then answer the questions below.

a) Our subcontractors **employed** a lot of illegal immigrants last year.
b) A lot of illegal immigrants **were employed** by our subcontractors last year.

1 Which sentence are you more likely to hear in a spoken conversation? ☐
2 Which sentence are you more likely to read in a written report? ☐
3 Which sentence uses a passive verb? ☐
4 Rewrite sentence b so that the person or thing that did the action (the agent) is not mentioned.

____

2 Read the sentences a–d then answer the questions below.

a) A lot of production **has been moved** overseas to countries where labour is cheap.
b) New laws **have been introduced** to protect health and safety at work.
c) The company admitted that mistakes **had been made**.
d) It **was agreed** that compensation would be paid to the employees who lost their jobs.

1 Which sentence uses the passive because the agent is obvious (it is clearly 'the government')? ☐
2 Which sentence uses the passive because the agent is unknown? ☐
3 Which sentence uses the passive because we are not interested in the agent (it is a group of people, but exactly who is irrelevant)? ☐
4 Which sentence uses the passive because the writer does not want us to identify the agent? ☐

3 Compare two ways to end this sentence.

Many tourists enjoy taking a cruise along the Danube, but over recent years …

1 … **the river has been polluted** by raw sewage, agricultural chemicals and industrial waste.
2 … raw sewage, agricultural chemicals and industrial waste **have polluted the river**.

Which ending makes a better link to the topic of the first part of the sentence ('the Danube')? ☐

- The passive is used when the agent (the person who does the action) is obvious, unknown or uninteresting.
- The passive is also used to bring a topic to the front of a phrase so that it links to the same topic just mentioned.
- The passive is more common in writing, and gives a formal, impersonal style.

4 Complete the table. Do not mention the agent.

Active form	Passive form
1 We make car parts here.	Car parts ________.
2 They're polluting the river.	The river ________.
3 We obeyed the law.	The law ________.
4 They've offered me the job.	I ________.
5 They were selling fake goods.	Fake goods ________.
6 We can change this policy.	This policy ________.
7 They might fine us.	We ________.
8 I will decide this later.	This ________.

5 Rewrite the sentences using a passive form. Decide whether or not to mention the agent.

1 We have put the environment at the centre of our future planning.
The environment ______________________.
2 Johnson & Johnson introduced the idea of corporate social responsibility.
The idea of corporate social responsibility ________
______________________.
3 Someone services the elevator every week.
The elevator ______________________.
4 That guy with the crazy look in his eyes serviced the elevator last week.
The elevator ______________________.
5 The company is hiring 100 new employees this month.
A hundred new employees ______________________.
6 A problem delayed my flight.
My flight ______________________.
7 A major security alert involving 80 Chechnian terrorists delayed my flight.
My flight ______________________.
8 We must protect the environment.
The environment ______________________.

6 Rewrite the phrase in bold so that there is a better link to the first part of the sentence.

A terrible gas leak occurred in Bhopal in 1984 – it seems that **an act of sabotage caused the disaster.**

Reported speech

7 **Match reported speech 1–7 with the quotations a–h. One reported version is used twice.**

Telling a friend about the conversation later:

She said (that) ...
1 ... she does that. ☐
2 ... she would do that. ☐
3 ... she had done that. ☐
4 ... she was doing that. ☐
5 ... she might do that. ☐
6 ... she could do that. ☐
7 ... she must do that. ☐

The actual words she spoke:

a) 'I'm doing that.'
b) 'I'll do that.'
c) 'I've done that.'
d) 'I did that.'
e) 'I do that.'
f) 'I can do that.'
g) 'I may do that.'
h) 'I must do that.'

8 **Put a tick (✓) if the sentence is possible, and a cross (✗) if it is impossible. Think about if you are reporting something which is still true.**

1 He said he would be here this afternoon. I need to speak to him. ☐
2 He said he will be here this afternoon. I need to speak to him. ☐
3 He said he would be here this afternoon. But his secretary has just called to say that he can't make it. ☐
4 He said he will be here this afternoon. But his secretary has just called to say that he can't make it. ☐

9 **Read the actual words spoken then underline the correct words in bold in the reported version.**

Actual words spoken on Monday:
'We'll give you our answer tomorrow.'
Reporting to a colleague on Tuesday:
She said that **we'd** / **they'd** give **you** / **me our** / **their** answer **tomorrow** / **today.**

When you report what someone said earlier, the original verb tense moves back in time:
- present simple → past simple, etc. (see Exercise 7 above)
- *will* → *would*

Both the past simple and present perfect change to the past perfect. There is no change for *must, should, might, could, would.*
You don't have to change the verb tense if the statement is still true.
Sometimes a pronoun or time expression changes as well.

Reporting verbs: *say/tell/ask*

10 **Underline the correct form in bold.**

1 She **said** / **told** that she would do that.
2 She **said me** / **told me** that she would do that.
3 She **said to me** / **told to me** that she would do that.
4 She asked me **that** / **what** I would do.
5 She asked me **that** / **if** I would do that.
6 She asked me what **I was doing** / **was I doing.**
7 She asked me when **I would arrive** / **would I arrive.**

You *say* something.
You *tell* somebody.
You *say* something *to* somebody.
To report a question you use *ask* + a question word (*what, when,* etc.) or *if.*
The word order of a reported question is like a normal statement, not like a question.

Other reporting verbs

There are many other verbs to report what people say. Study the table.

- Verbs like *say*, followed by 'something':
  admit, announce, claim, explain, imply, reply, state.
  NOT *She explained ~~us~~ the situation.*
- Verbs like *tell*, followed by 'somebody':
  assure, inform, persuade, reassure, remind.
  NOT *She ~~informed that~~ the situation was under control.*
  (Correct: *informed me that*)
- A few verbs can be followed by 'something' or 'somebody': *guarantee, promise.*
  She guaranteed (us) that the goods would be here.

11 **Report the phrases in bold using the verbs in brackets. Include the word *me* where possible.**

1 **'It's a really good deal** – you won't find this price anywhere on the market.'
(persuade)
He *persuaded me that it was a really good deal*.
2 **'We're stopping all production** until we discover the cause of the pollution in the river.'
(announce)
She ______.
3 'Don't worry, **we have fitted new filters** to make sure that the system is clean and safe.'
(reassure)
He ______.
4 'Do you want to know what we can do about this situation? We **can do absolutely nothing**.'
(reply)
She ______.

will

1 Match the forms of *will* in sentences 1–5 with their best explanations a–e below.

a) The merger **will** take place next January.
b) I think the merger **will** probably take place sometime early next year.
c) I'**ll** open the window – it's a bit hot in here.
d) I'**ll** carry your suitcase to the car.
e) I'**ll** call you next week. Bye!

1 a prediction about the future based on an opinion or belief ☐
2 a future fact ☐
3 a promise about the future ☐
4 an instant decision – sometimes referring to something immediate, not in the future ☐
5 an offer of help – sometimes referring to something immediate, not in the future ☐

> *will* has two main uses:
> 1 predictions and facts about the future
> 2 decisions, promises and offers of help that we make at the moment of speaking
> - The second use is informal, and in this use *will* is usually contracted to *'ll*.
> - Decisions, promises and offers of help are often combined:
>   *OK, I'll email the information to you this afternoon.* (instant decision + promise)
>   *I'll speak to my boss and see if we can do that.* (instant decision + offer of help)

2 Read the extract from a presentation then add the word *will* in three places and *won't* in two places.

'Good morning, ladies and gentlemen. I've called this press conference because of the rumours circulating in the media about our M&A strategy. Over the next few years our bank become a major player in Central Europe, and naturally we look at strong local banks as possible targets for acquisition. But we make any decisions until we have studied the market carefully. There has been much comment about possible job cuts, but I want to reassure you that the staff of a bank are amongst its most valuable assets. When we do make a move, there be significant job losses at the bank we acquire. In any case, we deal with this issue at the time, and I have no further comment to add now.'

3 Read these two sentences.

1 There will be significant job losses.
2 There won't be significant job losses.

Now add the word *probably* in the correct place to both sentences (but not at the beginning).

4 Match comments 1–5 with responses a–e below.

1 Bye! ☐
2 Are you ready to order now? ☐
3 Can you send me a copy of your new brochure? ☐
4 I only have an hour to get to the airport. ☐
5 Are you going for a drink with your colleagues? ☐

a) Of course, I'll put one in the mail this afternoon.
b) Bye! I'll see you tomorrow.
c) Don't worry, I'll call a taxi.
d) Yes, but I don't think I'll be back late.
e) Yes, I'll have the roast lamb.

5 Look at the use of *'ll* in responses a–e in Exercise 4. Which one is the *best* example of:

1 a prediction?
2 a future fact?
3 an instant decision?
4 a promise?
5 an offer of help?

be going to

6 Read the information about *be going to* in the box.

> *Be going to* has two main uses:
> 1 predictions, especially where there is strong evidence in the present situation
>   *Look out! It's going to fall.*
> 2 plans and decisions we have already made.
>   *We're going to cut forty jobs next month.*

Now decide how *be going to* is used in each sentence. Write *prediction* or *plan*.

1 It says in this article that there are going to be job cuts in our banking sector because of all the foreign acquisitions. __________
2 I'm going to see my bank manager about the loan next week. __________
3 You want delivery by the end of the month? That's going to be difficult. __________
4 We're going to launch the new model at the Frankfurt Motor Show. __________
5 There's too much to do before the deadline. We're not going to have enough time. __________
6 We want to expand our operations in Central and Eastern Europe, so we are going to open new branches in Bratislava and Warsaw. __________

7 Read the evidence in the first sentence. Then use the words in brackets to make a prediction with *be going to*.

1 American banks want to expand in Slovakia. (Citibank/make a bid for Tatra Banka.)
____
2 There's too much to do before the deadline. (We/not have enough time.)
____

Present continuous

8 Read the information about the present continuous in the box.

The present continuous has a present time reference (see *Grammar and practice* 4 page 128).
It also has a future time reference: to talk about fixed arrangements.
The fixed arrangements are often social arrangements and appointments.
There is usually a time phrase.
I'm seeing my bank manager at 11:30 next Tuesday.

Now complete the text by putting the verbs into the correct form of the present continuous.

'I _________ (fly) to Paris on Thursday morning. Louis and Isabelle _________ (come) from Lyons to join us. We _________ (give) a presentation about the merger to institutional investors on Friday morning, at the offices of BNP Paribas.'

will or *going to*?

9 Read the information in the box.

Often either *will* or *going to* are possible, and you could use both in the same situation. However there are some small differences that can influence your choice.

Predictions:

- *Will* is more likely if the prediction is based on the speaker's thoughts and opinions.
- *Going to* is more likely if the prediction is based on evidence in the present situation.

Decisions:

- *Will* is more likely if the decision is spontaneous, made at the moment of speaking.
- *Going to* is more likely if the decision has been made previously, and so now it is a plan.

Now <u>underline</u> the form in bold that is more likely (but remember that both are possible).

1 Have you heard the news? Citibank **will make / are going to make** a bid for Tatra Banka.
2 The UK **will probably start / is probably going to start** using the euro eventually.
3 If you're busy, **I'll come back / I'm going to come back** later.
4 I was talking with my friends yesterday - **we'll go / we're going to go** skiing in the Alps.

going to or present continuous?

Read the information in the box.

Going to and the present continuous are both used for plans and arrangements. Nearly always both are possible in the same situation.
Going to is slightly more likely if it's just a plan.

The present continuous is slightly more likely if the arrangement is fixed, with a time and a place.
I'm going to see my bank manager next week.
I'm seeing my bank manager at 11:30 next Tuesday.

Expressing likelihood

10 Use these expressions to complete the sentences below. Match the expressions in the box with the degree of probability in brackets.

it's almost certain to   it's likely to   it might
it might just   it will definitely
there's no way it will   there's not much chance it will

1 (100%) _________________ be a success.
2 (90%) _________________ be a success.
3 (70%) _________________ be a success.
4 (50%) _________________ be a success.
5 (20%) _________________ be a success.
6 (10%) _________________ be a success.
7 (0%) _________________ be a success.

11 Rewrite each sentence with one of these words so that the probability changes as shown in brackets.

almost   definitely   definitely   fully
good   highly   just

1 There's a chance the merger will go ahead. (50%→70%)
<u>There's a good chance the merger will go ahead.</u>
2 The merger will go ahead (100%→100% with emphasis)
____
3 The merger won't go ahead. (0%→0% with emphasis)
____
4 The merger might go ahead. (50%→20%)
____
5 The merger is certain to go ahead. (100%→90%)
____
6 It's likely the merger will go ahead. (70%→90%)
____
7 We expect the merger to go ahead. (70%→90%)
____

12 Write *T* (true) or *F* (false) after each statement.

1 The three alternatives in **bold** below all have approximately the same meaning. ☐
The merger ***may/might/could*** *go ahead.*
2 The three alternatives in italics below all have approximately the same meaning. ☐
The merger ***may not/might not/could not*** *go ahead.*
3 The two alternatives in italics below have approximately the same meaning. ☐
The merger ***should/is likely to*** *go ahead.*

Prepositions of time

1 Complete the sentences with these prepositions.

after	at	by	during	for
from	on	until	within	

1 My flight gets in _________ 20:15, a few hours _________ yours.
2 I'll be away _________ Monday, 11 June, and I won't be back _________ Wednesday, 20 June.
3 My holidays begin _________ Monday, 11 June.
4 The meeting should have finished _________ 4.30pm at the latest.
5 I'll be away _________ about ten days _________ the month of June.
6 When I get back there are a few things I need to sort out, but you'll hear from me _________ a few days.

2 Cross out the *one* incorrect word in bold in each sentence.

1 I'm away from Monday **by** / **to** / **until** Wednesday.
2 What did you do **at** / **during** / **in** / **over** the holidays?
3 How long was his presentation? Oh, it lasted **during** / **for** about an hour.
4 **During** / **While** my time at university I learned a lot about economic theory.
5 **During** / **While** I was at university I learned a lot about economic theory.
6 **Last year** / **In the last year** sales were slightly better than this year.
7 **Last year** / **In the last year** sales have been improving; by the end of the year we predict growth of around 2%.

3 Cross out the *one* word or expression that is not used with the preposition at the beginning.

1 *in* April / 2006 / the 90s / lunch / the morning / the summer / the third quarter / the 21st century
2 *on* Friday / Friday morning / 2 April / Christmas Day / the summer / my birthday
3 *at* half past ten / the weekend / lunch / Christmas / the end of the week / the morning / night

4 Write at the beginning of each time expression either *in*, *on*, *at* or Ø if no preposition is used.

1 _________ this morning
2 _________ yesterday afternoon
3 _________ last night
4 _________ the day before yesterday
5 _________ a few days ago
6 _________ last week

5 Complete each sentence with *by* or *until*.

1 I need your report _________ Friday.
2 I'll be away _________ Friday lunchtime, but I'm free all Friday afternoon.
3 I waited _________ ten and then left.
4 _________ ten I had dealt with all my emails.

Now complete the explanation in the box by writing *by* or *until*.

_________ means 'up to'.
_________ means 'on' or 'before'.

6 Complete each sentence with *in time* or *on time*.

1 I got to the airport _________ – but another few minutes and I would have missed my flight.
2 I got to the airport _________, and had a chance to look at the stores.
3 If you order today, you'll get the goods _________ for Christmas.
4 You can trust us to deliver your goods _________ every time.

Now complete the explanation in the box by writing *in time* or *on time*.

_________ means 'with enough time' (usually: to do something else).
_________ means 'at the right time'.

7 Complete the explanation in the box by writing these phrases: *at the end*, *by the end*, *in the end*, *towards the end*, *at last*.

- _________ means 'eventually' or 'finally'.
  The negotiation was going nowhere, and _________ we just walked away.
- _________ refers to the last part of something.
  _________ *of the negotiation their line manager will have to sign the contract.*
- _________ means 'at' or 'before the end'.
  _________ *of the negotiation we had explored every possible option.*
- _________ means 'near the end'.
  _________ *of the negotiation our legal team will have to start preparing the contract.*
- _________ shows pleasure because something happens that you have been waiting for.
  _________ *the negotiations are finished! Let's all go out for a meal to celebrate.*

8 Look at the alternatives in bold and write *S* (same meaning) or *D* (different meaning).

1 We appointed a sales agent in October, and **the following month/the month after that** we started to get our first orders. ☐
2 We appointed a sales agent in October, and **soon after/shortly after** we started to get our first orders. ☐

Verb + preposition

9 Match the verbs on the left in each group of five with a construction on the right.

1 apologize	a) to something
2 succeed	b) somebody to do something
3 rely	c) in doing something
4 conform	d) on somebody to do something
5 convince	e) for (not) doing something
6 hear	f) to doing something
7 insist	g) about something from somebody
8 look forward	h) to somebody about something
9 complain	i) for something
10 wait	j) on doing something

10 Use a verb + preposition from Exercise 9 to complete these sentences.

1 My soup was cold, so I _________ _________ the waiter. He _________ _________ the poor service, and said he would bring some hot soup immediately.
2 While I'm away on business I _________ _________ my secretary to do everything. If anything important happens, she calls me or sends an email so that I _________ _________ it straight away.
3 The salaries in our company should _________ _________ those in other similar companies. I've been saying that for ages, and I've now _________ _________ convincing senior management. We all get a 10% pay rise next month!
4 I'll ask the waiter to bring the bill, and I _________ _________ paying. You can pay when I visit you in your country, and I _________ _________ to doing that very soon.

11 Use a verb from A and a preposition from B to complete the sentences. Sometimes it is necessary to add a third person *-s* to the verb.

A
agree apply comply consist depend insure invest suffer
B
against for from in of on with with

1 As well as owning stocks and bonds, a good way to diversify your portfolio is to _________ _________ property.
2 The shipping cost _________ _________ two figures: the transport itself, and the insurance.
3 Health and safety is a big issue these days, and the company has to _________ _________ all the regulations in this area.
4 It all _________ _________ what you mean by 'profit'. Are you talking about gross profit, or net profit?
5 If there was a fire in the factory, or a serious accident, it would be a disaster – we must _________ _________ these kinds of risks.
6 Ruth persuaded me to _________ _________ the sales job, but I'm not sure that I want my career to go in that direction.
7 Don't worry, I'm quite OK. I _________ _________ an allergy to dairy products, but it's nothing serious.
8 I _________ _________ you up to a point, but I think there are some important issues that you haven't considered.

Noun + preposition

12 Complete the sentences using these prepositions.

for for for for in on on to to with

1 A company's image can be seriously damaged by involvement ___ illegal trading practices.
2 Bills of exchange are no substitute ___ careful credit checks.
3 Credit insurance can eliminate the need ___ letters of credit.
4 Credit ratings are a solution ___ the problem of evaluating risk.
5 It's important to be transparent in dealings ___ foreign governments.
6 Late payment can have a damaging effect ___ a company's cash-flow.
7 Negotiators should show respect ___ other cultures.
8 Some countries levy a special tax ___ imports.
9 The seller's bank may have access ___ information about the buyer's creditworthiness.
10 The seller's bank takes responsibility ___ obtaining payment.

13 Find a word in Exercise 12 that means:

1 the act of taking part in an activity or event _________
2 something that is used instead of something else _________
3 measurements of how good something is _________
4 the business relationship that you have with another person or organization (plural) _________
5 harmful _________
6 to officially request payment, especially of a tax _________
7 an amount of money that you have to pay to the government _________
8 the degree to which an organization is likely to pay back money that they borrow _________

Recordings

Business fundamentals

Company types and structures

1:01–1:05

Mina: I'm a geologist with a well-known multinational corporation – maybe you even own shares in our company. Our core business is mining – gold, silver, copper, iron and so on. We have a complex structure; each geographical region has a local management structure, but individual product managers also report to different functional managers at HQ – R&D, finance, marketing, etc. It's a huge operation, so decision-making can be very slow!

Marty: I'm a freelance photographer, so I run my own business. I do a lot of weddings, parties and so on. Because I'm self-employed, I can do things my way, which is great; on the other hand, it's financially risky. For example, if the business got into trouble, I could lose my home.

Owen: We make furniture for firms like Ikea. I sort of supervise production, and my sister runs the office, but in fact my dad decides everything. He's the General Manager. It's a family business; there are six shareholders altogether, but we can't really do anything without Dad.

Isabelle: I share an office and an assistant with three other lawyers. I specialize in employment law, advising companies on HR issues. My partners each have their own specialization, and Sarah, our assistant, works for all of us. In theory, as managing partner, I'm the boss, but in practice we each look after our own clients. So it's a very flat structure, there's no real hierarchy.

Frank: I work for a hairdressing franchise – my job is to recruit and manage new franchisees; I report directly to the CEO. We help franchisees to set up salons, promote our products, and ultimately, increase our shareholder value. It's good business for them, but although they manage their own limited companies, they don't have any real say in how things are done; there's a procedure for everything – and I mean everything!

1 Corporate culture

1.1 About business Work culture and placements

1:06

I got my first placement in a PR firm in Paris. Our teachers had told us to be careful about dress code, being on time, and so on. But I had a problem I really wasn't expecting.

The first day, I arrived at eight thirty and I was a bit surprised because I had to wait an hour and a half for my supervisor to arrive. In fact, most people came in at about eleven o'clock. But everybody was very friendly. They gave me a project to work on and I thought, great, I can really do a good job here and, you know, make a good impression.

Well, for the first two weeks I worked from nine in the morning to about seven in the evening. I didn't really have a social life because I only got home about eight, but, like I said, I wanted to make a good impression. But then gradually, people became less friendly, and stopped talking to me. I couldn't understand why they were giving me these funny looks, especially when I went home in the evening.

Anyway, in the end, I went and asked my supervisor what I'd done wrong. And in fact the problem was that most people didn't go home until 9 or 10pm. So because I left at about seven, I was breaking the unwritten rules. They all thought I was lazy! I mean, I knew I was the first to leave, but I arrived at 9am, and I was working really hard, you know?! But as far as they were concerned, you couldn't do any real work before eleven, so arriving at nine in the morning didn't count!

1:07

I'm a department manager in the civil service. The department's actually very informal and friendly – we're all quite young and everyone's on first name terms. We all have lunch together in the canteen and we often go to the pub for a drink after work. We have one or two interns per year. We try to make them feel at home and part of the team, and usually it's fine.

But, a year or two ago, I had a problem with an intern I was supervising. At first, everything was fine. Monica was very bright and friendly, and got on well with everybody. But then one day we had a crisis in the office. My manager needed one of Monica's files for an important meeting at 10am. We couldn't find it, and unfortunately Monica wasn't in the office; she wasn't answering her phone, and she didn't arrive until ten fifteen! In fact, she'd been to the dentist's, but she hadn't told me that she'd be late. Well, as you can imagine, I was stressed out and I made it very clear that this was unacceptable. And Monica just burst into tears, so I had to tell her that, you know, that was unprofessional too.

Anyway, after that, things were never the same. She stopped socializing with the rest of the team; she wouldn't say anything in meetings and she didn't even eat in the canteen with us any more. I tried to explain that it was my job to tell her when there was a problem, and that it wasn't personal. But she couldn't accept that. For her, a boss was a boss, and a friend was a friend, and you couldn't be a boss and a friend.

1.2 Vocabulary Work organization and responsibility

1:08

Bertram: All right, Sam, welcome to San Antonio. Now, I just want to tell you who's who at Warndar, so you know who to go to when you have questions, OK?

Sam: OK.

B: Now, let's start here in Marketing; I'm the Business Development Manager, and I have a team of four reporting in to me; two salesmen, Jake Smith, our Art Director, and Saidah Hussain, who's our PR Officer. You'll be working mainly with Jake and Saidah in PR, but you're going to report directly to me.

S: All right.

B: As I told you, we're a small company, so the organization is simple for the moment, but we're growing fast, so that's going to change as we hire new staff. For example, right now we don't really have an HR department – Monica Overstreet, our Office Manager, takes care of HR.

S: Yes, I met Ms Overstreet last time I was here.

B: That's right. She also looks after finance, and she has two accountants working under her. Now then, as you probably know, Warndar Technologies was founded by Merilyn Warner, our CEO, and David Darren, who's now COO.

S: COO?

B: Yeah. Chief Operating Officer. Basically, David runs the business on a day-to-day basis. Merilyn deals with strategy; she's often away at our parent company in Houston.

S: Uh-huh – so Warndar is a subsidiary of the Irysis group, right?

B: That's right. They took us over a couple of years ago. Anyway, there are three other department heads who all report to David. Roxane Pawle is our IT Manager in charge of IT and Technical Support. She's new – she joined six months ago when our old IT Manager resigned.

S: Really?

B: Yeah. He was appointed Head of IT in a big firm up in Washington. Nice job, but too much stress. They fired him after only three months!

S: Wow!

B: Yeah. Anyway, Roxane has a web developer and two support engineers reporting to her. OK? Now, the biggest department here is R&D. Doug Pearson has seven research scientists in the lab. Doug coordinates our development programs; so he liaises with me in Marketing and with our Program Manager, Herb Monroe. Herb manages the Engineering Department, and he's responsible for building our product package. He has a team of three: two software engineers and a technical writer.

S: OK.

B: All right, I think that's everyone. So, let's go and meet Saidah – unless you have any questions?

1.3 Grammar Past tenses and advice structures

1:09

Do you know the one about the CFO an the crocodiles? Well, there was this CEO, who was giving a party for his executive team. Over the years, the boss had done very well for himself, so he was proudly showing the executives around his luxurious country house. Anyway, at the back of the house, he had built the largest swimming pool any of them had ever seen. Absolutely huge, you know? But the pool was full of very hungry crocodiles. So, the CEO said to his executives,

'The most important quality for an executive is courage. Without it, you will never become a CEO like me. So, this is my challenge to each of you: if anyone can dive into the pool, swim through those crocodiles and reach the other side, I will give them anything they want. My job, my money, my house, anything!'

Well, of course, everyone laughed at the challenge and nobody took it very seriously. Anyway, they had just started to follow the CEO towards the barbecue when suddenly there was a loud splash. Everyone turned around and ran back to the pool where the Chief Financial Officer was swimming for his life. The crocodiles had almost caught him when he reached the edge of the pool. He'd just managed to climb out of the pool when he heard the mouth of the biggest crocodile close shut – snap – behind him.

Well, the CEO shook the CFO's hand and said,

'I'm really impressed. Until you dived into that pool, I never imagined you had such courage. You accepted my challenge and now anything I own is yours. Tell me what I can do for you.' The CFO was still recovering from the swim. He looked up at the CEO and said, 'You can start by telling me who the hell pushed me into the pool!'

1.4 Speaking Meetings one-to-one

1:10

Version 1

Simon: Morning, Tiffany. Good weekend?

Tiffany: Oh, yes, it was cool. And you?

S: No, not really. Listen, Tiffany, come into my office, I need to talk to you.

T: Oh no, what now?

S: Look, I hear you had a problem with Maureen on Friday.

T: Oh, that. Yeah. That idiot refused to help me! Who does she think she is?!

S: You mustn't talk about your colleagues like that. Maureen is a very experienced assistant and a valuable member of the team.

T: Maybe, but she still refused to help me.

S: Yes, but she had a good reason to refuse. Maureen was very busy on Friday and you didn't ask for help; you demanded her immediate attention. As a future manager, you should show respect to all the staff.

T: But I was just trying to finish the job.

S: Well, you won't get results from people like Maureen if you're rude.

T: Look, I was tired. I had a difficult week, OK?

S: Tiffany, everyone gets tired, and I'm getting tired of your attitude. You apologize, or there'll be trouble. Do you understand?

T: Me? Apologize to some stupid little secretary? No way!

1:11

Version 2

Simon: Morning, Tiffany. Good weekend?

Tiffany: Oh yes, it was cool and you?

S: Yeah I had a good weekend too – apart from having to finish off this report. How about you? What did you do?

T: I went to the swimming pool yesterday. Gorgeous weather.

S: Sounds good. Er, Tiffany, have you got a minute?

T: Sure.

S: Come in. I just wanted to have a quick word. Erm, I hear you had a problem with Maureen on Friday.

T: Oh, that. Yeah. That idiot refused to help me! Who does she think she is?!

S: Well, Tiffany, I think perhaps you should be more careful about how you talk about your colleagues. Maureen is a very experienced assistant and a valuable member of the team.

T: OK, but she still refused to help me.

S: Well, you might want to think about why she couldn't help you. Maureen was very busy on Friday, and I understand you didn't really ask for help so much as demand her immediate attention. We try hard to respect all our staff here. As a future manager, I think you ought to do the same.

T: But I was just trying to finish the job.

S: Well, I understand that, and I appreciate that you work hard and that you expect other people to show the same commitment. But, don't you think you might get better results from people like Maureen by being a little more diplomatic?

T: Yeah, OK. I'm sorry, you're right. I was tired. I didn't mean to be rude.

S: OK. It can happen to anyone. Why don't you ask Maureen to have a coffee with you, and just clear the air? OK?

T: OK. Thanks, Simon.

1.5 Writing A placement report

1:12

Jason: Hi, Jason!

Alex: Oh hi, Alex.

J: Do you feel like going out tonight? There's a new Will Smith movie on at nine fifteen!

A: Oh yeah. Look, I'd love to, but I've got this essay to finish, and then I've got to write my placement report.

J: Placement? Oh, that's interesting, I didn't know you did a placement. What did you do?

A: I spent three months near Birmingham at a place called Diftco. They export construction equipment.

J: Oh yeah, good job was it?

A: It was all right. They're a bit crazy there. People worked really hard, sometimes from eight in the morning to nine or ten in the evening.

J: Hmm. Sounds like school!

A: Yeah! Anyway, I was in charge of preparing shipping documents. It was lucky we did international trade last semester. It really helped me understand what was going on.

J: Preparing shipping documents, eh? Sounds boring. Didn't like international trade much myself. Did you get on well with your boss?

A: Oh, she was very strict. But, OK, I suppose. She didn't scream at me or anything when I did something wrong.

J: Why, did you get things wrong a lot?

A: Nah. Only once when I sent a container to Austria instead of Australia.

J: You're joking!

A: Well, it wasn't my fault. This guy on the phone had a really strong accent. I didn't understand half of what he said.

J: So you sent a container to Austria? What an idiot!

A: Well, I bet you wouldn't do any better. Anyway, it was interesting, 'cos they had this really sophisticated automatic system, but you can't ever eliminate human error completely.

J: Yeah, right, the guys at IBM only tested their systems with monkeys, they didn't expect you to be using them!

A: OK, OK … Now, if you've finished taking the mickey, I've got an essay to write.

J: No, come on. I'm just joking. I'm really interested in Diftco. I need to find a placement for next summer.

A: Well, it's a good placement for first-years, but I think second-years should have more responsibility. I was hoping to get some management experience but I mostly worked alone, so it wasn't that great.

J: You wouldn't recommend it, then?

A: No. I learned quite a lot in three months, but I certainly wouldn't like to work there.

J: Mm, I see what you mean.

A: Listen, now I've told you all about it, you couldn't help me with the report, could you? If we finish by nine, we can still make it in time for the movie. Look, I've already made these notes. You just have to write them up for me …

1.6 Case study Counselling

1:13

Now, before we go on, I'll just summarize the three points we've already discussed. Firstly, the goal of counselling is to help another person manage a personal problem using their own resources. Secondly, counselling is about listening, not about telling. It's about talking to someone and helping, not about persuading or manipulating. And, counselling is about assisting and exploring problems. It's not about reassuring someone or solving their problems for them. Thirdly, the three phases of counselling:

Phase one, talk. This is where you encourage the problem holder to talk about the problem, and to start to understand how they feel about the problem and why they feel that way. Phase two, think. This is where you encourage them to think about the problem and reassess it. You help them to see their situation from a new perspective, so that they can consider the different options for dealing with the situation. And phase three, act. This is where you help them to choose their own solution and to establish an action plan to manage the problem. OK, are there any questions?

2 Customer support

2.1 About business Call centres

1:14

Interviewer: Groupon is currently the world's fastest growing company, with 35 million registered users all around the world. How do you keep so many customers happy?

Manager: Well, one of the key factors has been cloud computing. We're now in 45 countries around the world, and we got there in about a year and a half. If it wasn't for the cloud architecture we have in place, we could never have done that.

I: Can you give us an example?

M: Well, we've recently adopted Natterbox. Basically, it's software that decides how valuable or how urgent a call is, and then transfers that call to the best person to answer it. If an important client calls and the salesperson is not at their desk, the call is pushed through to their mobile. If they don't pick up, the system records a voicemail that can be accessed online.

I: So if the salesperson is on the road, or in a restaurant …

M: They still get the call. Yes.

I: And where do your call centre staff work?

M: Well, from our call centre in London we provide customer service for England, Wales, Scotland, Ireland and Denmark. But we employ agents who come from all those regions, each with their own cultural familiarity and local knowledge. Natterbox recognises the location of the incoming phone numbers and directs the call to a customer service agent from the right region.

I: So if I'm calling from Scotland, the person who answers the phone will be Scottish, and if I'm calling from Denmark …

M: The agent will be Danish.

I: Excellent!

M: Yes. It also means we answer every call. Before we had Natterbox, our customer service department wasn't handling around 50% of the calls – they were just coming in and getting lost. And people hate it when a machine answers their call, it's very frustrating. With Natterbox, they get through to the right person straight away.

I: So, in theory, the sales person or the customer service agent could be anywhere in the world; in London, in India or in the Philippines, in a call centre or working from home?

M: Exactly.

2.2 Vocabulary Customer service and telephoning

1:15–1:22

1 **Operator:** Now, don't worry, madam. This is just a minor problem that a few customers experience at first. It will only take a few minutes to resolve.

2 … or if you would like more information about our products, please press four.
Customer: All I want is to speak to a human being, not a stupid, condescending, brainless piece of … silicon!

3 **Operator:** All right, sir. Yes, it is an unusual problem, and it's a little complicated, but you'll be pleased to know there is a solution.

4 **Customer:** Oh, that's wonderful. You're so clever! Thank you so much!

5 **Operator:** I fully understand your position, sir, and I would feel exactly the same way myself.

6 **Operator:** Alternatively, the simplest solution is to upgrade to the professional version of the software. The extra cost is only around one euro per month. I think you'd agree that that's excellent value, wouldn't you?

7 **Customer:** Oh, thank you so much. You're so patient. I bet nobody else has these problems. I just feel so stupid!

8 **Operator:** A very good morning to you, and thank you for calling the helpline. How I can help you today?

2.3 Grammar Asking questions and giving instructions

1:23

A: Welcome back to *Guess the Product*. Our next mystery product is a fairly simple but extremely useful piece of technology. Panel, you've just ten questions to help you 'guess the product'!

B: OK. Is it advertised on TV?

A: No, it isn't.

C: Do you use it for work?

A: Yes, you do.

D: Would you find one in every office?

A: Yes, you would.

C: Can you put it in your pocket?

A: Yes, you can.

D: Did it exist twenty years ago?

A: No, it didn't.

C: Does it use electricity?

A: Yes, it does.

B: Do you use it to speak to people?

A: No, you don't.

C: Is there a connection with computers?

A: Yes, there is.

B: Does it cost more than $30?

A: No, it doesn't.

D: Can you use it to store data?

A: Yes, you can. All right, that's ten questions. Now, have you 'guessed the product'?

D: We think it's a USB memory stick.

A: Yes! Well done! You've correctly 'guessed the product'!

1:24

Steve: OK, Pete. First of all, you open the printer. No, wait a minute, don't just open it, select 'change cartridge' from the menu.

Pete: From the menu? Do I have to switch the printer on?

S: Er, yes, of course you have to switch it on, otherwise you can't use the menu!

P: Oh, right. What about the computer?

S: No, that's all right, you needn't switch the PC on, just the printer.

P: All right. So, the printer's on, select 'change cartridge', OK, and open the printer. What now?

S: So now you gently remove the old cartridge. Don't force it. If it's difficult, you might have to pull it back first, then upwards.

P: Backwards, then upwards. All right, I've got it.

S: OK. So now you can install the new cartridge. You'll need to remove the adhesive tape first, but be careful you don't touch the printed circuits – they're very fragile.

P: You needn't worry. I'm being very careful. OK, that's it.

S: Right. It'll ask you if you want to align the new cartridge, but you needn't bother. Usually it's fine as it is.

P: OK. What about the old one? Can I just throw it in the trash?

S: Oh no, don't throw the old cartridge away. You can recycle them.

P: Oh yes, right. Listen, that's great. I really appreciate your help. Is there anything I can do for you?

S: No, that's all right, Pete. You needn't worry. Just buy me a coffee some time!

2.4 Speaking Dealing with problems by telephone

1:25

Helpline: Thank you for calling the Superword helpline. Please hold the line.

Dean: Good morning. Dean speaking. How can I help you?

Customer: Oh, good morning. Yes, I'm afraid your program isn't working properly.

D: Oh, I'm sorry to hear that. What exactly seems to be the problem?

C: Well, the thing is, I can't put those automatic table thingies in my documents.

D: I'm sorry, it's not a very good line. Could you speak up a little?

C: Yes, sorry. I'm on my mobile. Is that better?

D: Yes, that's much better, thank you.

C: All right. Anyway, I was just saying, I can't insert those tables.

D: Oh, I see. You're having trouble importing spreadsheets into a Superword document?

C: Yes, that's right.

D: All right, I'll put you through to our spreadsheet specialist.

C: Thank you.

D: Hello?

C: Yes?

D: I'm sorry, the number's busy. Could I ask her to get back to you in a few minutes?

C: Yes, that's fine.

D: OK, then. So, you're on 0680 425232?

C: That's right.

D: And could I have your name please?

C: Wyndham. Delia Wyndham.

D: Is that Wyndham with a 'y'?

C: That's right. W-Y-N-D-H-A-M.

D: Thank you, Ms Wyndham. I'm sure we'll be able to sort it out.

C: Thank you very much.

D: Not at all. Goodbye.

1:26

Operator: Customer support. May I help you?

Customer: Yes, well, I'm having trouble with Word.

O: Well, let me sort that out for you. What exactly seems to be the problem?

C: It doesn't work. It won't accept anything when I type.

O: I see. How long have you been having this problem?

C: Well, about ten minutes.

O: And was it working properly before that?

C: Sure. I was just typing away, and all of a sudden the words went away.

O: You mean they just disappeared?

C: Yes. Just like that.

O: So what does your screen look like now?

C: Nothing.

O: Nothing?

C: It's blank. Like I said, it won't accept anything when I type.

O: Uh-huh. Have you tried hitting 'Escape'?

C: Yes. Nothing happens.

O: OK. Did you quit Word?

C: I don't know. How do I tell if I quit?

O: Can you see the toolbar on the screen?

C: What's a toolbar?

O: OK, never mind. Can you move the cursor around on the screen?

C: There isn't any cursor. I told you, I can't type anything.

O: I see. Does your monitor have a power indicator?

C: What's a monitor?

O: It's the thing with the screen on it that looks like a TV. Does it have a little light that tells you when it's on?

C: I don't know.

O: Well, could you look on the back of the monitor and find where the power cord goes into it? Can you see that?

C: Yes, I think so.

O: Great. Now you just have to follow the cord to the plug, and tell me if it's plugged into the wall.

C: Er, yes, it is.

O: All right. Now, when you were behind the monitor, did you notice that there were two cables plugged into the back of it, not just one?

C: No.

O: Well, there are. I need you to look back there again and find the other cable.

C: … OK, here it is.

O: Good. Could you tell me if it's plugged securely into the back of your computer?

C: I can't reach.

O: Uh-huh. Well, you don't have to touch it. Can you just see if it's plugged in?

C: No. It's too dark.

O: So, you mean the lights are off?

C: Yes.

O: Well, couldn't you just turn on the light?

C: I can't.

O: No? Why not?

C: Because there's a power cut.

O: A power … A power cut? Ah, OK. I can handle this now. Listen, for the power cut, I'll have someone call the electricity company. For your Word problem, do you still have the boxes and manuals and packing stuff your computer came in?

C: Well, yes. I keep them in the closet.

O: Good. I'd like you to go and get them, to

unplug your system and to pack it up just like it was when you got it. Then I want you to take it back to the store you bought it from.

C: Really? Is it that bad?

O: Yes, I'm afraid it is.

C: Well, all right then, I suppose. What do I tell them?

O: Tell them you're too stupid to own a computer.

2.6 Case study Cybertartan Software

1:27

Interviewer: So, Laurie, these recruitment and turnover problems we're having – is it just a question of money?

Laurie McAllister: Well of course salaries are not terribly attractive these days. They were quite good a few years ago when the centre opened, but they haven't really increased with the cost of living, especially now house prices are so expensive here, so we're finding it more difficult to attract people from outside the area. But, actually, salaries are not the biggest problem. Basically there are two reasons why our turnover is high: working conditions and job satisfaction.

I: I see. What's the matter with working conditions? We give them free coffee, don't we?

LM: Well, things are very different now from when we started. In the past, the volume of calls was much lower, so things were more relaxed. Advisers had time to chat or have a cigarette between two calls. Now, the workload is much heavier, and the supervisors have to be very strict about breaks. Two bathroom breaks per day, and twenty minutes for lunch. There's a lot of unhappiness about that. And punctuality, well, the bus service here is totally inadequate. A lot of advisers can't afford a car, so transport is a real problem, especially at night.

I: Yes, I can see why that's a problem.

LM: And there are little things, you know, like having your own personal space. When you share your desk with your colleagues on the other shifts, you can't really personalize anything.

I: Hm. Maybe there are things that can be improved there. What's the problem with job satisfaction?

LM: Time, mostly. Our software products have become so complex that customers need more and more help. There are more calls than we can answer, so advisers have to keep them as short as possible. That's frustrating because there isn't time to build a relationship with the customer; sometimes there isn't even time to explain the solution properly. And then of course they say if they can't spend longer on the phone, they would like to send out instructions by email.

I: Yes, well, the customers would like that too, but we can't charge them for it like we can phone calls!

LM: Exactly. And we really need to give the advisers more training, especially the new people, but there just isn't time. They often have to read out instructions from the manual; it's not much fun answering questions when you don't really understand the answers yourself!

I: No. I can see that.

LM: Of course the thing they really don't like is the shift system. They work one week in the morning, from 6am to 2pm, one week in the afternoon from 2pm to 10pm, and one week nights, 10pm to 6am. I mean, it's OK for young, single people, but it's impossible for women with children, so that's a whole category of the population we have virtually no chance of employing. And some people actually like working nights, so they would happily swap their day shifts with other colleagues who don't want to work nights – but the company won't let them. It's company policy, but it's too rigid, it's just not realistic … Anyway, perhaps you should talk to the advisers themselves – get it straight from the horse's mouth, as they say.

3 Products and packaging

3.1 About business Packaging

1:28

Interviewer: Mr. Wang, you often say that packaging is 'the manufacturer's last chance to seduce the customer.' Why is that?

Wang: Yes. In today's highly competitive marketplace, many products are almost identical. So branding is not enough. That's especially true here in Asia, where there may be literally hundreds of competitors making the same product in the same city. You have to differentiate; you have to communicate the difference which makes your product a better choice. I agree with Jack Trout when he says, 'Every aspect of your communications should reflect your difference. The bottom line is: you can't overcommunicate your difference.'

I: So, packaging is the best way to communicate your difference?

W: Exactly. You know, 75% of purchasing decisions are made at the point of sale. And because most stores are self-service, your product is alone on the shelf, surrounded by its competitors. According to Wal-Mart – and they're the world's largest retailer, so they should know! – your product has to pitch its promise to the customer in three seconds or less, from up to fifteen feet away. If your packaging is not attractive, effective and distinctive, how are you going to communicate its difference?

I: OK, so packaging is critical, and manufacturers spend millions of dollars on it. So why are there so many failures?

W: The big problem is a lack of communication. Typically there are several different groups of experts, all working in their own specialized field: market research people who know nothing about design, designers who know nothing about manufacturing, and production people who know nothing about consumer needs. Traditionally, you keep your design team well away from business and manufacturing constraints because you don't want to limit their creativity. Unfortunately, the result is inevitably a compromise. You start out with an original, creative idea, but then you find out it's impractical, for reasons of cost or technical limitations. So, it gets watered down, simplified, adapted. In the end, you are left with a package which is easy to make, easy to transport and within budget, but it's no longer what the consumer wanted! So, you get focus groups where consumers don't really like any of the concepts that are presented. That means, either you start all over again, or you have to choose the least unpopular option!

I: How do you avoid this problem at New China Packaging?

W: Well, basically, what we do is build what we call a 'task force'. This is a cross-functional team with people from all the different departments involved in the project. We put them all together in a hotel, with all the tools they need to produce mockups and prototypes. Then we literally lock the door and we don't let them out until they produce something that everybody is enthusiastic about!

I: And do you include consumers in the task force?

W: Yes, indeed. We need the end user's input right from the beginning. Everything is consumer-led. And, because we know that what consumers say they need and what they really need are frequently two different things, we also observe them using the product. Frequently, we can detect behaviours and needs that the consumer is not even conscious of.

I: Really? Uh-huh. So, who else is involved?

W: Marketing, manufacturing, designers, consultants – everyone who has a stake in the product.

I: And how long does the process take?

W: Traditionally, months or sometimes years. But today, our task forces can usually deliver an optimal solution in one week, sometimes less. And remember, when they deliver, every aspect of the package is consumer-validated, realistic and feasible. So, this extremely short turn-around means that the manufacturer can react very, very quickly to changes in the market, almost in real time.

3.2 Vocabulary Specifications and features

1:29–1:34

1

A: I want to listen to English while I go jogging. Is that possible?

B: Oh, yeah. Jogging, cycling, skiing … whatever you like. Nothing can stop it. I even dropped mine down two flights of stairs, and when I picked it up, it was still working.

2

C: I hear you bought one of those new robots. What do you think of it?

D: It's fantastic! I used to spend hours cleaning the flat. Now I can just program the robot and sit back and watch it work.

C: That's incredible! I must get one …

3

E: I really like the colour. It's a beautiful car!

F: Yes, and it's an interesting shape, too. Quite unusual. Very different from other cars in this category, isn't it?

4

G: Mom, what's in this bottle? I can't open it!

H: Give that to me, dear. You mustn't touch that. It's for cleaning the kitchen, and it's dangerous. Fortunately, they put it in a special bottle that children can't open …

5

I: Quick, it's starting to rain and there's a pallet of those electronic toys outside!

J: OK, I'll move it straight away. But don't worry – the boxes are made of special paperboard. A little rain won't do any damage.

6

K: Are you sure I'll be able to record TV programmes? I mean, I'm not very good at anything technical.

L: Oh, yes. No worries. My five-year-old can operate this model. It's dead easy.

1:35

Good afternoon everybody. Imagine you're on a fishing trip. It's the middle of the night. It's dark, it's foggy, and you're sailing your boat between dangerous rocks. Are you afraid? Not at all. You are supremely confident, checking and adjusting your route with just a touch of a finger on a screen. How do you do it?

Well, I'm here today to tell you about the ChartTech i3, an extraordinary, nautical information system, where a touch-controlled screen enables you to operate several different navigation functions with the touch of a finger.

Let's start with the Touch Screen Command. Just by touching the screen, you can view and change charts, calculate distances, create a route and a lot more. The large colour display screen automatically shows you a bird's-eye view of where you are and where you're going.

Moving on to what's below the water. Thanks to the radar overlay, you see exactly what the fish are seeing. And the Touch Screen 3D Fishfinder, will help make your fishing trips considerably more successful!

Now, can I just turn to communications? The ChartTech i3 can send fax, email and voice messages. You can request and receive weather reports based on your actual GPS position. And you can even automatically monitor vital onboard systems when you're away from your boat.

So, I'll just sum up the ChartTech i3's main features. Let's just go back to our midnight fishing trip. First, Touch Screen Command lets you navigate between the rocks with just one finger and a bird's-eye view. Secondly, the underwater radar and fishfinder shows you where the rocks are, and where the fish are hiding. Finally, the communications function mean you can receive and send important data on the weather, your location and your boat at any moment.

I'd like to finish by inviting you to try the ChartTech i3 for yourself. Our website has an incredibly realistic simulation that you can try out without ever getting your feet wet. Thank you very much.

3.3 Grammar Articles, relative clauses and noun combinations

1:36

Synth voice: Please record your product review and your rating out of five after the beep. Thank you for your feedback.

Customer: This is easily the best phone I've had so far. It's the perfect phone for the basic user. I have already bumped it and dropped it a few times but it's still going strong. The battery life is incredible. Overall, it's a real workhorse – there are no frills, but it does what a cellphone needs to do. I rate it five out of five.

1:37

1

Synth voice: Please record your product review and your rating out of five after the beep. Thank you for your feedback.

Customer: I hate this phone. It's too small – I can't open the flip cover with one hand. There's no screen on the outside to see the caller identity. The reception is horrible. It drops calls probably 30% of the time. There is a very long key delay, which is incredibly annoying. I am anxiously awaiting the day I can upgrade and get rid of this monstrosity. I rate it zero out of five.

1:38

2

Synth voice: Please record your product review and your rating out of five after the beep. Thank you for your feedback.

Customer: I've had the phone for about three weeks. I like the size and the design. The features are good too. It's easy enough to use, and it has survived a couple of drops. However, the alarm clock won't work anymore. I'm not too sure about the internal antenna. I hate having a full signal when making a call, only to have a dramatic drop when I put the phone to my head. Everybody says it's the telecom company's fault, not the phone, or maybe I just got a bad one. We'll see. I'm going to try the 9200 next. I would give it a rating of three out of five.

3.4 Speaking Presentations – structure

1:39

Version 1

A: Um, shall I start then? OK, I know, erm, I know you're going to be very excited by the Pingman, like me! So, I'm sure you'll have lots of questions. And, perhaps we'll take questions after the demonstration.
OK, um, we've done lots of tests, which have all been very positive, and, er, there are lots of different markets for the Pingman, children, adults, dogs, businesses, and so on. We think there's an enormous potential for this product …
Until now, GPS tracking systems have been too bulky, too heavy and too unreliable indoors to be used as personal tracking devices. Our Pingman weighs only 75g, and, well, we'll show you how it works in a few minutes … on the, er, the Internet. So, you know, you can connect to the Internet from anywhere in the world, and just ping your user to know exactly where they are. Within … er, one metre. Nobody else has a product like this on the market, so we want you to approve the investment, because there's a huge market.

B: What do you mean by 'ping'?

A: Oh, yes, on the Internet, you tell a satellite to send a signal to the device, and the device answers the signal, and then the satellite can calculate the device's exact location. Anyway, it only weighs 75g, did I say that already? Yes, er, 75g, it's five centimetres in length and about three point five centimetres wide, so, about half the size of a cellphone, and there are different models for children or adults. Tests were really positive, and our sales forecasts are excellent. There's also a model for animals; it's built into a collar so, if you lose your dog, for example, you just ping it from the Internet to know where it is. So, er, unless you want to ask questions, I think we'd better have the demonstration. Um. Oh, I forgot to mention profitability. We think it will, er, will be profitable. Very profitable. OK, are there any questions? No? No questions? Um, OK then, let's have the demonstration. It's, er, at the back of the room. Yes. Er, …

1:40

Version 2

A: Good morning everybody. Would you like to know at all times exactly where your young child or teenager is? How comforting would it be to know that your elderly mother is safely back home from the shops? How much would it be worth to know precisely where your sales reps or technicians were? And how much time would you save if you knew where your dog was hiding? Well, here's the answer. I'm here this morning to present the Pingman, a revolutionary new personal GPS tracking device and to ask you, members of the Board, to approve the investment needed to start production.
Now, I know you're going to be very excited by the Pingman, so I'm going to give you a quick overview of the product in about fifteen minutes. After that, there'll be a hands-on demonstration, and I've allowed some time for questions and discussion after that. But if you have any questions that can't wait, feel free to interuput me, OK?
I've divided my presentation into three sections. First of all, I'm going to talk to you about the background to this project and the current offers on the market. After that, I'll be talking about the prototype, the specifications and the data we've collected from tests and focus groups. Finally, I'd like to present a business plan which will show you why we expect the return on investment in this product to be condsiderable.
OK, so, let's start with the background. Now, GPS tracking systems are not new, but until now they've been too heavy, and too unreliable indoors to be used as a personal tracking device. What's new about the Pingman is that we can build it into a wrist strap or collar small and light enough to be worn comfortably by a small child or a dog. For the first time, it will be possible to locate the wearer via the Internet, anywhere in the world, indoors or out, 24 hours a day….
… does that answer your question?
OK, so, I'd like to wrap up the presentation and move on to the demonstration. Let me just summarize what I've already told you. Firstly, I explained why there is a huge market just waiting for this product. Secondly, I presented the different specifications for the child, adult and animal versions we intend to launch, and the positive reactions we've had during trials. Last, but not least, I have given you the strongest possible reasons why you should approve this investment: extraordinary sales forecasts, strong cash flow and unprecedented profitability.
Now, if you'd like to move to the back of the room, our R&D staff are ready to start the demonstration and to answer your questions. Thank you very much for your attention.

1:41

I've divided my presentation into three sections. First of all, I'm going to remind you of the background to this project and the current offer on the market. After that, I'll be talking about the prototype, the specifications and the data we've collected from tests, focus groups and market studies. Finally, I'd like to present a business plan; this will show you why we expect a return on investment that is without precedent for our company. Is everybody happy with that agenda?

3.6 Case study Big Jack's Pizza

1:42

Jack Jr: OK, so, we all agree on that then? A completely new range of pizzas for the 21st century, featuring fusion cuisine with the best of contemporary Chinese and Western influences? Great. We'll need at least five really new recipes, so see what you can come up with.

Mick: We'll need new names for each new pizza, then, Jack ...

J: Of course, but we can come back to that later. OK, so, can we move on to point two – new promotional ideas? What suggestions do we have? Billie?

Billie: Well, obviously with the new pizza range we should do a re-launch. And what about doing specials at different times in the year? You know, New Year, National Day, Dragon Boat Festival ...

J: Well, Billie, it's been done before, but I guess we could do that. Why not? Mick?

M: What about BOGOF?

J: I'm sorry?

M: You know, B-O-G-O-F – buy one, get one free. Two pizzas for the price of one. And another idea would be to have a two-pizza box. The pizzas stay hotter when you have two in a box.

J: Hmm ... I'm not sure that's a direction we really want to go in. The franchisees won't like it, and we want to get away from the idea that Big Jack's is just good for filling your stomach.

M: Well, what about a gourmet club? Customers get special privileges if they become members. Or feature different national cuisines each month – Indian in the first month, Thai in the second, and so on?

B: Yes, that's good, Mick. And don't forget the Internet – what if you could build your own pizza and order your take-out or delivery online?

J: Sounds like it might be expensive, Billie, but yeah, that's more the kind of thing I had in mind. Anyway, let's go on to points three and four on the agenda. I think we can take them together, because the box depends very much on the logo and the colour scheme. Billie, I think you feel strongly about this?

B: Yes, Jack, I do. We've had our current logo ever since your dad started the business. The Big Jack logo was perfect 30 years ago, but a lot of things have changed since Big Jack's time. Apart from anything else, the symbolism is all wrong, and remember, people are very sensitive to that kind of thing here.

J: What do you mean, the symbolism is all wrong? Green and red are the colours of Italy, it's what pizza is all about!

B: Maybe, but the green chequered table-cloth on the round table – it symbolizes old-world values that people in Hong Kong just don't identify with. And it's well-known that green isn't a good colour for packaging for Chinese people.

M: Oh, really? Why's that?

B: Oh, you know, it's that thing about green hats – it means your wife is, you know, seeing another man ...

J: Billie, this is all very interesting, but ...

M: No, hang on, Jack. I think Billie's right. We have to take this kind of thing into account. And the box; the box is really important. It's easily the best way we have to communicate with our customers. Couldn't we have a more exciting box, as well as new colours and graphics? I mean, every baker in the city sells pizza in the same standard box as us. We need to differentiate! An octagonal box would be good, maybe with a window so you can see the delicious hot pizza you're carrying?

J: Well, as long as it doesn't complicate storage or delivery, I don't see why not. But it seems to me we need to get more advice on this. I trust you'll agree that we need to have some brand-building and packaging consultants work on this ... we'll consider their proposals at our next meeting.

4 Careers

4.1 About business Career choices

1:43

Part 1

Basically there are just five things you need to know about choosing a career. Two of those are things you really <u>shouldn't</u> do; two of them are things you absolutely <u>have</u> to do, and then the last thing is something only you <u>can</u> do.

OK, let's start with the two things you really <u>shouldn't</u> do. The first sounds very simple, but can actually be very difficult to avoid: you shouldn't let other people decide. Don't choose a career just because your parents, or your teachers, or your friends want you to do it, or think you'd be good at it. Choosing the right career is one of the biggest decisions you'll ever have to make, so don't choose for other people, choose for yourself. You'll have lots of opportunities to make other people happy, but this one is for you; this is maybe the one time in your life when you need to be totally selfish and choose what feels right for you.

Secondly, you shouldn't choose a career just because it's something you're good at. Now don't get me wrong; if you're good at something, and you genuinely love doing it, well that's great, so go for it! But all too often I meet people who chose a career in science, for example, just because they were good at science in school. And although they're still good at it, actually they hate it. So please, don't choose something that you're good at but that <u>isn't</u> going to make you happy.

Now, what about the two things you really <u>have</u> to do? Well, the first one sounds like something from a Kung Fu movie, but it's true: before you can choose a career, you need to to <u>know yourself</u>. Now, you can go to the Himalayas and spend a couple of years learning martial arts if you like, but there are also a lot of simple, very practical personality tests you can use at home. Tests like Myers Briggs or Keirsey are not a hundred per cent reliable, but they really can help you identify what sort of person you are. You'll find lots of tests online, or you can ask your career advisor for help.

The second thing you <u>have</u> to do is to find out what sort of work is available, and what it involves. Your personality test results will guide you towards the kind of careers that should suit your profile; then, you need to find out as much as you can about them, preferably from people who are already working in the sector. Social media sites like Facebook and Google+ are a great way to contact people who can share their experience.

1:44

Part 2

That brings us to the last thing, the thing only <u>you</u> can do: understanding what makes <u>you</u> happy. Now, you're probably thinking, that's easy; money - the more, the better! [laughter] Well, actually there's a great deal of research that shows that, although having <u>enough</u> money is very important, having <u>more</u> money doesn't actually make you any happier. In fact, people who believe that happiness depends on being rich, famous or beautiful are <u>more</u> likely to suffer from depression than the rest of us.

What <u>does</u> seem to make most people happy is surprisingly simple; things like contact with other people, variety, autonomy and recognition. Working with people you like and respect, having a wide range of different activities, and being able to decide what you do and when you do it are major sources of satisfaction. The feeling that you're doing something useful, that you're making the world a better place is also a big motivator. It's interesting that people who run their own businesses, or who work in small companies where they feel they are in control are usually happier than average, even though they probably earn lower salaries and have less job security than they would in a larger organisation.

Now, just before I finish, let me ask you this: do you ever get so involved in what you're doing that you just forget everything else, and time just flies? Yeah? It's a feeling you often get when you do things like team sports, playing or listening to music, writing, painting, repairing or inventing things. These are times when most people say they are happiest, and they're called 'flow' activities. If you know what makes you happy, and if you can identify jobs that let you experience that 'flow', then you have almost certainly found the key to choosing your ideal career.

4.2 Vocabulary Careers, personal skills and qualities

1:45

B: All right. So that brings us to Rachel Ratcliff. You've flagged her as a high-flier. She's certainly very committed to her work.

A: Absolutely. Rachel is doing a terrific job for us. She's an excellent team-player, and she really enjoys taking initiative. The problem is that she's ambitious and we don't have any ways to satisfy her ambition for the moment. We planned to make her a department manager in a couple of years' time, but there are no openings right now. She's obviously had other offers, perhaps from a headhunter, and she's thinking about resigning.

B: Hmm ... It would be a shame to lose her. Solutions?

A: Well, we could offer her a two-year assignment in Germany. I know there's a vacancy over there for someone with her profile, and she'd certainly be able to make a valuable contribution. But I don't know whether she'd agree. She has a fiancé, so it may be difficult. Another possibility would be to send her on an MBA course, and start preparing her for senior management.

B: You really think she's that good? A

potential MBA? Well, let me think about that one. I'll come back to you in a couple of days.

A: OK.

B: By the way, how is young Paul Stevens getting on? I believe he had a problem with his manager?

A: Yes, that's right. He was working to very strict deadlines, and just needed a break. I'm working closely with him now, and everything's fine. He's back on the high-fliers' list. He has strong negotiating skills, and I think he'll be an excellent engineer.

B: Good. OK, then, let's move on to Michael Diegel. He's a new hire too, isn't he?

A: Yes. Michael's been with us almost a year now, and we've marked him as a concern because he's not really delivering the goods. He arrived with a fantastic résumé, lots of skills and some good experience, but he's consistently underperformed, he just isn't able to manage the workload.

B: Hmm ... Any idea why?

A: Well, I'm not too sure. Some people in the department feel that it's a problem of motivation; he doesn't like Seattle, and he wants to move east. But others of us feel that perhaps he just doesn't have the strengths that his résumé claimed. At the moment he seems to have more weaknesses than strengths.

B: So, what do we do, give him an official warning? Tell him we'll fire him if he doesn't deliver?

A: Maybe. But we've already invested too much time and money to just dismiss him. How about offering him an easier position in Chicago? Something that won't be so difficult. If he realizes that the job here in Seattle is too much for him, perhaps he'd be more motivated to perform at his real level. Moving to Chicago would be a good way to save face.

B: Yes, that's not a bad idea. Could you liaise with his manager, and see what's available in Chicago or Boston, then come back to me?

A: OK.

B: Good. Now then, we come to our old friend Shane Garney, Mr Wannabe himself. Is he still on the high-fliers' list?

A: Not really. He's more of a concern now. He certainly has the skills, but he's getting greedy. We gave him a big raise six months ago when he was promoted, but now he says it's not enough. He says he's had a much better offer from the competition.

B: Well, I think it's time we had a serious talk with Mr Garney. He needs to understand that, although we appreciate ambition, our corporate policy is to reward achievement, not potential.

A: Hm. The problem is, of course, that he's very well- connected. You remember that his father's a senator. Wouldn't it be easier to give Shane a small raise to keep him happy?

B: Yes, I'm fully aware of that, and I'm aware that government contracts are very important to this company. But if Shane is only interested in money, he should join his father in Washington. The answer is 'no'. If he thinks he can get a better deal somewhere else, then fine, he can resign. We have a lot of good people like Rachel Ratcliff who would be happy to take his place.

4.3 Grammar Present tenses

1:46–1:55

1

A: Well, the job's yours if you want it.

B: Well, thank you very much, I'm delighted to accept.

2

C: Congratulations! Don't forget, the degree ceremony's next Friday!

D: Thank you, sir!

E: Thank you very much!

3

F: Nearly finished now.

G: Wow! Seventeen candidates in one day! And it's almost dinner time. What time did you start?

F: Eight o'clock this morning!

4

H: Ten kilometres! Phew! When they said 'recruitment tests', I thought they meant IQ and graphology, not an army assault course!

5

I: Have you seen the results, Jon?

J: Yeah.

I: Oh. Oh, I'm so sorry.

J: It's all right. It's not the end of the world.

6

K: I still think Ms Brown has more relevant experience than the others.

L: Look, we're not getting anywhere like this. Why don't we meet again tomorrow? And, remember, we can always ask all four candidates back for a second interview if we still can't decide.

7

M: Nick? Are you coming out for a drink?

N: Nah. Gotta finish my CV.

M: You still working on that CV?! I mean, how long can it take to say you've got no skills, no qualifications, and you've never done an honest day's work in your life?!

N: Very funny.

8

O: Hey, Paula, how did the interview go today?

P: Oh, so-so. Pretty much the same as the last 26.

O: Ah. Well, I've got to hand it to you Paula, you certainly don't give up easily.

9

Q: Look out!

R: Ooh, too late. Oh dear, it's all over your papers. Sorry about that, these cups are very easy to knock over, aren't they?

Q: Never mind.

R: Hope it wasn't anything important. Er, are you here for the interviews, then?

Q: Yes, as a matter of fact I am. I'm conducting the interviews, actually. It's Mr Singh, isn't it?

R: Ooh!

10

S: ... 98, 99, 100! There we are! Finished!

T: Finished what, Sally? You don't mean ...?

S: Yep. Job applications. Started this morning.

T: One hundred job applications?! You're kidding!

4.4 Speaking Job interviews

1:56–1:59

A

Interviewer: Where do you see yourself in five years' time?

A: Well, that's a difficult question to answer; let's just say that I see myself as a top performing employee in a leading company, like this one. I plan to gain experience and learn new skills. Hopefully, in five years' time, I would be ready to move up to a position with more responsibility.

B

Interviewer: How do you motivate people to do their best?

B: Well, I think there are two important aspects to this question. The first is to create a positive atmosphere. If people feel happy about what they're doing, they're much more motivated to work towards a common goal. So making sure they understand the objectives and the process, and that the atmosphere is pleasant and relaxed – those are really important. The second thing is to give feedback, especially when somebody does a good job, not just when they get something wrong. When I worked in a restaurant a couple of years ago, I realized that knowing how well you're doing is essential to staying motivated.

C

Interviewer: What are your weaknesses?

C: Well, of course, I'm aware that there are areas that I can improve on, but I have to say, as far as this job is concerned, I don't feel that I have any significant weaknesses. And if I do identify a problem, I take action to resolve it. Take time management, for instance. A couple of years ago, I realized I wasn't the most organized person in the world, so I followed a time management course. I applied what I learned, and now I would say that organization is one of my strengths.

D

Interviewer: Can you give an example of a situation you found stressful, and how you coped with the stress?

D: Yes. Last term, for example, I was on a work placement where my supervisor had to go off sick for three weeks, so the company asked me to take over responsibility for the project. It meant a huge workload, which was pretty stressful. Anyway, I sat down and planned out exactly what I had to do each day for those three weeks. I also planned an hour each evening in the gym. That really helped to ease the stress. I managed to finish the project on time, and in much better shape than when I started! Does that answer your question?

4.6 Case study Gap years and career breaks

2:01–2:06

1

My gap year? Oh yes, it was a fantastic experience. It was between my second and third years at university. I went to Nepal to teach English. I think I learned more in that year than in three years at university. It was incredible. Everybody should do it.

2

I went to live with a family in Dublin for a year before starting my degree course. Of course, it was really good for my English, and interesting from a cultural point of view. But it was pretty boring going back to school for another year, even if it was in English.

3

I've had a great year. I've been around the world, working for two or three weeks, then moving on to the next place. I've just gone back to my job, and now I have a much clearer idea of where I'm going and what I want to achieve. My only regret is not doing something to help people. If I could do it again, I'd definitely volunteer for charity work, probably in Africa.

4

Yeah, I took a gap year before starting business school. I needed to earn some money, so I worked in a car factory. It was hell. I've never been so bored in my life. I suppose I learned some valuable lessons, but now I wish I'd done something more exciting, gone somewhere exotic. I feel I wasted a year of my life.

5

I'd been in the same job for about twenty years, and I decided I needed to step back and think about what I wanted to do with the rest of my life. So I took a sabbatical. Fortunately my company was very understanding. I travelled in India for six months, then I wrote a book about my experiences. It completely changed my outlook on life. I'd recommend it to anybody.

6

I've just started studying medicine. I wanted to get away from my parents and see the world, so I've just come back from nine months in East Africa. It was really hard. I almost came home after the first week. I'm glad I stayed, because I felt I made a difference to people's lives – a very small difference, but a difference all the same. But if I'd known what it would be like, I'm sure I wouldn't have gone.

5 Making deals

5.1 About business Retailing

2:07

Interviewer: Excuse me, madam, could I ask you a few questions?

Shopper: It's miss actually, but all right then, if it doesn't take too long.

I: Thank you, miss, only a couple of minutes. I'd like you to tell me how interested you are in some of the opportunities offered by Internet services like Facebook and Foursquare.

S: Oh, I'm on Facebook, of course! Jessica Johnson, Miss Basildon twenty-twelve!

I: Really? Actually, I don't need your name, just a rating between zero and five. Zero means you're not interested at all, five means you're very interested.

S: OK.

I: So, how interested are you in checking in to shopping venues and letting your friends know where you are?

S: Oh, can you do that? So you can meet up for coffee, or go and try on some shoes together? Oh, yes, that sounds cool!

I: So that's a five then? Right. And what about winning gift certificates or prizes after a certain number of check-ins?

S: Ooh, wow! I love free stuff, don't you?

I: Uh-huh. Now, how about receiving information on special deals from stores?

S: Well, yes, I s'pose so. But not too many, you know what I mean? I can never resist a special offer! I end up spending more than I can afford!

I: OK. And how interested are you in checking in to a product by scanning a UPC?

S: Scanning a what?

I: A UPC. You know, a bar code.

S: What, on my iPhone?

I: Yes.

S: Why would I want to do that? Anyway, I wouldn't know how. I'm not really into technical stuff.

I: All right. Last question then; how interested are you in becoming the mayor of your favourite coffee-shop, or the queen of lipstick?

S: A lipstick expert? Nah, not really my thing. But wait a minute, what about shoes? Jessica Johnson, the queen of shoes? Oh, yes, I can see it now!

5.2 Vocabulary Negotiating and retailing

2:08–2:15

1 So that's five hundred at 12 euros a box, then. And you need them by Wednesday, you say?
2 Considering this would be a regular order, I think two and a half thousand is still a bit expensive.
3 How about if we paid cash? Could you give us an extra 2%?
4 No, I'm sorry, that's my final offer. I can't go any lower than that.
5 And then we'd need you to be available five or six weeks a year. Or maybe a bit less. Anyway, we can talk about it. Nothing's decided yet.
6 Yes, we usually ask for 20% now, and the balance on delivery.
7 Look, this just isn't good enough! If you don't deliver until tomorrow morning, it'll be too late!
8 Well, there's not much between us now. What do you say we split the difference?

2:16–2:20

1 five hundred at 12 euros a box
2 two and a half thousand
3 an extra 2%
4 five or six weeks a year
5 We usually ask for 20% now.

5.3 Grammar Conditionals and recommendations

2:21

Petra: OK, we have to decide how to divide this list of responsibilities between us. What are your priorities?

Jan: Well, I'd really like to go the conference in Madagascar. Could I suggest that you go to Siberia? If you agreed, I'd be willing to take my holidays in January and let you take yours in August.

P: I'm sorry, but I'd really like to go to Madagascar too. I couldn't agree to your proposal, unless you were prepared to take your holidays in January and go to the exhibition in Kazakhstan.

J: Hmm … Well, I might consider going to Kazakhstan. I've got an uncle who lives there …

P: Great!

J: … providing you looked after the foreign customer at the tennis tournament – I know nothing about tennis.

P: OK, we're making progress. So, can I just summarize the position so far? You can go to Madagascar, as long as you also go to Kazakhstan, and you let me take my holidays in August. OK?

J: OK. But only if you do the tennis weekend.

P: All right, no problem, I'll handle the tennis, if you take your holiday in January.

J: And you go to Siberia.

P: Oh, now wait a minute, I never agreed to that! I couldn't possibly go to Siberia unless you were able to …

5.4 Speaking Negotiations – bargaining

2:22

Part 1

Ingrid: So, Harry, you want to set up an e-business to sell music – mp3s and so on?

Harry: No, not mp3s – sheet music. You know, printed music for musicians to play, like song books, orchestral parts, and so on. At the moment we sell through our network of shops in Denmark, but I'd like to set up an e-business .

I: To reach customers worldwide?

H: Exactly. But the problem is, we don't have the skills, the staff, or the money to do it ourselves.

I: Well, Harry, Holman Multimedia can offer a complete package solution. We design, build and manage your website, and process your sales. We deal with the payments, we can even handle the logistics for you if you want. Although I suppose you'll send most of the music electronically, right?

H: Yes – as PDF files. It's much easier for us, and the customer gets immediate delivery.

I: Exactly. So all you have to do is make sure you have the product in stock, and count your profits!

H: And pay you a monthly fee, is that right?

I: That's right, Harry. No capital investment, no new staff, no overheads. And once you start selling music all over the world, that monthly fee is going to look very small.

H: All right then, Ingrid, I think we're in business. So what's next?

I: That's terrific, Harry! OK, well, can you tell me exactly what you want the site to do? You see, it all depends …

2:23

Part 2, Version 1

H: So, how soon can you deliver, and how much is it going to cost?

I: OK, look. I'm going to write down a figure per month here, just so it's clear, then you can tell me what you think. There, how do you feel about that?

H: Wow! No, there's no way I could pay that!

I: Well, I might possibly be able to bring it down a little, but only if we had a three-year contract.

H: A three-year contract! No, I can't agree to that.

I: Well, in that case, I can't bring the monthly fee down, I'm afraid.

H: And I can't commit myself to three years.

I: Well, Harry, you have my phone number. If you change your mind, just give me a call.

2:24

Part 2, Version 2

H: So, how soon can you deliver, and how much is it going to cost?

I: OK, look. I'm going to write down a figure per month here, just so it's clear, then you can tell me what you think.
There, how do you feel about that?

H: Wow! Is there any way we could bring it down, say 10%?

I: Well, I might possibly be able to bring it down a little, but only if we had a three-year contract.

H: Well, I'd be reluctant to agree to a three-year contract unless you could guarantee a maximum down time of 24 hours per month. Could you do that?

I: Let me reassure you on that point, Harry. Our sites and servers are very, very stable, and average down time is less than 24 hours per year. So we're happy to guarantee less than 24 hours per month, as long as you choose our platinum service level – but of course, it's more expensive.
H: Well, I don't really want to increase the budget. Hmm … What about lead time? Can you have the site up and running by next month?
I: Not unless we hire another developer. I suppose we could do it, providing you paid a year's fees in advance.
H: Hmm …
I: Normally, development time is around three months.
H: Look, let's split the difference. I can pay six months in advance, on condition that you have the site online in two months. And if you can bring the monthly fee down 5% and include the platinum service, I'll agree to the three-year contract.
I: You're a tough negotiator, Harry. But, OK, I think we can agree to that.
H: Excellent!

2:25–2:27

1 I might possibly be able to bring it down a little, but only if we had a three-year contract.
2 I might consider reducing the price, if you increased your order.
3 I'd be reluctant to agree to a three-year contract, unless you could guarantee a maximum down time of 24 hours per month.

5.6 Case study St John's Beach Club

2:28

Loretta: Oh, Malcolm, there you are. I just wanted a quick word.
Malcolm: Sure. Shall we use my office?
L: No, here is fine. I think I'll have a coffee too.
M: Black, no sugar?
L: Yes. Thanks, Malcolm. I saw your memo about the incentive trip – it sounds great. I wish I was going!
M: Well, why don't you? It would be an excellent opportunity to get to know the sales team better.
L: Yes, it would, wouldn't it? But I just don't have the time, I'm afraid. Anyway, the reason I wanted to catch you was to confirm the budget.
M: Ah, yes.
L: I spoke to Charles. I've asked him to allocate a global budget of $28,000. That's for everything except travel, which is a separate budget. That's up about 5% on last year. How does that sound?
M: That sounds great. Thanks, Loretta. I'm going to get one of our best negotiators to talk to a couple of travel agents, and see what sort of deal we can get. The hotels usually work with several agents, and some of them are prepared to negotiate better terms than others.
L: Uh-huh. Try to persuade them to throw in some extra benefits too. After all, if we use the full budget, we're giving them a lot of business. Sometimes you can get a free upgrade to an executive suite, that kind of thing. How many people are you taking?
M: Well, the top ten sales people, plus myself, and partners – that makes 22. But if we can negotiate a really good package, I'd like to take one or two more sales reps along. They've all worked fantastically hard this year.
L: Yes, I agree. It would encourage the reps who almost made it into the top ten. I always think it's hard on number eleven! It'll be about a week, like last year, I suppose?
M: Well, again, if we can squeeze a couple more nights out of the budget, that would be great. But we'll see.
L: OK, Malcolm. Let me know what you decide.
M: Sure. Thanks, Loretta.

6 Company and community

6.1 About business Corporate social responsibility

2:29

Part 1

Interviewer: My guest today is Estela Maldonaldo who is the co-founder and Chief Executive of 'Beach Hut', Argentina's most successful chain of beach cafés. Estela, Beach Hut is not only a very profitable business, but it's also famous for its ethical principles. Are profit and social responsibility really compatible?
Estela: Absolutely. I opened the first Beach Hut in Pinamar in 1998 with a close friend who, like me, had just lost her job. We both felt we'd been badly treated, and we wanted to prove a point. Unlike the multinationals we used to work for, we set out to treat our employees well, to look after the environment, and to support the local community. And of course we also wanted to make a little money!
I: And today you have, how many, thirty-seven cafés?
E: Yeah, number thirty-eight opens next month.
I: OK, so you've grown incredibly quickly, and you've won a number of awards along the way. How exactly have you managed that?
E: We've always felt that our employees should come first. Of course we love our customers, and we're very grateful to our shareholders. But our philosophy is this: if you make your staff your first priority, if you make sure they're happy and motivated, then they're going to look after your customers and so the business is going to do well. And when the business does well, shareholders are rewarded too.

2:30

Part 2

I: So, Estela, tell us something about your environmental policies, how have they helped you?
E: Right from the start, we wanted to be the greenest café in town. We do everything we can to reduce our carbon footprint: we have solar panels on the roof, we recycle, we use biodegradable packaging …
I: And all your food and drink is locally sourced?
E: Yes. We work with local businesses as much as possible, we want to be part of the local community, not a big brand that just takes people's money without giving anything back. But it makes good business sense too because it means we get quality produce and minimise our transport and logistic costs.
I: Right, so this is not just about altruism, then? The bottom-line is just as important?
E: Everything is linked. We can only give something back to the community if we make a profit, but taking care of the environment and the local community is very good P.R. – and that makes it easier to attract customers and to recruit good staff. It's a virtuous circle!
I: I understand you also run educational programmes for children in schools. How does that help your business?
E: Argentina's beaches are an incredibly beautiful and precious resource – but they're also very fragile. We send volunteer staff members to teach schoolchildren how to protect our natural environment. Of course, it doesn't have an immediate impact, and it doesn't bring customers through the door the next day. But in the medium and long term, having the environmental awards, and displaying the logos on our website and on our packaging really helps to build a positive image. The market is extremely competitive, but our customers are very loyal because they know we share the same values. They know we're not short-term driven; we have to think more long-term about building sustainable businesses, and it's the same for society in general. If you want a society that cleans up the beaches and plants trees and uses hybrid vehicles, you have to think long-term. The short-term model just doesn't work – not for business, and not for society.

6.3 Grammar The passive and reported speech

2:31–2:36

1
Leila Belabed: Mr Bullard, the mayor is very upset. You've just dismissed 500 people from the factory! Have you forgotten that when your company arrived, you promised to create jobs for our town?
2
Geoffrey Bullard: Well, of course I understand that you are upset, Ms Belabed. Unfortunately, new technologies have revolutionized our industry. You must understand that with new automated machinery, we will no longer need so many operators.
3
LB: I know that it is difficult to remain competitive, but what about these people and their families? It's a disaster for them. What are you intending to do to help them, Mr Bullard?
4
GB: Please call me Geoffrey. Of course we share your concerns. We are setting up an outplacement service to help people find new jobs, and I'm confident that most of them will find work very quickly.
5
LB: But what about those who don't, Mr Bullard? How will they survive? These people don't have a lot of savings, you know! Are you offering them financial help?
6
GB: Yes, of course, Ms Belabed, you don't need to worry about that. Each person has already received a generous redundancy payment. And we're also making interest-free loans and advice available for those who want to start their own businesses.

6.4 Speaking Meetings – teamwork

2:37

Anna: Do we all agree on that, then? All right. The next point on the agenda is company policy on gifts. What's your feeling? Personally, I tend to think that we need …

Stan: Sorry to interrupt, but …

A: Yes, Stan. Go on.

S: Well, in my opinion, accepting any kind of gift from a supplier is unwise. Would you agree, Anna?

A: Well, Stan, on the whole, yes, I would. Now, recently we had a major problem with our packaging suppliers. They were sending 'thank-yous' to our buyer's home.

S: Sorry, Anna. I don't see what you mean.

Jon: Gifts, Stan. Cases of champagne, I believe.

S: Champagne? Oh, that was nice of them!

A: Well, I agree up to a point, but unfortunately our buyer, Mr Vieri, not only accepted the gifts, but also actively encouraged the supplier to send more.

S: Well, I feel strongly that we should dismiss Mr Vieri! It's bad for the company's image.

J: Stan, I see your point, but you can't just dismiss someone for making one mistake!

S: So are you saying that we should keep him? I'm afraid I can't agree, Jon! It's not right, and he should leave the company.

J: But Stan, don't you think that everyone should have a second chance? I mean …

A: Jon, Stan, can we stick to the agenda? We're not here to talk about Mr Vieri; we're here to decide on a clear company policy for the future.

S: Yes, but wouldn't you agree that his behaviour was unethical? So he should be dismissed.

Magali: Could I just come in here?

A: Yes, Magali, do you have any views on this issue?

M: I'm sorry, Anna. When you say this issue, do you mean just our policy on gifts, or the wider issue of corporate ethics? It seems to me that we need to go further than just …

A: Sorry, Magali, but perhaps we should break for coffee. I think we're all a bit tired. Could we come back to this later?

6.5 Writing Reports and minutes

2:38

Jan: All right, then. Let's move on to point two on the agenda; diversity. As you know, our workforce is still 80% male. What's more, we have very few employees from ethnic minorities. The general feeling within the group is that we need to take measures in order to reflect the increasing diversity …

Ines: Sorry to interrupt, Jan, but when you say 'measures', do you mean positive discrimination? Hiring women in preference to men, for instance? Because that's all very well in sales and admin, but I really, really can't see women doing the heavy jobs in production. And anyway, I'm not sure that positive discrimination is the right way to approach the problem.

Christopher: No, I don't think it is either. It seems to me that we would just go from one extreme to another – you know, all our employees would be middle-aged female.

J: Point taken, Christopher. But, seriously, that's what we want to avoid – extremes. In fact, what we need are measures to ensure that we don't discriminate against anyone on whatever criteria, whether it's their age, their race, their gender, their religion, or anything else.

C: But Jan, don't you think that's just an HR problem? I mean, they're the people who interview the candidates, not us. Nine times out of ten, we only see a short-list of the people they've already approved. It's even worse when we recruit from the agencies. That's another problem, by the way: half of the people they send us are absolutely hopeless.
I don't know how they select them, but honestly …

J: Yes, Christopher. I know the agencies are a problem, but I think we're getting side-tracked here. Could we agree that we'll talk about the agencies next Monday?

C: OK.

J: Good. So, getting back to diversity. Ines, what can we do to attract more applications from women?

I: Well, for a start, we should offer more part-time positions. Flexible hours, longer holidays when the schools are closed, a four-day week. You know, jobs that women with families can manage. That's really obvious. I've been saying this for years! I mean, why don't we start by allowing our present staff to go part-time if they want to? I can think of at least four women who'd be delighted to work part-time! That would mean we could offer more part-time jobs to new candidates.

J: Yes, Ines, thank you. That's an excellent idea. Shall we get HR to work on it? Christopher?

C: That's fine by me.

J: All right, that's decided then. All right, shall we break for coffee now, or take point three first?

6.6 Case study Phoenix

2:39

Justin: … so we all agree that we need to keep an eye on that one. All right, that just leaves point six on the agenda; the new site for the South West. Helen, can you bring us up to date?

Helen: Yes, Justin. There's good news: we've identified three possible sites in a place called Port Katherine.

Glenn: Never heard of it!

H: Well, it's a small town about 30 miles south of Perth. It's exactly what we were looking for; close to Perth, but far enough away not to attract too much attention from the environmentalists.

G: Well, that's good news! We don't want another disaster like Cairns. Those Greens have absolutely no idea what this country would look like if we didn't recycle cars!

J: Yes, all right, Glenn. Shall we let Helen finish?

G: Oh, yes. Sorry, mate.

J: Helen?

H: Thank you. Port Katherine's population is only about three and half thousand, so Glenn will be happy to know that there shouldn't be too much local resistance. And the local authorities are desperate to attract new business and jobs to the area.

J: Sounds good. You said there were three possible sites?

H: Yes, that's right. I've put all the details in this handout. There you are, Glenn.

G: Oh, yeah. Thanks.

H: Now, Site A is a good one. It's a greenfield site just on the edge of town. There are several plus points. Firstly, it's close to the highway, so access for our trucks is easy. Secondly, the price of land is reasonable. And thirdly, it's a nice flat site to build on.

J: Any negatives?

H: Well, just one. It's right next to the local school.

G: Uh-oh!

H: But I don't think it's going to be a problem. I spoke to someone at the planning department, and they were very enthusiastic. Sites B and C are also possible, but they have other problems. Site B is on a business park, so no problems with residents, but it's a bit expensive and taxes will be higher. Site C is actually in the town centre.

G: Oh, yeah, perfect! 20-ton trucks in the high street!

H: Actually, Glenn, it's not that bad. It's on a big old factory site near the harbour. We'd have to demolish the old building, and access would be a bit of a problem, but they could build a new road. It's possible.

J: OK, thanks, Helen. Excellent work. I'll send somebody out there to start talking to the locals.

G: 'Operation Charm and Diplomacy', eh?

J: Yes.

H: Hmm … Better not send Glenn, then!

7 Mergers and acquisitions

7.1 About business Risks and opportunities in M&A

2:40

Interviewer: If mergers are so difficult to do well, why bother with external growth at all? Why not just grow internally?

Bernard Degoulange: Well, the most common reason, and probably the best reason for a merger, is that your customers are asking you for something you can't deliver. Let's say you sell champagne. If people are satisfied with your champagne, they're going to start asking you for whisky, simply because everybody would like to be able to get the solution to all of life's problems from the same place. Now, if you can't give your customers the whisky they're asking for, you have a problem. Because however satisfied they are with your champagne, they're going to go somewhere else for whisky, and that's when you risk losing those customers.

I: What advice would you give on finding the right company to acquire?

BD: Personally, I have five points that I want to examine when looking at a possible acquisition: the five Gs. If I don't get good answers to at least four of them, I don't do the deal. The first of the five Gs is Goals. Are our goals compatible? Are both companies trying to achieve something similar? If not, keep looking.
Secondly, Gains. I want to know if there will be real gains in terms of economies of scale. And will these gains compensate for perhaps not being able to react as quickly to new trends in the market because of the size of the organization? Being bigger is not always better.
The third point is Genes – and by that I mean company culture. There's no point in trying to merge a traditional, hierarchical family business with a fast-moving start-up with a relaxed management style. It just

won't work, the cultural genes are too different. It's not enough to find a partner whose strengths compensate for your weaknesses, and vice versa; there has to be a real synergy in culture and personality.

I: OK, so, Goals, Gains and Genes. What are the other two Gs?

BD: Geography and Growth. Are the companies based in the same city or geographical area? If not, communication between headquarters is much more difficult, and the Gains are harder to achieve.

I: And Growth?

BD: Will the merger provide technology or skills that you don't have now, which would take too long to develop yourself, and which will unquestionably allow your company to grow? If the merger will open new markets, which would otherwise be inaccessible, then it makes sense.

I: When you've identified the right partner, how can you make sure the merger goes smoothly?

BD: The most important thing is to look after your people: employees, management and of course customers, but especially employees. First of all, you have to keep them focused and productive. A merger is a wonderful opportunity for everybody to take their eye off the ball – and so it's a great opportunity for the competition to jump in and take market share from both companies in the merger.
Secondly You have to help employees get over their feelings of loss and perhaps anger as quickly as possible, and accept the new situation. Whenever there is a merger, two companies die and a new company is born. It's essential to help people get through that traumatic period, to explain how things will change and what their new roles will be, and to get them to accept the new organization and their new identity. It's essentially about communication, sometimes counselling, and compensating those who leave the company, whether by choice or not.

7.2 Vocabulary Business performance

2:41

Oxter Holdings today confirmed that they have increased their bid for Fraxis Corp. to $98 per share. Fraxis Corp. was floated in 1993 at just $15 per share. After a sudden drop of $3 in 1994, the stock rose gradually over the next two years to reach $50 in early 1996, when Fraxis acquired one of their smaller competitors, Nimmco. The market was not enthusiastic about the takeover, and Fraxis fell sharply by over 40%. It then recovered slightly and levelled off around the $30 dollar mark for the next three years. In 2000, Fraxis CEO Alex Firman announced an alliance with the European market leader Haffmann; the reaction was immediate. The stock price climbed to $65 as institutional investors rushed to share in the profits. The alliance has been a great success; with the exception of temporary falls to $50 in 2006 and $59 in 2011, Fraxis has climbed steadily to peak at $95, shortly after Oxter's first offer of $90 a share was rejected last week. Analysts believe that Fraxis are unlikely to accept anything less than $110, so expect to see the price jump to $100 plus when trading opens on Monday.

7.3 Grammar Future forms and expressing likelihood

2:42

Ashley: Emma, Happy New Year!

Emma: Happy New Year!

A: What are you doing all alone over here? I haven't had a chance to talk to you all evening. Have some more champagne!

E: No, I shouldn't. I'm going to give up smoking and drinking this year. It's my New Year's resolution.

A: Really?! Well, you can start tomorrow. Come on, Em, it's New Year!

E: Oh, all right, just a drop. Thanks. Anyway, what about you, Ashley? What's the New Year going to be like for you? Have you made any resolutions?

A: No, not really. But I'm definitely going to find a new job. There's no way I'm staying at that company for another year.

E: Right. Have you got anything in mind?

A: No, but I'm going to read the job ads until I find something good. I'm bound to find something better than what I do now.

E: Oh, I'm sure you'll find something easily. Or you could go freelance, with the talent you've got …

A: Freelance?! Well, I suppose I could, but I think it's unlikely. It's far too complicated. No, I'm just going to choose about ten or 12 jobs to apply for, go along to the interviews, and we'll see what happens. I'm going to take my time, not rush into anything.

E: Right. I think that's very sensible.

A: So, what about you? Are you going to stay at Artip?

E: I doubt it.

A: Really?! Are you going to leave, or are they going to throw you out?

E: Well, both of those are quite likely, actually. The company's being taken over in February, so we don't know what will happen. I mean, they're bound to make redundancies, we just don't know how many. Anyway, I'm starting evening classes next week. I'm going to retrain as a marketing assistant.

A: Excellent! Well, here's to a successful New Year for both of us!

E: Yes, cheers! But, Ashley, isn't there another New Year's resolution you've forgotten to tell me about? Is that a real diamond? Who's the lucky man, then?

7.4 Speaking Presentations – visuals

2:43–2:46

A Now, my next slide shows how the number of takeovers is likely to increase over the next decade. This one gives a breakdown by sector. This next slide highlights the probable effect on company performance. And this one, this one and now this third slide show how share prices will fall.

B Now, the next slide shows some very interesting data. As you can see – oh, perhaps you can't see – I'm sorry, the figures are rather small. Anyway, the forecast is particularly good, in contrast to the data for the last three years, which was in the, ah, smaller table, over here, which you, ah, can't read either.

C If you look at the next slide, you'll see that we collected data using a Grossman scheduled EMTI questionnaire modified from the standard CDF rapid assessment surveys procedure, and compensated for statistical significance using an unbiased reflex standard deviation algorithm.

D OK, customer reactions to price and service levels after mergers: 30% of customers noticed an improvement; 49 said things had got worse. Erm, customer satisfaction by sector: almost 9% down in retail; stable in the service and financial sector; and 5% up for manufacturing companies.

2:47

How will our customers react to a merger? My next slide shows two charts which illustrate the problem. Recently, customers of large Spanish companies were asked if they felt that prices and service had improved, remained the same or deteriorated as a result of a merger. As you will notice in the pie-chart, only a third of customers noticed an improvement, compared to almost half who said that things had got worse.

Let's look at the bar chart, which shows customer satisfaction by sector. As you can see, after a merger, customer satisfaction falls by an average of almost nine per cent in the retail sector, whereas it remains about the same in the service and financial sector, and rises by five per cent on average for manufacturing companies.

The figures seem to suggest that, on the whole, customers are always likely to react negatively to mergers. This is due to a perceived drop in levels of service after a merger. The results indicate that retailers, where service is crucial to customer satisfaction, are particularly affected, as opposed to manufacturers, who benefit from mergers. Of course, this is the result of improved product quality and design, which are the most important factors for their customers.

7.5 Writing Presentation slides

2:48

Good morning everyone, and thank you for coming. Two months ago, you asked me to conduct a strategic analysis of the company's strengths, weaknesses, opportunities and threats. I'm here today to present my findings, and to make recommendations on the basis of those findings. I intend first to give a short summary of the company's position, and then to invite you to ask questions and give your reactions to my proposals. If anything is not clear, please feel free to interrupt me.

First of all, I'd like to remind you of the company's main strengths. Galway Software has a reputation for innovation and quality in developing highly-specialized customer applications. We are able to provide excellent service thanks to our small team of expert engineers and developers. What's more, our finances have been carefully and cautiously managed: as you can see from the figures on this slide, today the company is in good financial health with practically no debt.

However, there are also a number of weaknesses which must be considered. The first, small weakness is office space. We just don't have enough. The second, more significant weakness is costs. As this graph shows, our development costs have risen steadily, whereas market prices are falling. It is becoming increasingly difficult to maintain our profit margins. The principal explanation for these high costs is the high salaries we have to pay to attract experienced developers. A third, associated problem is recruitment: in spite of high salaries, we are finding it increasingly difficult to attract young engineers who prefer to join large international companies. This brings me to perhaps the most significant weakness, and a problem which I want to come back to in a few moments when I talk about threats, and that is our size. As a small company in a very specific niche market, we are vulnerable. If things went wrong with just a few of our big customers, we could have serious difficulties.

But before looking at the threats, let's move on to opportunities. In particular, new technologies and a changing world economy are opening up exciting ways of re-thinking our business activities. For example, the new member states of the European Union in Eastern Europe have excellent schools and universities: their young engineers are talented, well-trained and keen to acquire experience in companies like ours. Another possibility is to do part of our development work offshore, in countries like India where labour costs are significantly lower than in Europe. Last, but certainly not least, we must look at opportunities in our own industry: competition is fierce, and a process of consolidation is under way. Many firms are forming alliances or launching takeover bids in order to exploit synergies, to make economies of scale and to diversify into new market segments. I believe these are opportunities we should not ignore and I will be making a specific recommendation in the last part of my presentation.

So, I've talked about our strengths, our weaknesses and our opportunities. I want now to explain why one of the opportunities I have just described is also a serious threat.

And finally, to look at threats: in the context of the consolidation I referred to earlier, Galway Software, as a small, successful, well-managed company with no debt, is a perfect target for a takeover. It is only a matter of time before a big international firm comes knocking at the door with its cheque book open. ... Unless we move first.

In the last part of this presentation, I am going to recommend that Galway Software should itself launch a takeover bid. There are many good reasons for this. Firstly, external growth with a reasonable amount of debt will make us less vulnerable. Secondly, a takeover will allow us to diversify into new markets, to expand our customer base and spread our risks, and to make economies of scale. And thirdly, the ideal candidate, Oranmore Video Games, which is based just 20 miles away, currently has more developers than it needs, and has a lot of unused office space.

I'm going to give you a handout which gives more details of why I believe we should acquire Oranmore ...

7.6 Case study Calisto

2:49

President: As you know, this year Calisto has lost one point five million dollars. Obviously this situation cannot continue. Unless we take action now, we will go out of business next year. We have several options to consider. Our first option is to adopt the same strategy as IMM. IMM have reduced their operating expenses by 20% over the last two years. However, they have achieved this by ruthlessly cutting jobs: one fifth of IMM's staff have been made redundant. Here at Calisto we have a long tradition of looking after our staff, and I do not wish to choose this option unless there is no other alternative.
Our second option is to follow the example of our friends at Reysonido, and buy European technology which would reduce our cost of sales by 10–15%. However, we estimate that this investment would increase our operating expenses by half a million dollars a year.
A third option is to cut our prices in order to increase sales. We estimate a price cut of 10% might increase next year's sales to \$16.5 million – assuming, of course, that our competitors do not reduce their prices. However, our cost of sales would increase to just under nine million dollars.
My friends, there are three more options which I have not yet discussed with you, but which I would like you to consider carefully. Option number four is a merger. IMM have offered us three million dollars, which, in view of our desperate situation, is a very reasonable offer. If we agreed to a merger with IMM, the new company would be the new market leader, and be in a far better position to compete with Dylan. However, there would no doubt be some redundancies in order to make economies of scale.
Now, option five. This is a high-risk strategy, but we must consider all possible solutions. In order to compete with Dylan, we need to be bigger; one way to obtain that critical size is by acquisition. Our fifth option is to acquire Reysonido. Reysonido are likely to accept a takeover bid of around four million dollars. As well as synergy and economies of scale, this acquisition would also give us another bonus: access to the technology which means Reysonido's cost of sales is 10% lower than our own. Of course, we would need to borrow the money, and the repayments would represent around half a million dollars per year over ten years: not so unrealistic with combined sales of 25 million, I believe.
The final option is one which I sincerely hope you will not choose. That is, to close the company, and sell off our assets to pay our debts. I have kept it until last in order to stress that it is a serious option.
All right, I'm sure you are anxious to ask questions. After that, I would like us to consider all the options in detail; everybody's contributions will be valuable. Thank you.

8 International trade

8.1 About business Export sales and payment

2:50

Interviewer: Mr Sullivan, can you tell us first what exactly credit agencies do?
James Sullivan: Well, basically, we offer a range of services in two main areas: information and insurance. Some of our clients are interested in information to help them manage credit risk, and others come to us for insurance. But many companies, like Eisenhart Games, need both information and insurance.
I: What sort of information can you provide?
JS: We have details of over 50 million businesses in countries all over the world. So, for example, we can help Daryl by telling him how businesses and countries in the Middle East are doing financially; we can tell him if his prospective customers pay, and how quickly they pay; and, in particular, we can warn him if one of his customers gets into financial difficulty.
I: And you give each company a rating which indicates how reliable they are?
JS: Yes, companies – and also countries – are given a rating. This gives us a quick guide to how safely you can do business with a particular company or in a particular country. Actually, there's much more than just the rating. Clients like Daryl receive detailed credit reports which help them decide if and how to work with different companies.
I: I see. Now, what about credit insurance? Is that something new?
JS: Well, it's relatively new over here in the States, but not in Europe. European companies have been using it for a long time. Seventy per cent of European companies use credit insurance, whereas in the States the figure is below 5%.
I: Why is that?
JS: Essentially because European firms have to export, because their internal markets are too small. Until now, the majority of American firms have done most of their business in America, so they didn't need credit insurance unless the customer was very risky. Nowadays, companies like Eisenhart need to export, so they're discovering the advantages of credit insurance. For example, it means that in Saudi Arabia, Daryl can trade on open account, with no need for letters of credit, which take a lot of time and are relatively expensive.
I: I see. Talking of expense, what does credit insurance cost?
JS: Well, of course, it depends on the contract. The more risk the insurer takes on, the higher the premium will be. But, on average, I would say, for international credit insurance, between a quarter and 1% of sales.

8.2 Vocabulary International deals and payments

2:51–2:55

1
A: Bruno, have you seen this letter from those people in Slovakia?
B: No, what do they want?
A: Well, they say they're ready to place a large order now if they can pay next year.
B: Well, you'd better do some research on the company. Make sure they can pay! But be discreet. We don't want to upset them.

2
C: I'm still worried about sending these parts by sea. They're quite fragile, you know.
D: Well, don't worry. We're meeting the insurance people tomorrow. If anything goes wrong, we'll be covered.
C: But the insurance premium will be expensive, won't it?
D: Probably. But we have to do it anyway. It's one of the conditions in the contract. No insurance, no deal.

3
E: Francesca, have we received a payment from Kawasaki?
F: No. And I've already sent two reminders.
E: Two? Listen, could you give them a call?

If we're not careful, they'll be late every month, and I don't want to have the same problems we had last year.

4

F: So, could you send the payment as soon as possible, Mr Takahashi?

G: Well, it's just that there seems to be a small problem with your invoice. It's more expensive than we expected.

F: I'm sorry, Mr Takahashi, but the invoice is for exactly the same amount as our quote, which you accepted.

G: Ah, yes. Well, as we are regular customers, could you perhaps wait two or three weeks? We just have a small cash-flow problem at the moment. I'm sure you understand, Ms Trevi. It's nothing to worry about ...

5

H: Well, we'll accept your terms providing you deliver direct to our factory.

I: Hmm ... Our customers normally collect the goods from the port of entry.

H: But you said yourself these parts are fragile, so surely it would be better for the same forwarder to deliver all the way to the door? That way there's less risk of damage.

I: Well, you have a point there, I suppose.

H: And this will be a regular order, so it means a lot of business for the forwarder. I'm sure you can negotiate good terms with them.

I: Yes. Yes, you're right. OK, then. It's a deal.

8.3 Grammar Prepositions

2:56–2:65

1

A: It seems to me that with interest rates so low, property is still a better choice than the stock market.

B: Yes, you're right. I think a small flat in the town centre should give a good return.

2

C: I think you should talk to her. She's still upset.

D: OK, OK. I'll call her and tell her I'm sorry. I didn't mean what I said.

3

E: What state is it in after the accident?

F: Well, it could have been worse. Apart from a broken windscreen and headlights, there are only a few scratches on the paintwork. I was lucky.

4

G: It's amazing. She already speaks seven different languages, and she's picking up Chinese really fast!

H: Yeah, some people just have a gift, I guess.

5

I: You desperately need to get some more contracts. Relying on just one big firm is so dangerous.

J: Yes, I know. But we've always done most of our turnover with them.

6

K: The Americans are much more demanding. The Food and Drug Administration are terribly strict. But if you want to sell in the States, there's no other way.

L: Yes, there's no choice. We'll have to adapt the product to their norms.

7

M: What if we deliver the goods but they don't pay?

N: Well, we have a policy which covers that risk. For a small percentage of the value of the goods, we will guarantee to pay you if the customer defaults.

8

O: Well, sales are up 300%, we've reduced costs, our stock price has almost doubled and shareholders are delighted! Everything's worked out perfectly!

P: Yes. It doesn't get any better than this.

9

Q: Have you had any news from Taiwan?

R: No, not a word. It's strange. Usually they're in touch at least once a week.

10

S: Hey, Terry. Have you changed the passwords? I can't get into the database!

T: No, I'm having the same problem. I've tried everything but the system won't let me in.

2:66

Paul: Oh, Jenny, did you pick up my tickets?

Jenny: No, I'm picking them up this evening. I have to be there before six, so I'll be able to drop them off here by 6.30.

P: That's great! What time's the flight?

J: It's at 23.10. But it's OK – check-in doesn't open until 21.15. You've got plenty of time.

P: Hmm ... I've got the finance committee tonight. That usually goes on until at least half seven. I'll only just have time to go home and pick up my suitcase. I probably won't see the kids for a week now. They'll be in bed by quarter to eight. When do I get back from the States again?

J: On Sunday morning. You've got six meetings between tomorrow morning and Friday. That leaves you a day to visit New York, and you fly back late on Saturday evening.

P: Well, I don't think I'll have much time to visit New York. I've got the Merosom pitch to prepare for next Monday. I'm going to be jet-lagged on Sunday, so I'll have to do it before flying back.

J: Oh, yes, that's right. When do you expect Merosom to announce their decision?

P: Well, they said within three weeks. By the way, have you got the files for the New York meetings?

J: Yes, they're all ready. Do want to look at them now?

P: No, I've got another meeting!

J: Well, you'll have to read them during the flight, then.

P: Hmm ... I suppose so.

J: OK. Well, I'll get on, then, unless you've got any other questions?

P: Er, yes, just one. When am I going to sleep?

8.4 Speaking Negotiations – diplomacy

2:67–2:69

1

A: I'm afraid I think we might need more time to explore all the implications, and perhaps to include some of our senior management in the discussions.

B: Look, Mr. Yamada, I've already been here a week, and I have a plane to catch this evening. If you don't want to do this deal, just say so! I mean, when I get back, I have to tell my boss we have a contract, or explain why I failed to get one!

2

C: We feel that there are still quite a large number of difficulties to face in this project, and these will take a very considerable amount of time and money to resolve.

D: OK, Amal, let's sit down and work out a schedule.

C: I am not sure that at this stage a schedule is appropriate, in view of the considerable ... cultural differences between our companies.

D: Well, we need to start work soon if we want to meet the deadlines.

C: Frau Meier, perhaps we should talk again in a few days, by telephone?

D: Are you saying you're quitting the project?!

C: If you insist on putting it in those terms, then, yes, I think probably that is best.

3

E: And you pay the shipping costs.

F: No, as I told you, our prices are ex works. You pay for shipping.

E: So you don't want to sell us your machine tools?

F: No, why do you say that? I never said that!

E: Your terms with Auckland Industries last year included shipping, I believe.

F: Yes, but that was a much larger contract.

E: So our order is not very important for you?

2:70–2:72

1

A: I'm afraid I think we might need more time to explore all the implications, and perhaps to include some of our senior management in the discussions.

B: Uh-huh. Yamada-san, correct me if I'm wrong, but you seem to be saying that you're not completely convinced by this deal.

A: I'm afraid there seems to be a slight misunderstanding, Mr Bryson. Let me put it another way. We are as enthusiastic about this deal as ever, but here in Japan, it is very important to take the time to consult everybody, and to be sure there is a consensus.

B: Ah, yes, I understand. It's important for me to keep my board informed too.

2

C: I'm afraid we feel there are still quite a large number of difficulties to face in this project, and these will take a very considerable amount of time and money to resolve.

D: OK, Amal, have I got this right? You're saying that you're not sure we have the time or the money to make this project a success?

C: That's right. Especially in view of the considerable, er, cultural differences between our companies.

D: So, would I be right in saying that you are considering withdrawing from the project?

C: No, I'm sorry, Sabine, that isn't quite what I meant. What I was trying to say was, we need to take our different approaches to these problems into account, but I'm sure we can find solutions.

D: Yes, I'm sure we can. Perhaps we should talk again in a few days, by telephone?

C: Yes, that would be fine.

3

E: And if I've understood correctly, you will pay the shipping costs.

F: I'm sorry, perhaps I haven't made myself clear. The price we quoted was ex works. But we can quote including shipping if you like.

E: But didn't you say you would give us the same terms as for Auckland Industries last year?

F: Ah, I see, yes. Well, allow me to rephrase that. What I meant was, we would be very happy to give you the same terms as Auckland, if you were in a position to order the same volume.

8.6 Case study Jeddah Royal Beach Resort

2:73

Frederick: Good evening, Riaz!
Riaz: Oh, hello Frederick. Everything OK?
F: Yes, fine, thanks. I just wanted to give you these applications, if you've got a moment?
R: Yes, of course. Have a seat.
F: Thanks.
R: OK, so what have we got here?
F: Well, first of all, there's Ms Koepple in room 406. She's with Cool Breeze. It's a record label based in Buenos Aires. Now, I know you don't like record companies, but …
R: Yes, Frederick, and you know very well why I don't like record companies and those vulgar rock groups they send us, always causing damage and disturbing the other guests. Argentina, you say?
F: Yes. But Ms Koepple says they want to organize a big conference for their executives. There won't be any rock groups or that kind of thing, just corporate executives. So, they're applying for our credit card.
R: Well, it's true we need to develop in the conference market. It's good business, and it often brings in more business by word of mouth. But Argentina … OK, leave it with me and I'll look into it. How big is Ms Koepple's bill?
F: Well, she's been here for four nights. Leaving on Saturday. She's spending a lot of money – maybe six thousand dollars so far. But she's very nice, very friendly. I'm sure she won't leave without paying.
R: Hmm … she's applying for a credit limit of twenty thousand. Let's keep an eye on her, anyway. Let me know if her account goes over ten thousand dollars, OK?
F: Sure.
R: What else have you got there?
F: The next one is Mr Kobayashi from Tokyo. Remember him?
R: Oh, yes. The second-hand car salesman?
F: Yes. He's a really difficult customer. We've had to move him to a different room three times this week because he didn't like the view, or it was too far from the restaurant …
R: Well, he may be difficult but his credit's good. He seems to have built himself quite an empire over there. Kobayashi Auto Sales is doing very well. We've never had any problem with his people.
F: Well, I wouldn't buy a car from him. He never looks you in the eye, never smiles, never says 'thank you'. He wants us to raise his credit limit, but I don't trust him.
R: Let me see. From fifty up to a hundred thousand, eh? All right, I'll think about it.
F: Right. And this last one is our old friend Mrs Saman and her team from Egypt.
R: Oh, no. Are they still coming here? I thought we stopped their credit last year.
F: No, the company paid up in the end, remember?
R: Yes, I do now. Charming lady, of course, but that company – what's it called? Black Nile, that's it. They invented the concept of the slow payer! I think it took 18 months to get them to pay their last invoice. What does she want now?
F: Well, she wants us to raise their credit limit to a hundred thousand, too.
R: Oh, no way!
F: But there are ten of them this time, and she's such a wonderful little old lady!
R: I should really suspend their credit and insist on cash in advance. They're on, let's see … thirty thousand dollars. It's just too big a risk. Have you seen the latest cash-flow figures? Our customers are taking longer and longer to pay, and uncollectibles have gone over 3%! I'm getting a lot of pressure from management to take firm action.
F: Well, be careful; Mrs Saman told me yesterday that her brother is a very senior government official. And remember, we have a lot of guests from Egypt now. We don't want to upset them.
R: Yes, that's true. You never know who Mrs Saman might talk to. She's a very influential old lady. All right, leave it with me, Frederick. I'll let you know what I decide tomorrow.

Glossary

The definitions for the words in this glossary are from the *Macmillan Dictionary*. The red words are high-frequency words, that is to say that they are among the 7,500 which native speakers use for 90% of what they speak or write. See http://www.macmillandictionary.com for more information.

1 Corporate culture

1.1 About business
Work culture and placements

assignment /ə'saɪnmənt/ noun [count or uncount] task given as part of your studies or your job: *His first assignment as a reporter was to cover the local election.*

autonomy /ɔː'tɒnəmi/ noun [uncount] the power to make your own decisions: *New regulations have severely restricted the autonomy of doctors.*

beating /'biːtɪŋ/ noun [count] the act of hitting someone hard a number of times as a punishment: *The man had been given a severe beating.*

dress code /dres kəʊd/ noun [count] a set of rules about what you should wear in a particular place or at a particular event: *The dress code in our office is very formal: everybody wears a suit.*

etiquette /'etɪket/ noun [uncount] a set of rules for behaving correctly in a particular situation: *Office etiquette demands that you don't read other people's messages.*

initiative /ɪ'nɪʃətɪv/ noun [uncount] the ability to think of ideas and take decisions independently. **Take the initiative**: to take the first step or be the first to take action: *She would have to take the initiative in order to improve their relationship.*

intern /'ɪntɜː(r)n/ noun [count] a student or recently qualified person who works in a job in order to get experience: *Most employers prefer interns who already have some work experience.*

pick up /ˌpɪk 'ʌp/ phrasal verb [transitive] to learn information or a new skill without trying or without meaning to.

1.2 Vocabulary
Work organization and responsibility

on a day-to-day basis /ɒn ə deɪ tə deɪ 'beɪsɪs/ phrase used for saying how often something happens. On a daily/monthly/annual, etc. basis: *Safety equipment was checked on a daily basis.*

organigram /ɔː(r)'gænəgræm/ noun [count] a drawing or plan that gives the names and job titles of all the staff in an organization or department.

predecessor /'priːdɪˌsesə(r)/ noun [count] the person who had the job before: *Alexander seems to have learned nothing from the faults of his predecessors.*

take over /teɪk 'əʊvə(r)/ phrasal verb [transitive] to take control of something: *IBM is taking over a much smaller company.*

1.5 Writing
A placement report

appendix /ə'pendɪks/ noun [count] a section giving extra details at the end of a book or document: *Technical specifications are included in the appendix to Chapter 9.*

gearbox /'gɪə(r)ˌbɒks/ noun [count] a metal box that contains the parts of a vehicle or a machine that change engine power into movement.

mailshot /'meɪlˌʃɒt/ noun [count] a letter or advertisement sent to many people at the same time.

rapport /ræ'pɔː(r)/ noun [singular or uncount] good relationship and understanding between people.

take the mickey /teɪk ðə 'mɪki/ phrase British Informal to laugh at somebody, usually in a friendly way.

waste /weɪst/ noun [count or uncount] useless materials that are left or thrown away: *A bill was introduced to clean up toxic waste from local factories.*

1.6 Case study
Counselling

body language /'bɒdi ˌlæŋgwɪdʒ/ noun [uncount] the movements or positions of your body that show other people what you are thinking or feeling: *Their body language betrayed the tension between them.*

bounce back /ˌbaʊns 'bæk/ phrasal verb [intransitive] to become healthy, happy or successful again after something bad has happened to you.

echo /'ekəʊ/ verb [transitive] to express someone else's ideas or to say the same words that someone else has said: *Blake echoed the views of many employees.*

headache /'hedeɪk/ noun [count] a pain in your head: *I've got a splitting headache* (= an extremely bad headache).

open question /ˌəʊpən 'kwestʃ(ə)n/ noun [count] a question with a *wh-* question word, as opposed to a **closed question** which has a *yes/no* answer.

outlook /'aʊtˌlʊk/ noun [singular] your general attitude to things: **share an outlook**: *They shared the same kind of outlook on life.*

paraphrase /'pærəˌfreɪz/ verb [transitive] to express what someone else has said using different words: *It is particularly important when paraphrasing to be sure that you do not distort the meaning of the original statement.*

perspective /pə(r)'spektɪv/ noun 1 [count] a way of thinking about something: 2 [uncount] a sensible way of judging the importance of something in comparison with other things: **keep something in perspective**: *It's important to keep things in perspective and not dwell on one incident.*

2 Customer support

2.1 About business
Call centres

bus /bʌs/ verb [transitive] to take someone somewhere by bus.

copycat /'kɒpiˌkæt/ adjective similar to something else and considered to be a copy of it: *copycat crimes.*

tax break /tæks breɪk/ noun [count] a reduction in the tax that you must pay: *A tax break for college.*

tax holiday /ˌtæks ˈhɒlɪdeɪ/ noun [count] a temporary period, during which time the government removes certain taxes (usually sales tax) on certain items, in order to encourage the consumption or purchase of these items.

twentysomething /ˈtwentiˌsʌmθɪŋ/ noun [count] refers to the age of someone who is between twenty and twenty-nine.

2.2 Vocabulary
Customer service and telephoning

clip /klɪp/ noun [count] a small object that holds something in position: *hair clip.*

earth /ɜː(r)θ/ verb [transitive] BRITISH to connect a piece of electrical equipment to the ground so that it is safe: *Make sure the machine is earthed properly.*

retain /rɪˈteɪn/ verb [transitive] to keep someone or something.

side-panel /ˈsaɪd ˌpæn(ə)l/ noun [count] a flat part of a box or other object that can be removed.

slot /slɒt/ noun [count] a long narrow hole that you can fit something into.

upset /ʌpˈset/ adjective very sad, worried or angry about something: *Why are you so upset?*

2.4 Speaking
Dealing with problems by telephone

Come again? /kʌm əˈgen/ INFORMAL used for asking someone to repeat what they have just said.

crash /kræʃ/ verb [intransitive or transitive] COMPUTING if a computer or computer program crashes, it suddenly stops working.

freeze /friːz/ verb [intransitive or transitive] COMPUTING if a computer screen freezes or is frozen you cannot move anything on it because there is something wrong with the computer.

2.5 Writing
Formal and informal correspondence

accounts payable /əˌkaʊnts ˈpeɪəb(ə)l/ noun [plural] MAINLY AMERICAN a record of how much money a company owes other people or companies for goods and services.

ASAP /ˌeɪ es eɪ ˈpiː/ abbreviation as soon as possible.

crack /kræk/ verb [transitive] to damage something so that a line appears on its surface, but it does not break into pieces: *I dropped a plate and cracked it.*

duplicate /ˈdjuːplɪkeɪt/ adjective made as an exact copy of something else.

inconsistency /ˌɪnkənˈsɪstənsi/ noun [count] something that does not match something else.

patch /pætʃ/ noun [count] a piece of software that you add to a computer program to improve it or remove a fault.

Trojan (horse) /ˈtrəʊdʒ(ə)n hɔː(r)s/, noun [count] COMPUTING a program that seems useful but is designed to cause damage, for example by destroying information.

write-off /raɪt ɒf/ noun [count] a vehicle or machine that is so badly damaged that it cannot be repaired.

2.6 Case study
Cybertartan Software

come up with /ˌkʌm ˈʌp wɪð/ phrasal verb [transitive] to think of something such as an idea or a plan.

from the horse's mouth /frəm ðə ˈhɔː(r)sˌɪz maʊθ/ INFORMAL information from the horse's mouth comes from someone who is directly involved.

obsolescence /ˌɒbsəˈles(ə)ns/ noun [uncount] the state of something which is no longer used: **planned obsolescence** the practice of making products that will not last long, so that people will need to buy new ones.

shift /ʃɪft/ noun [count] a period of work in a factory or business where some people work during the day and some work at night: *a three-shift system.*

staff turnover /stɑːf ˈtɜː(r)nəʊvə(r)/ noun [count or uncount] the rate at which people leave jobs and new people arrive: *a high turnover of staff/personnel*

swap /swɒp/ verb [intransitive or transitive] to give something to someone in exchange for something else: *Do you want to swap seats?*

triple /ˈtrɪp(ə)l/ verb [transitive] to increase something so that it is three times bigger than before: *He helped triple the value of the company.*

3 Products and packaging

3.1 About business
Packaging

focus group /ˈfəʊkəs ˌgruːp/ noun [count] a small group of people who are interviewed together and give their opinions to help a company make decisions.

frustration /frʌˈstreɪʃ(ə)n/ noun [count or uncount] the feeling of being frustrated.

interface /ˌɪntə(r)ˈfeɪs/ verb [intransitive] interact and communicate with each other.

provocation /ˌprɒvəˈkeɪʃ(ə)n/ noun [count or uncount] the act of doing or saying something deliberately in order to make somebody angry or upset. *She bursts into tears at the slightest provocation.*

rage /reɪdʒ/ noun [count or uncount] a very strong feeling of anger: MAINLY JOURNALISM angry violent behaviour in a public situation: *It is clear that air rage is now on the increase.*

resistant /rɪˈzɪst(ə)nt/ adjective able to resist something: *a disease that is resistant to antibiotics.*

trigger /ˈtrɪgə(r)/ verb [transitive] to make something happen: *to trigger an alarm.*

wrap /ræp/ verb [transitive] to cover something by putting something such as paper or plastic around it. *I wrapped my present for my sister's birthday.*

3.2 Vocabulary
Specifications and features

attention-grabbing /əˈtenʃ(ə)n ˌgræbɪŋ/ adjective an attention-grabbing remark or activity is one that is intended to make people notice it.

bird's-eye view /ˌbɜːdz aɪ ˈvjuː/ noun [singular] a good view of something from a high position.

blueprint /ˈbluːˌprɪnt/ noun [count] a drawing that shows how to build something.

chart /tʃɑː(r)t/ noun [count] a map used for navigation in boats or planes.

foolproof /ˈfuːlˌpruːf/ adjective very well designed and easy to use so that it cannot fail and you cannot use it wrongly. *This recipe is foolproof: it works every time.*

mockup /ˈmɒkʌp/ noun [count] a model of a future product that is the same size as the real thing.

overlay /ˈəʊvə(r)ˌleɪ/ noun [count] a set of extra information that is added to a picture by a computer.

retardant /rɪˈtɑː(r)d(ə)nt/ adjective slowing down a process. *This door is fire retardant.*

tamper with /ˈtæmpə(r) ˌwɪð/ phrasal verb [transitive] to touch something and change it in a way that will damage it.

3.3 Grammar
Articles, relative clauses and noun combinations

bump /bʌmp/ verb [intransitive or transitive] to hit against something solid: *The car bumped into a tree.*

drop calls /ˈdrɒp kɔːlz/ phrase to fail to connect incoming calls.

empowerment /ɪmˈpaʊə(r)mənt/ noun [uncount] giving control or power over something.

flip cover /ˈflɪp ˌkʌvə/ noun [count] part of a mobile phone which folds over the keypad.

get rid of /ɡet ˈrɪd əv/ phrasal verb [transitive] to throw away, give away or sell a possession that you no longer want: *I have to get rid of my old computer.*

no frills /ˈnəʊ frɪlz/ expression used for something which is good enough but has no unnecessary extra features: *A simple meal with no frills.*

rating /ˈreɪtɪŋ/ noun [count] a measurement of how good or popular someone or something is: *The guide gives restaurants a rating out of ten.*

workhorse /ˈwɜː(r)kˌhɔː(r)s/ noun [count] a very useful piece of equipment that you use a lot: *My old car was a great workhorse.*

3.4 Speaking
Presentations – structure

hook /hʊk/ noun [count] a curved piece of metal for hanging things on; a method for getting people interested and attracted to something: *Hang your coat on the hook.*

lecture /ˈlektʃə(r)/ noun [count] a talk to a group of people about a particular subject, especially at a college or university: *This lecture about the Dark Ages was really fascinating.*

overwhelmingly /ˌəʊvə(r)ˈwelmɪŋli/ adverb very strongly: *They voted overwhelmingly against the proposal.*

ping /pɪŋ/ verb [transitive] COMPUTING to send an electronic signal requesting an answer from a device: *I'll ping it to you later.*

tracking /ˈtrækɪŋ/ noun [uncount] the act of following or looking for a person, animal or thing.

wrap up /ˌræp ˈʌp/ phrasal verb [intransitive or transitive] INFORMAL to finish something: *That just about wraps it up for today.*

3.5 Writing
A product description

alloy /ˈælɔɪ/ noun [count or uncount] a metal that is made from combining two or more metals.

benefit /ˈbenɪfɪt/ noun [count or uncount] an advantage you get from a product or situation.

feature /ˈfiːtʃə(r)/ noun [count] an important part or aspect of a product.

intuitive /ɪnˈtjuːɪtɪv/ adjective an intuitive system is easy to use because the process of operating it is very natural or obvious.

plug-in /ˈplʌɡɪn/ noun [count] COMPUTING a software addition which allows an application to perform additional functions.

quibble /ˈkwɪb(ə)l/ noun [count] a complaint or criticism about something that is not important: **no quibble guarantee** a promise to refund the customer without questioning their reasons for dissatisfaction.

stand out /ˌstænd ˈaʊt/ phrasal verb [intransitive] to be easy to see because of being different.

3.6 Case study
Big Jack's Pizza

BOGOF /ˈbɒɡɒf/ abbreviation buy one, get one free.

chequered /ˈtʃekə(r)d/ adjective a chequered pattern or design consists of squares in two or more different colours.

dine-in /ˌdaɪn ˈɪn/ adjective used to describe meals taken in a restaurant: *dine-in curry.*

franchisee /ˌfræntʃaɪˈziː/ noun [count] a person or company that has the franchise to sell a particular type of goods or services.

fusion cuisine /ˈfjuːʒn kwɪˈziːn/ noun [uncount] a particular style of cooking food combining Chinese and Western recipes.

gourmet /ˈɡʊə(r)meɪ/ noun [count] someone who knows a lot about good food and wine.

slide /slaɪd/ verb [intransitive] to move across a smooth surface.

strengthen /ˈstreŋθ(ə)n/ verb [transitive] to make something stronger.

threat /θret/ noun [count or uncount] something that could cause harm.

USP /juː es ˈpiː/ noun [count] BUSINESS unique selling point/proposition: the thing that makes a product or service different from others.

4 Careers

4.1 About business
Career choices

earth-shattering /ˈɜː(r)θ ʃæt(ə)rɪŋ/ adjective extremely surprising and important.

inertia /ɪˈnɜː(r)ʃə/ noun [uncount] a situation in which something does not change: a feeling of not wanting to change things.

jump in at the deep end /ˌdʒʌmp ˈɪn ˌæt ðə ˈdiːp ˌend/ phrasal verb [intransitive] to become involved in a difficult situation with little preparation.

pick someone's brains /ˌpɪk ˈsʌmwʌnz ˌbreɪnz/ expression INFORMAL to ask someone questions to get advice or information: *I wanted to pick your brains about this idea I've had.*

posse /ˈpɒsi/ noun [count] INFORMAL a group of friends.

start the ball rolling /ˌstɑː(r)t ðə ˈbɔːl ˌrəʊlɪŋ/ expression to make something start happening.

stay put /ˌsteɪ ˈpʊt/ verb [intransitive] to remain in one place or position.

treadmill /ˈtredˌmɪl/ noun [count] a situation that is very tiring or boring because you do the same things continuously.

4.2 Vocabulary
Careers, personal skills and qualities

controversial /ˌkɒntrəˈvɜː(r)ʃ(ə)l/ adjective a controversial subject, opinion or decision is one that people disagree about or do not approve of.

flag /flæg/ verb [transitive] to mark something so that you will be able to find it again.

headhunter /ˈhedˌhʌntə(r)/ noun [count] a person or company who searches for good staff and tries to persuade them to leave their jobs and go to work for another company.

liaise /liˈeɪz/ verb [intransitive] if one person liaises with another or people liaise, they talk to each other and tell each other what they are doing, so that they can work together effectively.

multitasking /ˌmʌltiˈtɑːskɪŋ/ noun [uncount] doing several things at the same time.

on the spot /ˌɒn ðə ˈspɒt/ expression immediately.

unconventional /ˌʌnkənˈvenʃ(ə)nəl/ adjective different from what most people consider to be usual or normal.

wannabe /ˈwɒnəbi/ noun [count] INFORMAL someone who wants to be famous or successful.

4.3 Grammar
Present tenses

assault course /əˈsɔːlt ˌkɔː(r)s/ noun [count] an exercise involving running, climbing and jumping, used in military training.

hand /hænd/ verb [transitive] to give something to someone with your hand; **you have to hand it to someone** expression SPOKEN used for saying that you admire someone for something they have done.

knock over /ˌnɒk ˈəʊvə(r)/ verb [transitive] to hit something so that it falls: *The car knocked him over.*

relevant /ˈreləv(ə)nt/ adjective directly connected to what is being discussed or considered.

undergraduate /ˌʌndə(r)ˈgrædʒʊət/ noun [count] a student who is studying for a first degree at a college or university.

You're kidding /ˌjɔː(r) ˈkɪdɪŋ/ expression mainly spoken used for saying that you do not believe what someone is saying.

4.4 Speaking
Job interviews

achievement /əˈtʃiːvmənt/ noun [count] a particular thing that you have succeeded in doing after a lot of effort.

cope with /ˈkəʊp ˌwɪð/ verb [intransitive] to deal successfully with a difficult situation or job.

rapport /ræˈpɔː(r)/ noun [singular/uncount] a relationship in which people like, understand, and respect each other: *Having good rapport with your clients is essential.*

regardless of /rɪˈgɑː(r)dləs əv/ phrase without being affected by.

strength /streŋθ/ noun [count] something that someone does well: *Ron's main strength is his ability to motivate players.*

weakness /ˈwiːknəs/ noun [count] a fault or problem that makes someone less effective or attractive.

4.6 Case study
Gap years and career breaks

eco- /iːkəʊ/ prefix relating to the environment: used with some nouns and adjectives.

find your feet /ˌfaɪnd jə(r) ˈfiːt/ expression to start to feel confident and familiar with something.

step back /ˌstep ˈbæk/ phrasal verb [intransitive] to stop for a moment in order to consider something objectively.

tangible /ˈtændʒəb(ə)l/ adjective important and noticeable: *tangible evidence.*

underprivileged /ˌʌndə(r)ˈprɪvəlɪdʒd/ adjective not having as many advantages or opportunities as most other people.

5 Making deals

5.1 About business
Retailing

bricks-and-mortar /ˌbrɪks ænd ˈmɔː(r)tə(r)/ expression a building, when you are thinking of it in connection with how much it cost to build or how much it is worth: *They put their money into bricks and mortar.*

claw /klɔː/ noun [count] the sharp curved part at the end of some animal's toes, for example a cat.

hit /hɪt/ noun [count] a piece of information that a computer program finds for you: *I searched for the name 'Mundy' and got over fifty hits.*

5.4 Speaking
Negotiations – bargaining

down time /ˈdaʊn ˌtaɪm/ noun [count or uncount] period during which equipment or a machine is not functional or cannot work.

lead time /ˈliːd ˌtaɪm/ noun [count or uncount] the time between starting and completing a production process.

package /ˈpækɪdʒ/ noun [count] a set of products or services that are sold together as one unit.

reluctant /rɪˈlʌktənt/ adjective not willing to do something.

tentative /ˈtentətɪv/ adjective not definite or certain.

5.5 Writing
A proposal

cash flow /ˈkæʃ ˌfləʊ/ noun [uncount] the rate at which a business takes in money through sales and pays it out for the things it needs to continue operating.

contingency plan /kənˈtɪndʒ(ə)nsi ˌplæn/ noun [uncount] a plan that helps you to prepare for possible bad events.

mail order /ˌmeɪl ˈɔː(r)də(r)/ noun [uncount] a way of buying goods in which you order them by post or by telephone and they are posted to you.

merchant account /ˈmɜː(r)tʃ(ə)nt əˌkaʊnt/ noun [count] a special account for performing e-business transactions.

set-up fee /ˈset ʌp fiː/ noun the price you have to pay to have a piece of equipment installed.

6 Company and community

6.1 About business
Corporate social responsibility

altruism /ˈæltruˌɪz(ə)m/ noun [uncount] a way of thinking and behaving that shows you care about other people and their interests more than you care about yourself.

biodegradable /ˌbaɪəʊdɪˈgreɪdəb(ə)l/ adjective biodegradable substances can be broken into very small parts by bacteria so that they are not harmful to the environment.

credo /ˈkriːdəʊ/ noun [count] a statement of your beliefs.

hybrid /ˈhaɪbrɪd/ noun [count] a mixture of different things or styles.

sustainable /səˈsteɪnəb(ə)l/ adjective capable of continuing for a long time at the same level.

virtuous circle /ˈvɜː(r)tʃʊəs ˈsɜː(r)k(ə)l/ noun [singular] a process in which a good action or event produces a good result that also causes the process to continue so that more good results happen.

6.2 Vocabulary
Meetings, ethical behaviour and social performance

damage limitation /ˈdæmɪdʒ ˌlɪmɪˈteɪʃ(ə)n/ noun [uncount] the process of trying to limit the amount of damage that is caused by something.

extravagant /ɪkˈstrævəgənt/ adjective extreme, excessive or unreasonable.

misleading /mɪsˈliːdɪŋ/ adjective giving the wrong idea or impression and making you believe something that is not true.

settlement /ˈset(ə)lmənt/ noun [count] an official agreement that ends an argument between two people or groups.

6.3 Grammar
The passive and reported speech

leakage /ˈliːkɪdʒ/ noun [uncount] an amount of liquid or gas escaping through a hole in something.

protracted /prəˈtræktɪd/ adjective FORMAL continuing for a long time, especially longer than is normal or necessary.

stakeholder /ˈsteɪkˌhəʊldə(r)/ noun [count] a person or company that is involved in a particular organization, project, system, etc., especially because they have invested money in it.

6.4 Speaking
Meetings – teamwork

civil servant /ˌsɪv(ə)l ˈsɜː(r)v(ə)nt/ noun [count] someone who works for a government department.

disabled /dɪsˈeɪb(ə)ld/ adjective someone who is disabled is unable to use part of their body or brain properly because of injury or disease.

ethnic minority /ˌeθnɪk maɪˈnɒrəti/ noun [count] a group of people who have a different culture and different traditions to most people living in a place.

misconduct /mɪsˈkɒndʌkt/ noun [uncountable] unacceptable behaviour.

6.5 Writing
Reports and minutes

derive /dɪˈraɪv/ verb [transitive] to get a feeling from something, e.g. pleasure, satisfaction: **derive something from something**: *They derive great enjoyment from these simple games.*

greenfield site /ˈgriːnfiːld ˌsaɪt/ noun [count] a piece of land that has never been built on before.

paternalism /pəˈtɜː(r)nəˌlɪz(ə)m/ noun [uncount] governing like a father, by looking after people but also taking away their freedom and responsibilities.

positive discrimination /ˌpɒzətɪv dɪˌskrɪmɪˈneɪʃ(ə)n/ noun [uncount] the practice of giving special benefits to people from a group that was treated in an unfair way in the past.

6.6 Case study
Phoenix

hazardous /ˈhæzə(r)dəs/ adjective dangerous, especially to people's health or safety: *These chemicals are hazardous to human health.*

resident /ˈrezɪd(ə)nt/ noun [count] a person who lives in a particular place.

resistance /rɪˈzɪst(ə)ns/ noun [uncount] dislike of or opposition to a plan, an idea, etc.

7 Mergers and acquisitions

7.1 About business
Risks and opportunities in M&A

due diligence /ˌdjuː ˈdɪlɪdʒ(ə)ns/ noun [uncount] investigation of a company's activities and finances before investment or acquisition.

gene /dʒiːn/ noun [count] information in cells that determines a person's characteristics: *He believes that shyness is in the genes.*

homogenize /həˈmɒdʒənaɪz/ verb [transitive] to make things the same, often so that the result is boring.

open enrolment /ˌəʊpən ɪnˈrəʊlmənt/ noun [count] a university class which anybody can join.

prestigious /preˈstɪdʒəs/ adverb respected and admired as very important or of a very high quality.

susceptible /səˈseptəb(ə)l/ adjective easily influenced or affected.

takeover bid /ˈteɪkˌəʊvə(r) ˌbɪd/ noun [count or uncount] an offer to buy the shares in a company and take control of it: *Shareholders have accepted a takeover bid.*

turmoil /ˈtɜː(r)mɔɪl/ noun [uncount] a state of excitement or uncontrolled activity.

7.2 Vocabulary
Business performance

be in the black /biː ɪn ðə ˈblæk/ expression to have money in your bank account or more money than you owe: *We've been in the black for over a year now.*

bid /bɪd/ noun [count] an offer to give a particular amount of money for something, for example at an auction: *We received a bid of £5,000 for the table.*

filter through /fɪltə(r) ˈθruː/ verb [intransitive] if news or infomation filters through to people, they receive it gradually or after a period of time: *News of the decision filtered through to reporters.*

flotation /fləʊˈteɪʃ(ə)n/ noun [count or uncount] BUSINESS the sale of shares in a company for the first time.

FTSE 100, the /ˌfʊtsi wʌn ˈhʌndrəd/ noun [uncount] the Financial Times Stock Exchange index; an average of the prices of shares from the top 100 companies on the London stock exchange.

rumour /ˈruːmə(r)/ noun [count or uncount] unofficial information that may or may not be true: *He'd heard rumours about some big financial deal.*

7.4 Speaking
Presentations – visuals

crucial /ˈkruːʃ(ə)l/ adjective extremely important; **crucial to**: *Listening to customers' needs is crucial to designing good products.*

deteriorate /dɪˈtɪəriəreɪt/ verb [intransitive] to become worse: *The economic situation is deteriorating.*

disposable income /dɪˈspəʊzəb(ə)l ˈɪnkʌm/ noun [uncount] money that you have left to spend after you have paid your bills.

highlight /ˈhaɪˌlaɪt/ verb [transitive] to emphasize or underline part of something: *The presenter highlighted the need for a quick decision.*

overload /ˌəʊvə(r)ˈləʊd/ verb [transitive] to put too much of something on something; to present people with too much information for them to understand easily.

7.5 Writing
Presentation slides

bullet points /ˈbʊlɪt pɔɪnts/ noun [count] a circle printed before each item on a list.

distracting /dɪˈstræktɪŋ/ adjective preventing you from concentrating on something: *This noise outside the classroom is very distracting.*

font /fɒnt/ noun [count] TECHNICAL the style of letters and numbers used in a document.

vague /veɪg/ adjective not clearly explained or very detailed: *Witnesses gave only a vague description of the driver.*

7.6 Case study
Calisto

charismatic /ˌkærɪzˈmætɪk/ adjective a charismatic person has a strong personality that makes other people like them and be attracted to them.

meteoric /ˌmiːtiˈɒrɪk/ adjective becoming very successful very quickly.

ruthless /ˈruːθləs/ adjective willing to make other people suffer so that you can achieve your aims.

slick /slɪk/ adjective done in a very impressive way that seems to need very little effort.

trumpet /ˈtrʌmpɪt/ verb [transitive] to announce something publicly in a way that is intended to make it seem very important.

8 International trade

8.1 About business
Export sales and payment

chase /tʃeɪs/ verb [transitive] to try hard to get something you want: *Many companies are still chasing debts that are more than five years old.*

creditworthiness /ˈkredɪtˌwɜː(r)ðinəs/ noun [uncount] ability to repay debts.

level playing field /ˌlev(ə)l ˈpleɪŋ fiːld/ noun [singular] a situation that is fair for everybody involved.

take on board /ˌteɪk ɒn ˈbɔː(r)d/ expression to consider an idea, to accept criticism and learn from past mistakes.

think outside the box /ˈθɪŋk autˌsaɪd ðə ˈbɒks/ expression to find new and unusual ways of doing things, especially solving problems.

without a trace /wɪðˈaʊt ə ˈtreɪs/ expression no sign that someone has been present; **disappear without trace**: *She was seen last week, then disappeared without trace.*

wizard /ˈwɪzə(r)d/ noun [count] someone who is very good at something.

8.2 Vocabulary
International deals and payments

file a claim /ˌfaɪl ə ˈkleɪm/ verb [transitive] to present a claim so that it can be officially recorded and dealt with.

forwarder /ˈfɔː(r)wə(r)də(r)/ noun [count] firm specializing in arranging storage and shipping of merchandise on behalf of its shippers.

frequent-flyer scheme /ˌfriːkwentˈflaɪə(r) ˌskiːm/ noun [count] a system to encourage people to travel with the same airline by giving them reductions or gifts.

get behind with /ˌget bɪˈhaɪnd ˌwɪð/ phrasal verb [intransitive] if you get behind with work or payments, you have not done as much work or made as many payments as you should have: *She'd been ill so often that, she was getting behind with her schoolwork.*

8.3 Grammar
Prepositions

drop off /ˌdrɒp ˈɒf/ phrasal verb [transitive] to take something to a place and not stay there long: *Is it OK if I drop the documents off later?*

jet-lagged /ˈdʒetˌlæɡd/ adjective feeling tired and sometimes confused after a long flight.

pitch /pɪtʃ/ noun [count] an oral proposal designed to persuade someone to buy your product or support you.

8.4 Speaking
Negotiations – diplomacy

consensus /kənˈsensəs/ noun [uncount] an opinion that all members of a group agree with.

implication /ˌɪmplɪˈkeɪʃ(ə)n/ noun [count usually plural] a possible effect or result: *We need to consider the financial implications.*

quit /kwɪt/ verb [intransitive or transitive] to leave a job or project: *She quit after only six months in the job.*

8.5 Writing
Requests and reminders

disregard /ˌdɪsrɪˈɡɑː(r)d/ verb [transitive] to pay no attention to something.

extend /ɪkˈstend/ verb [transitive] FORMAL to agree to lend someone money or give them credit.

factoring /ˈfæktərɪŋ/ noun [uncount] selling a company's receivable invoices in order to obtain funds more quickly.

outstanding /aʊtˈstændɪŋ/ adjective an amount of money that is outstanding has not yet been paid.

overdue /ˌəʊvə(r)ˈdjuː/ adjective if a payment is overdue, it should have been paid before now.

oversight /ˈəʊvə(r)ˌsaɪt/ noun [count] something you do not think of which causes problems later.

settle /ˈset(ə)l/ verb [transitive] to pay all the money you owe someone: *He has thirty days to settle his bill.*

8.6 Case study
Jeddah Royal Beach Resort

armoury /ˈɑː(r)məri/ noun [usually singular] a set of skills, equipment or powers that is available for someone if they need it.

loyalty /ˈlɔɪəlti/ noun [uncount] continued use of the products or services of a particular business: *A high level of brand loyalty.*

uncollectible /ʌnkəˈlektəb(ə)l/ noun [count] a bad debt which cannot be recovered.

vulgar /ˈvʌlɡə(r)/ adjective someone who is rude, unpleasant, and offensive.

word of mouth /ˌwɜː(r)d əv ˈmaʊθ/ expression information communicated by people speaking informally to each other.

Macmillan Education Limited
4 Crinan Street
London N1 9XW

Companies and representatives throughout the world

ISBN 978-0-230-43788-3

This edition published 2013
First edition published 2007

Original design by Keith Shaw, Threefold Design Ltd
Page make-up by Keith Shaw, Threefold Design Ltd
Illustrated by Mark Duffin, Peter Harper, NAF and Keith Shaw
Cover design by Keith Shaw, Threefold Design Ltd
Cover image: Getty Images/Steve Coleman
Picture research by Susannah Jayes

Author's acknowledgements
Thanks first of all to everybody at Macmillan Oxford for making the project not only efficient, but also fun.
Special thanks to Roger Miller of ESDES Lyon for his invaluable input on the syllabus.
Once again I have to thank my partners and colleagues at Infolangues for their patience, help and encouragement, especially Tessa Wisely, Peter Wheeler and Jeremy Townend.
Last but not least, many thanks to my wife and family for allowing me to spend so much time in front of the computer or with my head in the clouds.

The publishers would like to thank the following people for piloting and commenting on material for this coursebook:
Paul Bellchambers, Business and Technical Languages, Paris, France; Bunmi Rolland, Pôle Universitaire Léonard de Vinci, Paris, France; Prof. Vanessa Leonardi, Faculty of Economics, University of Ferrara, Italy; Prof. Paola De La Pierre, Faculty of Economics, University of Turin, Italy; Elżbieta Typek, Cracow University of Economics, Poland; Marlena Nowak, Cracow University of Economics, Poland; Lucyna Wilinkiewicz-Górniak, Cracow University of Economics, Poland; Jolanta Regucka-Pawlina, Cracow University of Economics, Poland; Sebastian Florek-Paszkowski, Cracow University of Economics, Poland; Bożena Bielak, Cracow University of Economics, Poland; Małgorzata Held, Cracow University of Economics, Poland; Anna Wróblewska-Marzec, Cracow University of Economics, Poland; Lidia Zielińska, Cracow University of Economics, Poland; Olga Druszkiewicz, Cracow University of Economics, Poland; Maciej Krzanowski, Cracow University of Economics, Poland; Lubov Kulik, Moscow Lomonosov State University, Russia; Irina Ekareva, The Russian Plekhanov University of Economics, Russia; Larisa Tarkhova, The Russian Plekhanov University of Economics, Russia; Irina Schemeleva, Higher School of Economics, Russia; Irina Matveeva, The Academy of Social and Labour Relations, Russia; Galina Makarova, Denis' School, Russia, Liam James Tyler, IPT, Russia; Tatiana Efremtseva, The Russian International Academy of Tourism, Russia; Tatiana Sedova, The University of Finance, Russia; Tony Watson and Kim Draper, MLS Bournemouth, Bournemouth, UK; Louise Raven, Marcus Evans Linguarama, Stratford-upon-Avon, UK.

The publishers would like to thank the following people for piloting and commenting on material for the original edition of this coursebook: Johan Strobbe, University of Leuven, Belgium; Elena Angelova, Pharos School of Languages and Computing, Sofia, Bulgaria; Markéta Černá, Prague University of Economics, Czech Republic; Dagmar Ryšavá, University of West Bohemia, Czech Republic; Kevin Gore, Helsinki Business Polytechnic, Finland; Irene Cros, ENSEEIHT, Toulouse, France; Marc Hyde, ENSEEIHT, Toulouse, France; Anne Britain, ENSEEIHT, Toulouse, France; Judit Szücs, Berzsenyi College, Szombathely, Hungary; Ilona Máthé, Tessedik Samuel College School of Business and Economics, Békéscsaba, Hungary; Terri Bland, Università Carlo Cattaneo, Castellanza, Italy; Anna De Angelis, Università Carlo Cattaneo, Castellanza, Italy; Elaine Jones, Università Carlo Cattaneo, Castellanza, Italy; Danuta Korta, Gdynia Maritime University, Poland; Delia Radulescu, ECHO, Bucharest, Romania; Brindusa Nicolaescu, University of Bucharest, Romania; Irina Ciobanu, Petre Andrei University, Iasi, Romania; Catalina Chiriac, Academy of Economic Studies, Bucharest, Romania; Irene Novikova, Moscow State University of Printing Arts, Russia; Lydia Korzheva, Moscow Diplomatic Academy, Russia; Tatiana Baranovskaya, Higher School of Economics, Moscow, Russia; Marina Fedotova, Plekhanov Russian Economic Academy, Moscow, Russia; Lucia Hlubenova, Bratislava University of Economics, Slovakia; Juan Carlos Palmer, Universitat Jaume I, Castellón de la Plana, Spain; Thomas Lavelle, Stockholm School of Economics, Sweden; Anette Nolan, Folkuniversitetet, Stockholm, Sweden; Preeyanuch Chanprasert, The University of the Thai Chamber of Commerce, Bangkok, Thailand.
And to all the other teachers around the world who took the time to complete Macmillan's tertiary Business English questionnaire — a big thank you.

The authors and publishers would like to thank the following for permission to reproduce their images: **Alamy**/Blend Images p56, Alamy/Peter Bowater p110cl, Alamy/Paul Bradbury p43, Alamy/Brownstock p18, Alamy/Corbis RF p13, Alamy/Cultura Creative p46, Alamy/Simon Dack p70, Alamy/Peter Dench: p58, Alamy/Fancy p88, Alamy/foodfolio p36tr, Alamy/Goodard New Era, p110br, Alamy/Imagebroker p59br, Alamy/ImageSource p79, Alamy/Christian Klein p23, Alamy/Dennis MacDonald p62, Alamy/Cro Magnon p99, Alamy/Chris North p110bl, Alamy/Olaf Speier p68, Alamy/Alex Serge p45, Alamy/Apisit Sriputtirut pp14-15b, Alamy/TravelStockCollection - Homer Sykes p82, Alamy/Carlos Villoch-MagicSea.com p72bl, Alamy/Zefa RF p16; **www.cartoonstock.com**/John Morris p77; **Comstock Images** p7; **Corbis**/ABM p80, Corbis/Jon Feingersh/Blend Images p102, Corbis/Rick Gomez p105tl, Corbis/JGI/Blend Images p63, Corbis/Bob Krist p72bc, Corbis/Beau Lark p65, Corbis/Morgan David de Lossy p28cr, Corbis/Moodboard: p28tl, Corbis/RTimages/Tetra Images p89, Corbis/Patrick Mac Sean/ès p76, Corbis/Klaus Tiedge p81br, Corbis/Whisson/Jordan p36tc; Photos p38: **Fedex** © Federal Express Corporation, all rights reserved; **Garmin** p39t; **Getty Images** pp 11tr & br, 39bl, 40cl & bl, 78, 81bl, Getty Images/Elie Bernager p67, Getty Images/bilderlounge p92; Getty Images/Blend Images p59bcr, Getty Images/Bloomberg pp 39br, 40c, Getty Images/Comstock p103cl, Getty Images/Digitalvision p24, Getty Images/Dorling Kindersley p82, Getty Images/George Doyle p12, Getty Images/Mark Evans p44, Getty Images/Fotosearch p15cl, Getty Images/Glow Images Inc p105cr, Getty Images/Robb Kendrick p33, Getty Images/Kord.com pp72–73, Getty Images/Ryan Lane p37, Getty Images/Marcus Lyon p19, Getty Images/NBC p26, Getty Images/Per-Gunnar Ostby p17, Getty Images/Push Pictures p109, Getty Images/Sakis Papadopoulos p72br, Getty Images/Ken Reid p101, Getty Images/Rubberball p57, Getty Images/Beowulf Sheehan p9, Getty Images/Steve Smith p59tr, Getty Images/Henrik Sorensen p54, Getty Images/Brent Stirton p107tr, Getty Images/Stockbyte pp 84–85, Getty Images/Thinkstock p22, Getty Images/VCL/Spencer Rowell p21, Getty Images/WireImage p40cr, Getty Images/Zero Creatives p97; **Glow Images**/daj p93, Glow Images/Chad Ehlers p32, Glow Images/Rubberball p66, Glow Images/Chuck Savage/Corbis p69; **Press Association Images**/Daniel Acker/Landov p39bc; **Reuters**/Jason Reed: p59cr; **Rex Features**/Action Press p49, Rex Features/c.Paramount/Everett p71.

The authors and publishers are grateful for permission to reprint the following copyright material:
Material used from *Unlocking Your People's Potential* by Eddie Davies (Fenman Training, 1995), copyright © Eddie Davies 1995, reprinted by permission of the publisher; Word definitions taken from *Macmillan English Dictionary For Advanced Learners* copyright © Macmillan Publishers 2002, reprinted by permission of the publisher; Material used from website - *www.openoffice.org Community*, reprinted by permission; Material from 'Ten Tips for Creating a Career That Lights Your Fire' taken from http://www.passioncatalyst.com/passioncatalyst/article1.htm, reprinted by permission of the publisher; Material used from 'Help Desk Call' taken from Funny.co.uk 08.02.03; Material used from 'Methods of Payment in International Trade' taken from www.sitpro.org.uk; Information from 'Groupon's call centre in the cloud' taken from website www.information-age.com; Material used from 'The Johnson & Johnson Credo' taken from www.jnj.com.; Material used from 'Good neighbours are good for business' copyright © OECD observer No. 248, March 2005 from http://www.oecdobserver.org/news/fullstory.phdaid/1583/Good-neighbours-are-good-for-business-html.

Printed and bound in the UK by CLOC Ltd
2023 2022
29 28